TEXTBOOK OF PHYTOCHEMISTRY

TEXTBOOK OF PHYTOCHEMISTRY

By
Dr. Syed Aftab Iqbal
M.Sc. , Ph.D., FICS
FICC, FIAEM, MNASc.
Professor
Department of Chemistry
Saifia Science College
Barkatullah University
Bhopal (India)
&
Dr. Noor Ahmed Khan
M.Phil., Ph.D.
Saifia Science College
Barkatullah University
Bhopal (India)

DISCOVERY PUBLISHING HOUSE PVT. LTD.
NEW DELHI-110 002

Published by:
Tilak Wasan
DISCOVERY PUBLISHING HOUSE PVT. LTD.
4831/24, Ansari Road, Prahlad Street
Darya Ganj, New Delhi-110002 (India)
Phone: +91-11-23279245, 43764432
Fax: +91-11-23253475
E-mail: parul.wasan@gmail.com
discoverypublishinghouse@gmail.com
info@discoverypublishinggroup.com
web: www.discoverypublishinggroup.com

***First Edition:* 2011**
ISBN: 978-81-8356-847-0

Textbook of Phytochemistry

Printed at:
Shree Balaji Art Press
Delhi

PREFACE

Phytochemistry is in the strict sense of the word the study of phytochemicals. These are chemicals derived from plants. In a narrower sense the terms are often used to describe the large number of secondary metabolic compounds found in plants. Many of these are known to provide protection against insect attacks and plant diseases. They also exhibit a number of protective functions for human consumers.

Phytochemistry is widely used in the field of Chinese medicine especially in the field of herbal medicine.

Phytochemical technique mainly applies to the quality control of Chinese medicine or herbal medicine of various chemical components, such as saponins, alkaloids, volatile oils, flavonoids and anthraquinones. In the development of rapid and reproducible analytical techniques, the combination of HPLC with different detectors, such as diode array detector (DAD), refractive index detector (RID), evaporative light scattering detector (ELSD) and mass spectrometric detector (MSD), has been widely developed.

In most cases, biologically active compounds in Chinese medicine or herbal medicine have not been determined. Therefore, it is important to use the phytochemical methods to screen and analyze bioactive components, not only for the quality control of crude drugs, but also for the elucidation of their therapeutic mechanisms. Modern pharmacological studies indicate that binding to receptors or ion channels on cell membranes is the first step of some drug actions. A new method in phytochemistry called biochromatography has been developed. This method combines human red cell membrane extraction and high performance liquid chromatography to screen potential active components in Chinese medicine.

Carbohydrates, sugars and gums - Carbohydrates (sugars) are the products of photosynthesis that plants use as starting material for most of the other compounds in plants. Cellulose is a carbohydrate that most plants make and contain that gives plants their structure and strength, some parts of plants may be more than 50% cellulose. Gums are polysaccharidic (made from sugars) compounds, where various different sugars are joined together to form polymer like structures. Some acacias produce quite large amounts of gum from injuries or insect attack, some are edible, they can vary greatly in their water solubility, some becoming gelatinous and not really dissolving.

Author

CONTENTS

1
INTRODUCTION

Phytochemistry is in the strict sense of the word the study of phytochemicals. These are chemicals derived from plants. In a narrower sense the terms are often used to describe the large number of secondary metabolic compounds found in plants. Many of these are known to provide protection against insect attacks and plant diseases. They also exhibit a number of protective functions for human consumers.

Techniques commonly used in the field of phytochemistry are extraction, isolation and structural elucidation (MS,1D and 2D NMR) of natural products, as well as various chromatography techniques (MPLC, HPLC, LC-MS). temperature is high, water will evaporate sooner.

Constituent Elements

The list of simple elements of which plants are primarily constructed—carbon, oxygen, hydrogen, calcium, phosphorus, etc.—is not different from similar lists for animals, fungi, or even bacteria. The fundamental atomic components of plants are the same as for all life; only the details of the way in which they are assembled differs.

Eastern Medicine

Phytochemistry is widely used in the field of Chinese medicine especially in the field of herbal medicine.

Phytochemical technique mainly applies to the quality control of Chinese medicine or herbal medicine of various chemical components, such as saponins, alkaloids, volatile oils, flavonoids and anthraquinones. In the development of rapid and reproducible analytical techniques, the combination of HPLC with different detectors, such as diode array detector (DAD), refractive index detector (RID), evaporative light scattering detector (ELSD) and mass spectrometric detector (MSD), has been widely developed.

In most cases, biologically active compounds in Chinese medicine or herbal medicine have not been determined. Therefore, it is important to use the phytochemical methods to screen and analyze bioactive components, not only for the quality control of crude drugs, but also for the elucidation of their therapeutic mechanisms. Modern pharmacological studies indicate that binding to receptors or ion channels on cell membranes is the first step of some drug actions. A new method in phytochemistry called biochromatography has been developed. This method combines human red cell membrane extraction and high performance liquid chromatography to screen potential active components in Chinese medicine.

All or a combination of the compounds below may be found in many flowering plants, including acacias. This is however a rather simplified treatment of a very complex subject, there being literally thousands of different compounds and metabolites in pl ants. The role or function, if any, is still debatable, protection against predation, end metabolites, plant hormones, pheromones, anti-fungal/viral etc.

Carbohydrates, sugars and gums - Carbohydrates (sugars) are the products of photosynthesis that plants use as starting material for most of the other compounds in plants. Cellulose is a carbohydrate that most plants make and contain that gives p lants their structure and strength, some parts of plants may be more than 50% cellulose. Gums are polysaccharidic (made from sugars) compounds, where various different sugars are joined together to form polymer like structures. Some acacias produce quite large amounts of gum from injuries or insect attack, some are edible, they can vary greatly in their water solubility, some becoming gelatinous and not really dissolving.

Terpenes, oils and resins - Generally water insoluble organic compounds, originally applied to substances made up of two 5-carbon units, the so called isoprene unit. Monoterpenes are two units, sesquiterpenes are three units, diterpenes are four units, triterpenes six units etc. Different oils and terpenes may be found in the flowers and foliage, some acacia flower essential oils are used in perfumery. Most essential oils are mono or sesqui terpenes, resins are often more complex terpenoid mixt ures that may also contain gums.

Tannins - Tannins are complex compounds based on tannic and gallic acid, very common in the wood, bark and foliage that are water soluble but react with proteins, this is what causes the astringency of many plants and is utilised to preserve lea ther in the tanning process. Acacia bark has been used as a source of tannins, some species having large amounts in the bark.

Glucoside - Is a general term for substances made up of of a sugar residue (glucose unit) and another compound, such as a flavanoid, coumarin, steroid or terpene, collectively known as the aglycone. Glycosides are common in plants, there are qui te a few that have a strong action on the body, including the heart, digestive and peripheral nervous system. 'Cyanogenetic glycosides' produce free HCN (cyanide) when reduced and along with other glycosides, like the cardioactive glycosides can produce toxic even fatal results if enough is ingested, which may not be very much. About forty species from sub-genus Phyllodineae have been recorded as being cyanogenetic.

The glycoside kaempferol has been isolated from the flowers of A. *discolour*, A. *linifolia*, A. *decurrens* and A. *longifolia*, kaempferol is water soluble and yellow, and in these cases responsible for the colour of the flowers and this may be the case with many, if not most acacia flowers. This compound has been found to be a diuretic (promotes urination) and natriuretic (causes sodium loss), increasing urine secretions and the functioning of the kid ney cells, increasing in turn, their permeability and circulation. The general result is that kidney function improves which helps the body to positively react to water retention and excessive blood glucose levels, both of which are secondary symptoms of diabetes (Winkelman, Ethnobotanical treatments of diabetes in Baja California norte. unpublished report, Arizona state uni, Flavanoids - This is a term that is applied to compounds common in many plants and quite often responsible for the colours in wood, fruit and flowers. The flavanoids of the heartwoods of Australian acacias has been the subject of some study. The se studies have found that Australian acacias can be broadly divided into different groups depending on the flavanoids present in the wood. These groupings did not correspond exactly with the classification based on morphological differences. There were h owever some correlations with the Botrycephaleae forming a distinct group and Phyllodineae species with flowers in racemes having a similar flavanoid pattern. The Juliflorae and Plurinerves had a similar flavanoid pattern, the Juliflorae being a fairly well defined group, with a further small group in the Juliflorae having unique but related flavanoids. There was also a distinct group in the Phyllodineae that had unique flavanoids that give members of this group distinctively purple heartwood. There were some mixed results for some species in sections Phyll odineae, Plurinerves and Juliflorae, especially the tropical northern species.

Other studies of the free amino acids in the seeds of different species found that sub-genus Acacia was a distinct group different to sub-genus Phyllodineae and Acueiliferum, a sub-genus of mostly Asian, African and Central American species. There seem ed to be some relationship between sub-genus Phyllodineae and Acueiliferum, with the addition of two more amino acids, one toxic, in the Acueiliferum species seeds compared to sub-genus Phyllodineae. Three extra Australian species of sub-genus Phyllodinea e, a. confusa, a. simplex and a. kuauiensis also have been found contain these extra amino acids.

Alkaloids - is a general term for basic (alkaline) nitrogen containing organic compounds, generally bitter in taste and strong physiological action, many plant derived drugs and medicines are alkaloids, eg quinine, scopolomine, codiene, morphine, ephedrine, tryptamines etc. A lot of them can be potentially toxic, even fatal, especially when in the form of purified alkaloids extracted from plants, quite often only a small amount of the alkaloids can have a strong effect. Obviously some, or at least the plants that contain them have proved immensely useful to people for disease and illness, for thousands of years.

Alkaloids are relatively common in the leguminosae as a whole, and within the genus acacia in Australia alkaloids that have been reported include N,N-dimethyltryptamine, N-methyltryptamine, tryptamine, tetrahydroharman, N-methyl-tetrahydroharman, b-phe nethylamine, N-methyl-b-phenethylamine, hordenine (N,N-dimethyl-4-hydroxy-b-phenethylamine), N-cinnamoylhistamine.

For the number of species, there has been little research on the alkaloids of Australian acacias, and like many studies of Australian plants there has been quite alot of variability in the results. For example the root bark of acacia holoserica is repo rted in a few publications as containing the β-phenethylamine alkaloid hordenine, up to 1.22% of the dry weight. Yet in a recent study of aboriginal medicinal plants all parts of this species were found to give a negative result for alkaloids. It was still used medicinally and another species, *Acacia auriculiformis,* which was used in a similar way was found to give a positive test for alkaloids, both are members of section Juliflorae. Other studies have found that there can not only be variation in the amount, but also in the type of alkaloids present, e.g. *A. baileyana* has been found to contain both β-carboline and tryptamine alkaloids at different times of the year.

Qualitative studies of the alkaloids have found that B-phenethylamine alkaloids are quite common in the uninerved members of section Phyllodineae with flowers in racemes, with some specimens found to contain more than 1% alkaloi ds. β-phenethylamines have been found in other species from section Phyllodineae. N-cinnamoylhistamine has been isolated from at least one member of section Juliflorae. Tryptamine or it's N-methyl and N, N-dimethyl derivatives have been found in a number of members of section Juliflorae, and a single species from the Botrycephalae. An extra-Australian member of sub-genus Phyllodineae is recorded as contain ing methylated tryptamine and β-carboline alkaloids together. A member of section plurinerves is reported to contain β-carboline alkaloids.

So the picture regarding alkaloids seems complex, with much variation from different areas or amongst types or chemical races. Other plants in the Australian flora exhibit this sort of phenomena, with great variation in the amount and even the constitu ents of the volatile oils (Eucalyptus, Melaleuca), alkaloids (Duboisia) or other compounds between types or localities. Many Aboriginal people recognised this trait in the Australian bush by using plants from one area, and claim that the same plant from a different spot would not be effective, or may even be toxic.

2

METABOLOMICS

Metabolomics is the "systematic study of the unique chemical fingerprints that specific cellular processes leave behind" - specifically, the study of their small-molecule metabolite profiles The metabolome represents the collection of all metabolites in a biological organism, which are the end products of its gene expression. Thus, while mRNA gene expression data and proteomic analyses do not tell the whole story of what might be happening in a cell, metabolic profiling can give an instantaneous snapshot of the physiology of that cell. One of the challenges of systems biology and functional genomics is to integrate proteomic, transcriptomic, and metabolomic information to give a more complete picture of living organisms.

Metabolome

Metabolome refers to the complete set of small-molecule metabolites (such as metabolic intermediates, hormones and other signalling molecules, and secondary metabolites) to be found within a biological sample, such as a single organism. The word was coined in analogy with transcriptomics and proteomics; like the transcriptome and the proteome, the metabolome is dynamic, changing from second to second.

Although the metabolome can be defined readily enough, it is not currently possible to analyse the entire range of metabolites by a single analytical method. In January 2007, scientists at the University of Alberta and the University of Calgary completed the first draft of the human metabolome. They catalogued approximately 2500 metabolites, 1200 drugs and 3500 food components that can be found in the human body, as reported in the literature This information, available at the Human Metabolome Database and based on analysis of information available in the current scientific literature, is far from complete. In contrast, much more is known about the metabolomes of other organisms, especially of plants, where over 50,000 metabolites have been characterized from the plant kingdom, and many thousands of metabolites have been identified and/or characterized from single plants. Metabolomics in today's world carries on its shoulders the huge responsibility of providing a detailed description of metabolic pathways and their workings, whether they be in humans, animals, or the plants we both eat and admire.

Metabolites

Metabolites are the intermediates and products of metabolism. The term metabolite is usually restricted to small molecules. A primary metabolite is directly involved in the normal growth, development, and reproduction. A secondary metabolite is not directly involved in those processes, but usually has important ecological function. Examples include antibiotics and pigments.

The metabolome forms a large network of metabolic reactions, where outputs from one enzymatic chemical reaction are inputs to other chemical reactions. Such systems have been described as hypercycles.

Metabonomics

Metabonomics is defined as "the quantitative measurement of the dynamic multiparametric metabolic response of living systems to pathophysiological stimuli or genetic modification". This approach was pioneered by Jeremy Nicholson at Imperial College London and has been used in toxicology, disease diagnosis and a number of other fields. Historically, the metabonomics approach was one of the first methods to apply the scope of systems biology to studies of metabolism.

There has been some disagreement over the exact differences between 'metabolomics' and 'metabonomics', although the term 'metabolomics' is more commonly used. The difference between the two terms is not related to choice of analytical platform: although metabonomics is more associated with NMR spectroscopy and metabolomics with mass spectrometry-based techniques, this is simply because of usages amongst different groups that have popularized the different terms. While there is still no absolute agreement, there is a growing consensus that the difference resides in the fact that 'metabolomics' places a greater emphasis on comprehensive metabolic profiling, regardless of species investigated, while 'metabonomics' is used to describe multiple (but not necessarily comprehensive) metabolic changes caused by a biological perturbation. The term 'metabonomics' is rarely used to describe research not directly related to human disease or nutrition. In practice, within the field of human disease research there is still a large degree of overlap in the way both terms are used, and they are often in effect synonymous.

History

Metabolic biochemists have arguably been 'doing metabolomics' for decades. The chromatographic separation techniques that made the initial detection of metabolites possible were developed in the late 1960s, which marks the technical origin of the field.

The development of metabolomics began in 1970 by Arthur Robinson investigating Pauling's ideas as to whether biological variability could be explained on the basis of far wider ranges of nutritional requirements than what was generally recognized. In analyzing the "messy" chromatographic patterns of urine from vitamin B6-loaded subjects, Robinson realized that the patterns of hundreds or thousands of chemical constituents in urine contained much useful information.

Although it was not called metabolomics, the first paper devoted to this topic was titled, "Quantitative Analysis of Urine Vapor and Breath by Gas-Liquid Partition Chromatography", by Robinson and Pauling in 1971 and published in the Proceedings of the National Academy of Sciences. Since then, Robinson has had nineteen more papers published on the quantitative patterns of metabolites in body fluids. Robinson and colleagues have identified several diseases, conditions, and physiological age based on this data. It was his expectation that body fluid analysis can be optimized to make a low cost, information-rich, medically-relevant means of measuring metabolically-driven changes in functional state, even when the chemical constituents are all in the "normal range".

The core idea that Robinson conceived is that information-rich data that reflects the functional status of a complex biological system resides in the quantitative and qualitative pattern of metabolites in body fluids. Twenty years later, others began to realize the value of this approach, and interest in this has mushroomed. The name metabolomics was coined in the 1990s. Systematic functional analysis of the yeast genome. Trends Biotechnol. 16, 373-378), and in 2004 a society was formed to promote its study. Many of the bioanalytical methods used for metabolomics have been adapted (or in some cases simply adopted) from existing biochemical techniques. What sets metabolomics apart from strictly analytical chemistry-based analyses is the scope of the work. Three characteristics common to metabolomic research are:

1. Effort is made to profile metabolites with as little bias as is possible towards a specific metabolite or group of

metabolites. Nevertheless, all profiling approaches require extraction of metabolites from biological tissues, and will therefore be biased due to solvent properties. This holds true, but is reduced, even if multiple solvent systems are used.

2. Large numbers of metabolites are profiled at the same time, instead of being analyzed one by one.
3. Relationships between the metabolites are characterized, currently mostly by multivariate methods, although other data analysis tools are being developed.

The field of metabolomics exploded in the early 2000s, particularly as a result of efforts by researchers from the Max Planck Institute for Plant Physiology, in Golm, Germany, under the direction of Prof. Dr. Lothar Willmitzer. Their research, while still more appropriately called 'metabolite profiling' because they analyzed only hundreds of compounds and not the entire complement of the plant cell, set the framework for metabolomics-scale investigations. Their review articles promoting the field and its potential applications to agriculture, medicine, and other fields in the biological sciences, definitely had a strong stimulatory effect on the field as a whole.

On January 23, 2007, the Human Metabolome Project, led by Dr. David Wishart of the University of Alberta, Canada, completed the first draft of the human metabolome, consisting of a database of approximately 2500 metabolites, 1200 drugs and 3500 food components. Similar projects have been underway in several plant species, most notably Medicago truncatula and Arabidopsis thaliana for several years.

Analytical Technologies

There are four important issues to be addressed for metabolite analysis:

1. Efficient and unbiased extraction of metabolites from biological tissues.

2. Separation of the analytes, usually by chromatography. Electrophoresis, particularly capillary electrophoresis, is also used.
3. Detection of the analytes, following separation by chromatographic or other methods.
4. Identification and quantification of the analytes.

Separation Methods

Gas chromatography, especially when interfaced with mass spectrometry (GC-MS), is one of the most widely used and powerful methods. It offers very high chromatographic resolution, but requires chemical derivatization for many biomolecules: only volatile chemicals can be analysed without derivatization. (Some modern instruments allow '2D' chromatography, using a short polar column after the main analytical column, which increases the resolution still further.) Some large and polar metabolites cannot be analysed by GC.

High performance liquid chromatography (HPLC). Compared to GC, HPLC has lower chromatographic resolution, but it does have the advantage that a much wider range of analytes can potentially be measured.

Capillary electrophoresis (CE). So far, there are only a relatively small number of publications on use of CE for metabolite profiling. This will no doubt change, as there are a number of advantages of CE: it has a higher theoretical separation efficiency than HPLC, and is suitable for use with a wider range of metabolite classes than is GC. As for all electrophoretic techniques, it is most appropriate for charged analytes.

Detection Methods

Mass spectrometry (MS) is used to identify and to quantify metabolites after separation by GC, HPLC, or CE. GC-MS is the most 'natural' combination of the three, and was the first to be developed. In addition, mass spectral fingerprint libraries exist or can be developed that allow identification of a metabolite according to its fragmentation pattern. MS is both sensitive (although, particularly for HPLC-MS, sensitivity is more of an issue as it is affected by the charge on the metabolite, and can be subject to ion suppression artifacts) and can be very specific. There are also a number of studies which use MS as a stand-alone technology: the sample is infused directly into the mass spectrometer with no prior separation, and the MS serves to both separate and to detect metabolites.

Nuclear magnetic resonance (NMR) spectroscopy. NMR is the only detection technique which does not rely on separation of the analytes, and the sample can thus be recovered for further analyses. All kinds of small molecule metabolites can be measured simultaneously - in this sense, NMR is close to being a universal detector. Practically, however, it is relatively insensitive compared to mass spectrometry-based techniques; additionally, NMR spectra can be very difficult to interpret for complex mixtures.

Other techniques. MS and NMR are by far the two leading technologies for metabolomics. Other methods of detection that have been used include electrochemical detection (coupled to HPLC) and radiolabel (when combined with thin-layer chromatography).

Key Applications

Toxicity assessment/toxicology. Metabolic profiling (especially of urine or blood plasma samples) can be used to detect the physiological changes caused by toxic insult of a chemical (or mixture of chemicals). In many cases, the observed changes can be related to specific syndromes, e.g. a specific lesion in liver or kidney. This is of particular relevance to pharmaceutical companies wanting to test the toxicity of potential drug candidates if a compound can be eliminated before it reaches clinical trials on the grounds of adverse toxicity, it saves the enormous expense of the trials.

Functional Genomics

Metabolomics can be an excellent tool for determining the phenotype caused by a genetic manipulation, such as gene deletion or insertion. Sometimes this can be a sufficient goal in itself — for instance, to detect any phenotypic changes in a genetically-modified plant intended for human or animal consumption. More exciting is the prospect of predicting the function of unknown genes by comparison with the metabolic perturbations caused by deletion/insertion of known genes. Such advances are most likely to come from model organisms such as Saccharomyces cerevisiae and Arabidopsis thaliana. The Cravatt laboratory at The Scripps Research Institute has recently applied this technology to mammalian systems, identifying the N-acyltaurines as previously uncharacterized endogenous substrates for the enzyme fatty acid amide hydrolase (FAAH) and the monoalkylglycerol ethers as endogenous substrates for the uncharacterized hydrolase KIAA1363.

Nutrigenomics is a generalised term which links genomics, transcriptomics, proteomics and metabolomics to human nutrition. In general a metabolome in a given body fluid is influenced by endogenous factors such as age, sex, body composition and genetics as well as underlying pathologies. The large bowel microflora are also a very significant potential confounder of metabolic profiles and could be classified as either an endogenous or exogenous factor. The main exogenous factors are diet and drugs. Diet can then be broken down to nutrients and non- nutrients. Metabolomics is one means to determine a biological endpoint, or metabolic fingerprint, which reflects the balance of all these forces on an individual's metabolism.

Metabolism is the set of chemical reactions that occur in living organisms in order to maintain life. These processes allow organisms to grow and reproduce, maintain their structures, and respond to their environments. Metabolism is usually divided into two categories. Catabolism breaks down organic matter, for example to harvest energy in cellular respiration. Anabolism, on the other hand, uses energy to construct components of cells such as proteins and nucleic acids.

The chemical reactions of metabolism are organized into metabolic pathways, in which one chemical is transformed into another by a sequence of enzymes. Enzymes are crucial to metabolism because they allow organisms to drive desirable but thermodynamically unfavorable reactions by coupling them to favorable ones, and because they act as catalysts to allow these reactions to proceed quickly and efficiently. Enzymes also allow the regulation of metabolic pathways in response to changes in the cell's environment or signals from other cells.

The metabolism of an organism determines which substances it will find nutritious and which it will find poisonous. For example, some prokaryotes use hydrogen sulfide as a nutrient, yet this gas is poisonous to animals. The speed of metabolism, the metabolic rate, also influences how much food an organism will require.

A striking feature of metabolism is the similarity of the basic metabolic pathways between even vastly different species. For example, the set of carboxylic acids that are best known as the intermediates in the citric acid cycle are present in all organisms, being found in species as diverse as the unicellular bacteria Escherichia coli and huge multicellular organisms like elephants These striking similarities in metabolism are most likely the result of the high efficiency of these pathways, and of their early appearance in evolutionary history.

Key Biochemicals

Most of the structures that make up animals, plants and microbes are made from three basic classes of molecule: amino acids, carbohydrates and lipids (often called fats). As these molecules are vital for life, metabolism focuses on making these molecules, in the construction of cells and tissues, or breaking them down and using them as a source of energy, in the digestion and use of food. Many important biochemicals can be joined together to make polymers such as DNA and proteins. These macromolecules are essential parts of all living organisms.

Amino Acids and Proteins

Proteins are made of amino acids arranged in a linear chain and joined together by peptide bonds. Many proteins are the enzymes that catalyze the chemical reactions in metabolism. Other proteins have structural or mechanical functions, such as the proteins that form the cytoskeleton, a system of scaffolding that maintains the cell shape. Proteins are also important in cell signaling, immune responses, cell adhesion, active transport across membranes and the cell cycle.

Lipids

Lipids are the most diverse group of biochemicals. Their main structural uses are as part of biological membranes such as the cell membrane, or as a source of energy. Lipids are usually defined as hydrophobic or amphipathic biological molecules that will dissolve in organic solvents such as benzene or chloroform. The fats are a large group of compounds that contain fatty acids and glycerol; a glycerol molecule attached to three fatty acid esters is a triacylglyceride. Several variations on this basic structure exist, including alternate backbones such as sphingosine in the sphingolipids, and hydrophilic groups such as phosphate in phospholipids. Steroids such as cholesterol are another major class of lipids that are made in cells.

Carbohydrates

Glucose can exist in both a straight-chain and ring form Carbohydrates are straight-chain aldehydes or ketones with many hydroxyl groups that can exist as straight chains or rings. Carbohydrates are the most abundant biological molecules, and fill numerous roles, such as the storage and transport of energy (starch, glycogen) and structural components (cellulose in plants, chitin in animals). The basic carbohydrate units are called monosaccharides and include galactose, fructose, and most importantly glucose. Monosaccharides can be linked together to form polysaccharides in almost limitless ways.

Nucleotides

The polymers DNA and RNA are long chains of nucleotides. These molecules are critical for the storage and use of genetic information, through the processes of transcription and protein biosynthesis This information is protected by DNA repair mechanisms and propagated through DNA replication. A few viruses have an RNA genome, for example HIV, which uses reverse transcription to create a DNA template from its viral RNA genome. RNA in ribozymes such as spliceosomes and ribosomes is similar to enzymes as it can catalyze chemical reactions. Individual nucleosides are made by attaching a nucleobase to a ribose sugar. These bases are heterocyclic rings containing nitrogen, classified as purines or pyrimidines. Nucleotides also act as coenzymes in metabolic group transfer reactions.

Coenzymes

Metabolism involves a vast array of chemical reactions, but most fall under a few basic types of reactions that involve the transfer of functional groups. This common chemistry allows cells to use a small set of metabolic intermediates to carry chemical groups between different reactions. These group-transfer intermediates are called coenzymes. Each class of group-transfer reaction is carried out by a particular coenzyme, which is the substrate for a set of enzymes that produce it, and a set of enzymes that consume it. These coenzymes are therefore continuously being made, consumed and then recycled.

One central coenzyme is adenosine triphosphate (ATP), the universal energy currency of cells. This nucleotide is used to transfer chemical energy between different chemical reactions. There is only a small amount of ATP in cells, but as it is continuously regenerated, the human body can use about its own weight in ATP per day. ATP acts as a bridge between catabolism and anabolism, with catabolic reactions generating ATP and anabolic reactions consuming it. It also serves as a carrier of phosphate groups in phosphorylation reactions.

A vitamin is an organic compound needed in small quantities that cannot be made in the cells. In human nutrition, most vitamins function as coenzymes after modification; for example, all water-soluble vitamins are phosphorylated or are coupled to nucleotides when they are used in cells. Nicotinamide adenine dinucleotide (NADH), a derivative of vitamin B3 (niacin), is an important coenzyme that acts as a hydrogen acceptor. Hundreds of separate types of dehydrogenases remove electrons from their substrates and reduce NAD^+ into NADH. This reduced form of the coenzyme is then a substrate for any of the reductases in the cell that need to reduce their substrates Nicotinamide adenine dinucleotide exists in two related forms in the cell, NADH and NADPH. The NAD^+/NADH form is more important in catabolic reactions, while NADP+/NADPH is used in anabolic reactions.

Minerals and Cofactors

Inorganic elements play critical roles in metabolism; some are abundant (e.g. sodium and potassium) while others function at minute concentrations. About 99% of mammals' mass are the elements carbon, nitrogen, calcium, sodium, chlorine, potassium, hydrogen, phosphorus, oxygen and sulfur. The organic compounds (proteins, lipids and carbohydrates) contain the majority of the carbon and nitrogen and most of the oxygen and hydrogen is present as water.

The abundant inorganic elements act as ionic electrolytes. The most important ions are sodium, potassium, calcium, magnesium, chloride, phosphate, and the organic ion bicarbonate. The maintenance of precise gradients across cell membranes maintains osmotic pressure and pH. Ions are also critical for nerves and muscles, as action potentials in these tissues are produced by the exchange of electrolytes between the extracellular fluid and the cytosol. Electrolytes enter and leave cells through proteins in the cell membrane called ion channels. For example, muscle contraction depends upon the movement of calcium, sodium and potassium through ion channels in the cell membrane and T-tubules.

The transition metals are usually present as trace elements in organisms, with zinc and iron being most abundant. These metals are used in some proteins as cofactors and are essential for the activity of enzymes such as catalase and oxygen-carrier proteins such as hemoglobin. These cofactors are bound tightly to a specific protein; although enzyme cofactors can be modified during catalysis, cofactors always return to their original state after catalysis has taken place. The metal micronutrients are taken up into organisms by specific transporters and bound to storage proteins such as ferritin or metallothionein when not being used.

Catabolism is the set of metabolic processes that break down large molecules. These include breaking down and oxidising food molecules. The purpose of the catabolic reactions is to provide the energy and components needed by anabolic reactions. The exact nature of these catabolic reactions differ from organism to organism, with organic molecules being used as a source of energy in organotrophs, while lithotrophs use inorganic substrates and phototrophs capture sunlight as chemical energy. However, all these different forms of metabolism depend on redox reactions that involve the transfer of electrons from reduced donor molecules such as organic molecules, water, ammonia, hydrogen sulfide or ferrous ions to acceptor molecules such as oxygen, nitrate or sulfate In animals these reactions involve complex organic molecules being broken down to simpler molecules, such as carbon dioxide and water. In photosynthetic organisms such as plants and cyanobacteria, these electron-transfer reactions do not release energy, but are used as a way of storing energy absorbed from sunlight.

The most common set of catabolic reactions in animals can be separated into three main stages. In the first, large organic molecules such as proteins, polysaccharides or lipids are digested into their smaller components outside cells. Next, these smaller molecules are taken up by cells and converted to yet smaller molecules, usually acetyl coenzyme A (CoA), which releases some energy. Finally, the acetyl group on the CoA is oxidised to water and carbon dioxide in the citric acid cycle and electron transport chain, releasing the energy that is stored by reducing the coenzyme nicotinamide adenine dinucleotide (NAD^+) into NADH.

Digestion

Macromolecules such as starch, cellulose or proteins cannot be rapidly taken up by cells and need to be broken into their smaller units before they can be used in cell metabolism. Several common classes of enzymes digest these polymers. These digestive enzymes include proteases that digest proteins into amino acids, as well as glycoside hydrolases that digest polysaccharides into monosaccharides.

Microbes simply secrete digestive enzymes into their surroundings while animals only secrete these enzymes from specialized cells in their guts. The amino acids or sugars released by these extracellular enzymes are then pumped into cells by specific active transport proteins

Energy from Organic Compounds

Carbohydrate catabolism is the breakdown of carbohydrates into smaller units. Carbohydrates are usually taken into cells once they have been digested into monosaccharides. Once inside, the major route of breakdown is glycolysis, where sugars such as glucose and fructose are converted into pyruvate and some ATP is generated. yruvate is an intermediate in several metabolic pathways, but the majority is converted to acetyl-CoA and fed into the citric acid cycle. Although some more ATP is generated in the citric acid cycle, the most important product is NADH, which is made from NAD^+ as the acetyl-CoA is oxidized. This oxidation releases carbon dioxide as a waste product. In anaerobic conditions, glycolysis produces lactate, through the enzyme lactate dehydrogenase re-oxidizing NADH to NAD^+ for re-use in glycolysis. An alternative route for glucose breakdown is the pentose phosphate pathway, which reduces the coenzyme NADPH and produces pentose sugars such as ribose, the sugar component of nucleic acids.

Fats are catabolised by hydrolysis to free fatty acids and glycerol. The glycerol enters glycolysis and the fatty acids are broken down by beta oxidation to release acetyl-CoA, which then is fed into the citric acid cycle. Fatty acids release more energy upon oxidation than carbohydrates because carbohydrates contain more oxygen in their structures.

Amino acids are either used to synthesize proteins and other biomolecules, or oxidized to urea and carbon dioxide as a source of energy. The oxidation pathway starts with the removal of the amino group by a transaminase. The amino group is fed into the urea cycle, leaving a deaminated carbon skeleton in the form of a keto acid. Several of these keto acids are intermediates in the citric acid cycle, for example the deamination of glutamate forms a-ketoglutarate The glucogenic amino acids can also be converted into glucose, through gluconeogenesis.

Energy Transformations

In oxidative phosphorylation, the electrons removed from food molecules in pathways such as the citric acid cycle are transferred to oxygen and the energy released is used to make ATP. This is done in eukaryotes by a series of proteins in the membranes of mitochondria called the electron transport chain. In prokaryotes, these proteins are found in the cell's inner membrane These proteins use the energy released from passing electrons from reduced molecules like NADH onto oxygen to pump protons across a membrane.

Pumping protons out of the mitochondria creates a proton concentration difference across the membrane and generates an electrochemical gradient. This force drives protons back into the mitochondrion through the base of an enzyme called ATP synthase. The flow of protons makes the stalk subunit rotate, causing the active site of the synthase domain to change shape and phosphorylate adenosine diphosphate - turning it into ATP.

Energy from Inorganic Compounds

Chemolithotrophy is a type of metabolism found in prokaryotes where energy is obtained from the oxidation of inorganic compounds. These organisms can use hydrogen reduced sulfur compounds (such as sulfide, hydrogen sulfide and thiosulfate) ferrous iron (FeII) or ammonia as sources of reducing power and they gain energy from the oxidation of these compounds with electron acceptors such as oxygen or nitrite These microbial processes are important in global biogeochemical cycles such as acetogenesis, nitrification and denitrification and are critical for soil fertility

Energy from Light

The energy in sunlight is captured by plants, cyanobacteria, purple bacteria, green sulfur bacteria and some protists. This process is often coupled to the conversion of carbon dioxide into organic compounds, as part of photosynthesis, which is discussed below. The energy capture and carbon fixation systems can however operate separately in prokaryotes, as purple bacteria and green sulfur bacteria can use sunlight as a source of energy, while switching between carbon fixation and the fermentation of organic compounds.

In many organisms the capture of solar energy is similar in principle to oxidative phosphorylation, as it involves energy being stored as a proton concentration gradient and this proton motive force then driving ATP synthesis. The electrons needed to drive this electron transport chain come from light-gathering proteins called photosynthetic reaction centres or rhodopsins. Reaction centers are classed into two types depending on the type of photosynthetic pigment present, with most photosynthetic bacteria only having one type, while plants and cyanobacteria have two.

In plants, algae, and cyanobateria, photosystem II uses light energy to remove electrons from water, releasing oxygen as a waste product. The electrons then flow to the cytochrome b6f complex, which uses their energy to pump protons across the thylakoid membrane in the chloroplast. These protons move back through the membrane as they drive the ATP synthase, as before. The electrons then flow through photosystem I and can then either be used to reduce the coenzyme NADP+, for use in the Calvin cycle which is discussed below, or recycled for further ATP generation

Anabolism

Anabolism is the set of constructive metabolic processes where the energy released by catabolism is used to synthesize complex molecules. In general, the complex molecules that make up cellular structures are constructed step-by-step from small and simple precursors. Anabolism involves three basic stages. Firstly, the production of precursors such as amino acids, monosaccharides, isoprenoids and nucleotides, secondly, their activation into reactive forms using energy from ATP, and thirdly, the assembly of these precursors into complex molecules such as proteins, polysaccharides, lipids and nucleic acids.

Organisms differ in how many of the molecules in their cells they can construct for themselves. Autotrophs such as plants can construct the complex organic molecules in cells such as polysaccharides and proteins from simple molecules like carbon dioxide and water. Heterotrophs, on the other hand, require a source of more complex substances, such as monosaccharides and amino acids, to produce these complex molecules. Organisms can be further classified by ultimate source of their energy: photoautotrophs and photoheterotrophs obtain energy from light, whereas chemoautotrophs and chemoheterotrophs obtain energy from inorganic oxidation reactions.

Carbon Fixation

Plant cells (bounded by purple walls) filled with chloroplasts (green), which are the site of photosynthesis. Photosynthesis is the synthesis of carbohydrates from sunlight and carbon dioxide (CO_2). In plants, cyanobacteria and algae, oxygenic photosynthesis splits water, with oxygen produced as a waste product. This process uses the ATP and NADPH produced by the photosynthetic reaction centres, as described above, to convert CO_2 into glycerate 3-phosphate, which can then be converted into glucose. This carbon-fixation reaction is carried out by the enzyme RuBisCO as part of the Calvin–Benson cycle. Three types of photosynthesis occur in plants, C_3 carbon fixation, C_4 carbon fixation and CAM photosynthesis. These differ by the route that carbon dioxide takes to the Calvin cycle, with C_3 plants fixing CO_2 directly, while C_4 and CAM photosynthesis incorporate the CO_2 into other compounds first, as adaptations to deal with intense sunlight and dry conditions.

In photosynthetic prokaryotes the mechanisms of carbon fixation are more diverse. Here, carbon dioxide can be fixed by the Calvin–Benson cycle, a reversed citric acid cycle or the carboxylation of acetyl-CoA. Prokaryotic chemoautotrophs also fix CO_2 through the Calvin–Benson cycle, but use energy from inorganic compounds to drive the reaction.

Carbohydrates and Glycans

In carbohydrate anabolism, simple organic acids can be converted into monosaccharides such as glucose and then used to assemble polysaccharides such as starch. The generation of glucose from compounds like pyruvate, lactate, glycerol, glycerate 3-phosphate and amino acids is called gluconeogenesis. Gluconeogenesis converts pyruvate to glucose-6-phosphate through a series of intermediates, many of which are shared with glycolysis However, this pathway is not simply glycolysis run in reverse, as several steps are catalyzed by non-glycolytic enzymes. This is important as it allows the formation and breakdown of glucose to be regulated separately and prevents both pathways from running simultaneously in a futile cycle.

Although fat is a common way of storing energy, in vertebrates such as humans the fatty acids in these stores cannot be converted to glucose through gluconeogenesis as these organisms cannot convert acetyl-CoA into pyruvate; plants do, but animals do not, have the necessary enzymatic machinery As a result, after long-term starvation, vertebrates need to produce ketone bodies from fatty acids to replace glucose in tissues such as the brain that cannot metabolize fatty acids. In other organisms such as plants and bacteria, this metabolic problem is solved using the glyoxylate cycle, which bypasses the decarboxylation step in the citric acid cycle and allows the transformation of acetyl-CoA to oxaloacetate, where it can be used for the production of glucose.

Polysaccharides and glycans are made by the sequential addition of monosaccharides by glycosyltransferase from a reactive sugar-phosphate donor such as uridine diphosphate glucose (UDP-glucose) to an acceptor hydroxyl group on the growing polysaccharide. As any of the hydroxyl groups on the ring of the substrate can be acceptors, the polysaccharides produced can have straight or branched structures. The polysaccharides produced can have structural or metabolic functions themselves, or be transferred to lipids and proteins by enzymes called oligosaccharyltransferases.

Fatty Acids, Isoprenoids and Steroids

Simplified version of the steroid synthesis pathway with the intermediates isopentenyl pyrophosphate (IPP), dimethylallyl pyrophosphate (DMAPP), geranyl pyrophosphate (GPP) and squalene shown. Some intermediates are omitted for clarity.Fatty acids are made by fatty acid synthases that polymerize and then reduce acetyl-CoA units. The acyl chains in the fatty acids are extended by a cycle of reactions that add the actyl group, reduce it to an alcohol, dehydrate it to an alkene group and then reduce it again to an alkane group. The enzymes of fatty acid biosynthesis are divided into two groups, in animals and fungi all these fatty acid synthase reactions are carried out by a single multifunctional type I protein, while in plant plastids and bacteria separate type II enzymes perform each step in the pathway.

Terpenes and isoprenoids are a large class of lipids that include the carotenoids and form the largest class of plant natural products. These compounds are made by the assembly and modification of isoprene units donated from the reactive precursors isopentenyl pyrophosphate and dimethylallyl pyrophosphate. These precursors can be made in different ways. In animals and archaea, the mevalonate pathway produces these compounds from acetyl-CoA while in plants and bacteria the non-mevalonate pathway uses pyruvate and glyceraldehyde 3-phosphate as substrate One important reaction that uses these activated isoprene donors is steroid biosynthesis. Here, the isoprene units are joined together to make squalene and then folded up and formed into a set of rings to make lanosterol Lanosterol can then be converted into other steroids such as cholesterol and ergosterol.

Proteins

Organisms vary in their ability to synthesize the 20 common amino acids. Most bacteria and plants can synthesize all twenty, but mammals can synthesize only the ten nonessential amino acids Thus, the essential amino acids must be obtained from food. All amino acids are synthesized from intermediates in glycolysis, the citric acid cycle, or the pentose phosphate pathway. Nitrogen is provided by glutamate and glutamine. Amino acid synthesis depends on the formation of the appropriate alpha-keto acid, which is then transaminated to form an amino acid.

Amino acids are made into proteins by being joined together in a chain by peptide bonds. Each different protein has a unique sequence of amino acid residues: this is its primary structure. Just as the letters of the alphabet can be combined to form an almost endless variety of words, amino acids can be linked in varying sequences to form a huge variety of proteins. Proteins are made from amino acids that have been activated by attachment to a transfer RNA molecule through an ester bond. This aminoacyl-tRNA precursor is produced in an ATP-dependent reaction carried out by an aminoacyl tRNA synthetase This aminoacyl-tRNA is then a substrate for the ribosome, which joins the amino acid onto the elongating protein chain, using the sequence information in a messenger RNA.

Nucleotide Synthesis and Salvage

Nucleotides are made from amino acids, carbon dioxide and formic acid in pathways that require large amounts of metabolic energy. Consequently, most organisms have efficient systems to salvage preformed nucleotides. Purines are synthesized as nucleosides (bases attached to ribose). Both adenine and guanine are made from the precursor nucleoside inosine monophosphate, which is synthesized using atoms from the amino acids glycine, glutamine, and aspartic acid, as well as formate transferred from the coenzyme tetrahydrofolate. Pyrimidines, on the other hand, are synthesized from the base orotate, which is formed from glutamine and aspartate.

Xenobiotics and Redox Metabolism

All organisms are constantly exposed to compounds that they cannot use as foods and would be harmful if they accumulated in cells, as they have no metabolic function. These potentially damaging compounds are called xenobiotics Xenobiotics such as synthetic drugs, natural poisons and antibiotics are detoxified by a set of xenobiotic-metabolizing enzymes. In humans, these include cytochrome P450 oxidases UDP-glucuronosyltransferases, and glutathione S-transferases. This system of enzymes acts in three stages to firstly oxidize the xenobiotic (phase I) and then conjugate water-soluble groups onto the molecule (phase II). The modified water-soluble xenobiotic can then be pumped out of cells and in multicellular organisms may be further metabolized before being excreted (phase III). In ecology, these reactions are particularly important in microbial biodegradation of pollutants and the bioremediation of contaminated land and oil spills Many of these microbial reactions are shared with multicellular organisms, but due to the incredible diversity of types of microbes these organisms are able to deal with a far wider range of xenobiotics than multicellular organisms, and can degrade even persistent organic pollutants such as organochloride compounds.

A related problem for aerobic organisms is oxidative stress. Here, processes including oxidative phosphorylation and the formation of disulfide bonds during protein folding produce reactive oxygen species such as hydrogen peroxide These damaging oxidants are removed by antioxidant metabolites such as glutathione and enzymes such as catalases and peroxidases.

Thermodynamics of living Organisms

Living organisms must obey the laws of thermodynamics, which describe the transfer of heat and work. The second law of thermodynamics states that in any closed system, the amount of entropy (disorder) will tend to increase. Although living organisms' amazing complexity appears to contradict this law, life is possible as all organisms are open systems that exchange matter and energy with their surroundings. Thus, living systems are not in equilibrium, but instead are dissipative systems that maintain their state of high complexity by causing a larger increase in the entropy of their environments. The metabolism of a cell achieves this by coupling the spontaneous processes of catabolism to the non-spontaneous processes of anabolism. In thermodynamic terms, metabolism maintains order by creating disorder.

Regulation and Control

As the environments of most organisms are constantly changing, the reactions of metabolism must be finely regulated to maintain a constant set of conditions within cells, a condition called homeostasis Metabolic regulation also allows organisms to respond to signals and interact actively with their environments Two closely-linked concepts are important for understanding how metabolic pathways are controlled. Firstly, the regulation of an enzyme in a pathway is how its activity is increased and decreased in response to signals. Secondly, the control exerted by this enzyme is the effect that these changes in its activity have on the overall rate of the pathway (the flux through the pathway) For example, an enzyme may show large changes in activity (i.e. it is highly regulated) but if these changes have little effect on the flux of a metabolic pathway, then this enzyme is not involved in the control of the pathway.

Effect of insulin on glucose uptake and metabolism. Insulin binds to its receptor:

1. which in turn starts many protein activation cascades;
2. These include: translocation of Glut-4 transporter to the plasma membrane and influx of glucose;
3. glycogen synthesis;
4. glycolysis;
5. fatty acid synthesis;
6. There are multiple levels of metabolic regulation.

In intrinsic regulation, the metabolic pathway self-regulates to respond to changes in the levels of substrates or products; for example, a decrease in the amount of product can increase the flux through the pathway to compensate. This type of regulation often involves allosteric regulation of the activities of multiple enzymes in the pathway. Extrinsic control involves a cell in a multicellular organism changing its metabolism in response to signals from other cells. These signals are usually in the form of soluble messengers such as hormones and growth factors and are detected by specific receptors on the cell surface. These signals are then transmitted inside the cell by second messenger systems that often involved the phosphorylation of proteins.

A very well understood example of extrinsic control is the regulation of glucose metabolism by the hormone insulin. Insulin is produced in response to rises in blood glucose levels. Binding of the hormone to insulin receptors on cells then activates a cascade of protein kinases that cause the cells to take up glucose and convert it into storage molecules such as fatty acids and glycogen. The metabolism of glycogen is controlled by activity of phosphorylase, the enzyme that breaks down glycogen, and glycogen synthase, the enzyme that makes it. These enzymes are regulated in a reciprocal fashion, with phosphorylation inhibiting glycogen synthase, but activating phosphorylase. Insulin causes glycogen synthesis by activating protein phosphatases and producing a decrease in the phosphorylation of these enzymes.

Evolution

The central pathways of metabolism described above, such as glycolysis and the citric acid cycle, are present in all three domains of living things and were present in the last universal ancestor. This universal ancestral cell was prokaryotic and probably a methanogen that had extensive amino acid, nucleotide, carbohydrate and lipid metabolism. The retention of these ancient pathways during later evolution may be the result of these reactions being an optimal solution to their particular metabolic problems, with pathways such as glycolysis and the citric acid cycle producing their end products highly efficiently and in a minimal number of steps The first pathways of enzyme-based metabolism may have been parts of purine nucleotide metabolism, with previous metabolic pathways being part of the ancient RNA world.

Many models have been proposed to describe the mechanisms by which novel metabolic pathways evolve. These include the sequential addition of novel enzymes to a short ancestral pathway, the duplication and then divergence of entire pathways as well as the recruitment of pre-existing enzymes and their assembly into a novel reaction pathway. The relative importance of these mechanisms is unclear, but genomic studies have shown that enzymes in a pathway are likely to have a shared ancestry, suggesting that many pathways have evolved in a step-by-step fashion with novel functions being created from pre-existing steps in the pathway. An alternative model comes from studies that trace the evolution of proteins' structures in metabolic networks, this has suggested that enzymes are pervasively recruited, borrowing enzymes to perform similar functions in different metabolic pathways (evident in the MANET database These recruitment processes result in an evolutionary enzymatic mosaic A third possibility is that some parts of metabolism might exist as "modules" that can be reused in different pathways and perform similar functions on different molecules.

As well as the evolution of new metabolic pathways, evolution can also cause the loss of metabolic functions. For example, in some parasites metabolic processes that are not essential for survival are lost and preformed amino acids, nucleotides and carbohydrates may instead be scavenged from the host. Similar reduced metabolic capabilities are seen in endosymbiotic organisms.

Investigation and Manipulation

Metabolic network of the Arabidopsis thaliana citric acid cycle. Enzymes and metabolites are shown as red squares and the interactions between them as black lines.Classically, metabolism is studied by a reductionist approach that focuses on a single metabolic pathway. Particularly valuable is the use of radioactive tracers at the whole-organism, tissue and cellular levels, which define the paths from precursors to final products by identifying radioactively-labelled intermediates and products. The enzymes that catalyze these chemical reactions can then be purified and their kinetics and responses to inhibitors investigated. A parallel approach is to identify the small molecules in a cell or tissue; the complete set of these molecules is called the metabolome. Overall, these studies give a good view of the structure and function of simple metabolic pathways, but are inadequate when applied to more complex systems such as the metabolism of a complete cell.

An idea of the complexity of the metabolic networks in cells that contain thousands of different enzymes is given by the figure showing the interactions between just 43 proteins and 40 metabolites to the right: the sequences of genomes provide lists containing anything up to 45,000 genes However, it is now possible to use this genomic data to reconstruct complete networks of biochemical reactions and produce more holistic mathematical models that may explain and predict their behaviour. These models are especially powerful when used to integrate the pathway and metabolite data obtained through classical methods with data on gene expression from proteomic and DNA microarray studies. Using these techniques, a model of human metabolism has now been produced, which will guide future drug discovery and biochemical research These models are now being used in network analysis, to classify human diseases into groups that share common proteins or metabolites.

A major technological application of this information is metabolic engineering. Here, organisms such as yeast, plants or bacteria are genetically-modified to make them more useful in biotechnology and aid the production of drugs such as antibiotics or industrial chemicals such as 1,3-propanediol and shikimic acid. These genetic modifications usually aim to reduce the amount of energy used to produce the product, increase yields and reduce the production of wastes

History

History of biochemistry and history of molecular biology.

The term metabolism is derived from the Greek – "Metabolismos" for "change", or "overthrow". The history of the scientific study of metabolism spans several centuries and has moved from examining whole animals in early studies, to examining individual metabolic reactions in modern biochemistry. The concept of metabolism dates back to Ibn al-Nafis (1213-1288), who stated that "the body and its parts are in a continuous state of dissolution and nourishment, so they are inevitably undergoing permanent change. The first controlled experiments in human metabolism were published by Santorio Santorio in 1614 in his book Ars de statica medecina He described how he weighed himself before and after eating, sleeping, working, sex, fasting, drinking, and excreting. He found that most of the food he took in was lost through what he called "insensible perspiration".

In these early studies, the mechanisms of these metabolic processes had not been identified and a vital force was thought to animate living tissue. In the 19th century, when studying the fermentation of sugar to alcohol by yeast, Louis Pasteur concluded that fermentation was catalyzed by substances within the yeast cells he called "ferments". He wrote that "alcoholic fermentation is an act correlated with the life and organization of the yeast cells, not with the death or putrefaction of the cells." This discovery, along with the publication by Friedrich Wöhler in 1828 of the chemical synthesis of urea proved that the organic compounds and chemical reactions found in cells were no different in principle than any other part of chemistry.

It was the discovery of enzymes at the beginning of the 20th century by Eduard Buchner that separated the study of the chemical reactions of metabolism from the biological study of cells, and marked the beginnings of biochemistry. The mass of biochemical knowledge grew rapidly throughout the early 20th century. One of the most prolific of these modern biochemists was Hans Krebs who made huge contributions to the study of metabolism He discovered the urea cycle and later, working with Hans Kornberg, the citric acid cycle and the glyoxylate cycle Modern biochemical research has been greatly aided by the development of new techniques such as chromatography, X-ray diffraction, NMR spectroscopy, radioisotopic labelling, electron microscopy and molecular dynamics simulations. These techniques have allowed the discovery and detailed analysis of the many molecules and metabolic pathways in cells.

Chemical Plants

'Every plant is a chemical factory for complex substances which exceeds any human capability. In their poisons, antibiotic agents, prickles and foul tastes, they developed defences against attack long before human stockades and pesticides.'

Plants provide us with an enormous array of chemicals essential to industry and to our daily lives. But why are the chemicals there and why does the plant produce them? Many of the chemicals are linked to the ingenious strategies that plants have developed to help them flourish and survive.

Plants can't run away from their enemies, be they animals or bacteria. Some of their defences include the thick, insulating bark of many trees, and the vicious thorns on roses. But what is it that makes the stem hairs on stinging nettles produce a rash. Why do some plants produce saps that have an extremely bitter taste; and why do others produce antibacterial substances?

Most plants can be regarded as complex chemical factories, since an astonishing array of compounds has evolved within them over millions of years. Scientists divide these compounds into two categories:

Primary Metabolites

Primary Metabolites are found in all plant cells. These include sugars (carbohydrates), fats, oils and proteins, which are involved in the fundamental biochemical reactions common to all life. However, we're not interested in primary metabolites here. We're more interested in the second category.

Secondary Metabolites

Secondary Metabolites tend to be more specialised, and are usually peculiar to only one plant or species. Their biological function is not always obvious, but they are not formed without a reason. They are important for the survival and propagation of the plant.

While some secondary metabolites are designed to attract creatures that can pollinate their flowers or distribute their seeds, others protect the plant from the sun's radiation, or serve as 'chemical signals' that enable the plant to respond to 'environmental clues'. Others are defensive compounds, designed to deter or kill disease-causing organisms, potential predators or competitors.

Oddly enough, it's among the plant chemicals that are generally poisonous to mammals, that so many of our medicines are found. Examples of such drugs in common use today include morphine and digitalis. These are both secondary metabolites, and still isolated from plant sources.

There are three major categories of secondary metabolite:

1. alkaloids;
2. phenols; and
3. terpenoids.

Alkaloids

Alkaloids are an important group of plant chemicals, of which nearly 10 000 have now been isolated. Many are extremely poisonous to humans but a number, like morphine, atropine and cocaine, are widely used in medicine. One alkaloid that is a powerful insecticide is nicotine.

Phenols

Phenols include the tannins, which are large molecules produced by almost all plants. Their ecological role is not fully understood, but some tannic acids interfere with the digestive processes of insects, and it's possible that they also inhibit microbial growth. Their astringent taste is repellent to insects and higher animals alike.

Terpenoids

Terpenoids are the largest class of secondary metabolites: over 22 000 have been described. They include compounds called steroids, which, like alkaloids, are particularly useful in medicine. Steroids are complex compounds that all have the same basic structure. Slight structural modification leads to different compounds with different properties, such as male and female sex hormones.

Resins and latexes are also mixtures of terpenoids and other complex substances, and they too have a protective function in the plants that produce them. The resin in the hemp plant helps protect its vulnerable parts from drying out in hot weather.

Latexes are fluids, which many plant anatomists believe are the by-products of chemical reactions in the plant. Latexes are secreted into special cells to stop them interfering with normal cell functions, but they may well deter predators too. Perhaps the best known plant latex is natural rubber from Hevea brasiliensis.

Probably the most familiar terpenoids are the essential oils, many of which are responsible for the distinctive tastes and smells of plants (like those used in perfumery or as herbs and spices). Examples are pinene, limonene and camphene. Unlike 'vegetable oils', which are mostly extracted from seeds and which are usually food sources for the germinating embryo, essential oils are found in any or all parts of the plant. Because they diffuse readily into the air, they are sometimes called volatile oils.

While many essential oils found in flowers are there to attract the animals or insects that will pollinate them, those found in leaves are there to stop insects eating them, and to prevent infestation by micro-organisms.

Rosemary oil, which we extracted on Capraia, is a mixture of complex chemicals. Although a number of other essential oils are better suited as insect repellents (notably geraniol produced by Pelargonium species), we could not find them on Capraia, so we chose rosemary (Rosmarinus officinalis) which has some insecticidal properties. Many essential oils are useful in medicine because of their important antiseptic, antibacterial, antibiotic or other properties.

How to Extract Compounds from the Plant

With such a large number of different plant compounds, it's not surprising that a variety of methods has to be used to extract them. The most appropriate method depends, among other things, on the part of the plant to be processed and the nature of the compound to be extracted. There are two methods:

1. Steam Distillation
2. Solvent Extraction

Steam Distillation

Essential oils are generally extracted by steam distillation, which involves passing steam through the plant material. As this happens, the essential oils vaporise and are carried away in the steam. As the vapour cools, it condenses and separates into water with a layer of the essential oil on top. This was the method we used to extract the rosemary oil on Capraia.

Solvent Extraction

Solvent extraction, the process we used to extract the antiseptic oil from myrtle (*Myrtus communis*) is used industrially to produce not essential oils, but highly concentrated perfume materials known as absolutes. In this process, the plant material is immersed in a solvent such as alcohol or petroleum ether until the essence is dissolved in the solvent. The solvent is then evaporated off to give the absolute.

3
PLANT SECONDARY METABOLITES

Secondary metabolites are molecules that are not necessary for the growth and reproduction of a plant, but may serve some role in herbivore deterrence due to astringency or they may act as phytoalexins, killing bacteria that the plant recognizes as a threat. Secondary compounds are often involved in key interactions between plants and their abiotic and biotic environments that influence them. Throughout history secondary metabolites of plants have been utilized by humanity. There are approximately 4 major classes of secondary compounds that are significant to humans. The classes are the alkaloids, phenylpropaniods, flavonoids, and the terpenoids.

The first stage in forming a secondary metabolite involves the formation of a branch-point enzyme, which directs a certain amount of the primary metabolism into secondary metabolism. The biosynthesis of alkaloids derived from different amino acids require different branch-point enzymes, and in opiate biosynthesis, the branch-point enzyme is tyrosine/dopa decarboxylase (TYDC), which converts L-tyrosine into tyramine, and also converts dopa

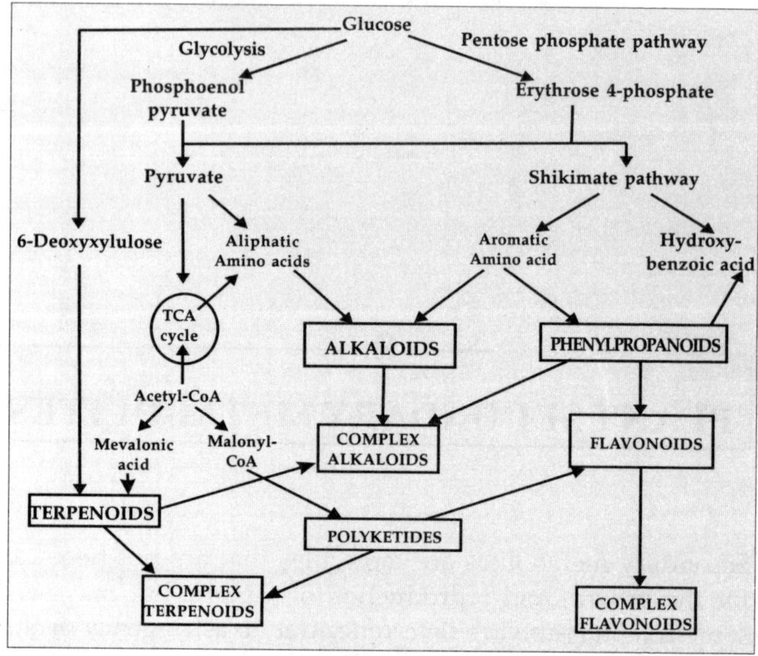

Fig. 3.1

into dopamine, which is required for the synthesis of the first committed intermediate in opiate biosynthesis; (S)-norcoclaurine, and is shown in this figure.

In secondary metabolism, many key steps require a molecule to become oxidized. The reactions that occur to oxidize compounds are commonly catalyzed by dioxygenases, which are haem-containing enzymes which utilize oxygen and a-ketoglutarate in oxidation reactions, and release CO_2 and succinate. Another common step of secondary metabolite biosynthesis is the methylation of potentially reactive carboxylic acid, amino, and hydroxyl groups that can spontaneously interact and form products that are undesireable to the plant. The universal methylating agent, S-adenosyl-L-methionine, or SAM, has been recognized to be active in seondary metabolism, and it is likely to be only one of many methyltransferases involved in methylating reactive groups in secondary metabolism.

Morphine, an alkaloid synthesized by the opium poppy has been recognized to most likely deter herbivores from feeding on the plant by causing a physiological change in the organism that is detrimental to the organism's survival. Codeine, also synthesized by the opium poppy may have a similar effect, causing the herbivore to have a lessened sensation of pain, which may in turn cause it to injure itself without realizing it, and at the same time, the nature of analgesic compounds would cause the herbivore to become drowsy, increasing its susceptibility to predators. As previously mentioned, sanguinarine most likely has a phytoalexin role, killing harmful bacteria, and may also have a fungitoxin role. Sanguinarine has been found to inhibit choline acetyltransferase activity, intercalate DNA, inhibit DNA synthesis, and it has also been found to inhibit reverse transcriptase activity. The DNA intercalation activity of sanguinarine would most likely cause it to be a fairly potent compound that would deter fungi and bacteria. The inhibition of reverse transcriptase activity would most likely effect retroviruses that utilize plants as hosts. It has been suggested that sanguinarine may also inhibit herbivore activity as well, however most herbivores feed on the foliage and do not feed on the roots. Unless sanguinarine is synthesized in other areas of the plant and subsequently translocated to the roots, the effect of sanguinarine on herbivores is most likely negligible.

Secondary metabolites, while valuable to humans, are often very difficult to isolate in large quantities. Biotechnology has not been very efficient in enabling scientists to upregulate the biosynthesis of many of the valuable secondary metabolites, and, as a result, some of the products of secondary metabolism can be very expensive to acquire, because they are available in such low amounts. The opium poppy, however, allows for relatively easy isolation of opiates and their derivatives, through mature laticifers, and they are an annual herbaceous plant, so a greater number of plants can be grown than in some of the woody species that are utilized for their secondary metabolites. Since the opium poppy has been cultivated for centuries, it has been bred to produce a large amount of opiates compared to the parent plant that P. somniferum arose from.

Biosynthesis of Opiate Alkaloids in P. somniferum

The alkaloid compounds synthesized by opium poppy can take a number of different forms, and follows different pathways as shown in this figure. TDC represents the enzyme L-tryptophan decarboxylase, which converts L-tryptophan into tryptamine, which combines with secologanin to form the first intermediate in secondary metabolism utilizing trp as a nitrogen source, strictosidine. Concurrently, L-tyrosine/dopa decarboxylase (TYDC) catalyzes reactions which leads to the synthesis of the first tyr intermediate in the tyr-derived alkaloid biosynthesis pathway.

Alkaloid biosynthesis can occur in a number of different methods . Within the monoterpenoid indole alkaloids further modifications are possible to modify alkaloids or to synthesize other secondary metabolites. Utilizing tyr as a source of nitrogen, it is possible to synthesize benzylisoquinoline alkaloids, which contain benzene rings and are shown in the figure, can undergo further modifications to form morphine and codeine, which are also benzylisoquinoline alkaloids. Tyramine can also combine with coumarin derivatives to give rise to cell wall-bound amides. (S)-nococlaurine is recognized as the common precursor for alkaloids, with over 2500 known benzylisoquinoline compounds being derived from it The versatiliy of alkaloid biosynthesis is one of the reasons that a diverse number of secondary metabolites exist. Alkaloid biosynthesis incorporates a number of different secondary metabolites to form many of the compounds that are found in the opium poppy and in other plants. The opium poppy utilizes unique biosynthetic pathways that enable it to produce compounds such as sanguinarine, morphine, and codeine, and is shown in fig. 3.2.

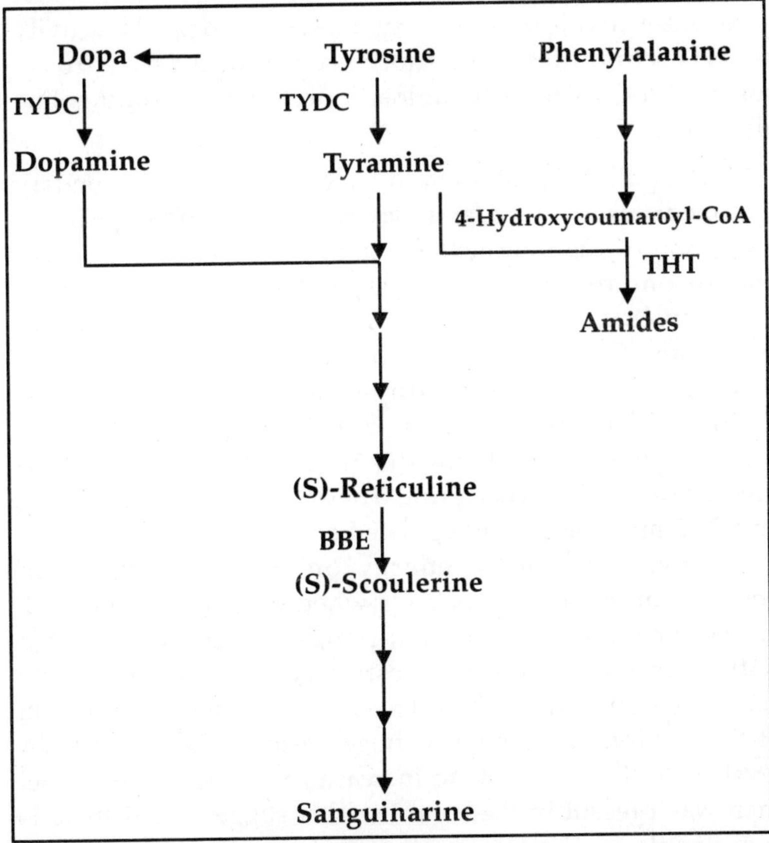

Fig. 3.2

BBE represents the berberine bridge enzyme, which is responsible for converting the last common intermediate (S)-reticuline into (S)-scoulerine in the morphine and sanguinarine biosynthetic pathways (adapted from Facchini,

1998). The synthesis of (S)-scoulerine represents the first committed step in sanguinarine biosynthesis. Since the conversion of (S)-reticuline to (S)-scoulerine is not a reversible reaction, BBE must have a regulatory function to moderate the resources that the opium poppy will use for sanguinarine biosynthesis. THT represents tyramine hydroxycinnamoyl transferase, and is utilized to synthesize amides. The activity of THT combines a phenolic compound, 4-hydroxy-coumaroyl-CoA with tyramine, a proto-benzylisoquinoline alkaloid to form amides.

The pathways all seem to have a primary to secondary intermediates involved, and may be rate-limiting steps in the formation of the intermediate compound between primary and secondary metabolite. All of the opiates and their derivatives are alkaloids derived from the amino acid tryrosine. The biosynthesis of dopamine from L-dopa, through the action of dopa decarboxylase and 4-hydroxyphenylacetylaldehyde are also important steps, as they are needed to form the first committed alkaloid intermediate (S)-norcoclaurine. The activity of TYDC, DODC, and BBE must be highly regulated so the opium poppy does not expend too much energy on the biosynthesis of benzylisoquinoline compounds when they are not needed. A study conducted on opium poppy cell cultures elicited with Botrytis ssp. mycelia responded with sanguinarine accumulation between five to ten hours after the addition of the elicitor. The fungal pathogen also caused the mRNA levels of BBE and TYDC to increase to a much higher level than was present in the controls. This suggests that there is a molecule in the fungus that induces the synthesis of sanguinarine. The BBE and TYDC induction pathways have not yet been elucidated, however, mycorrhizal fungi most likely do not cause an upregulation of BBE and TYDC gene transcription, so there must be a compound that is only present in pathogenic fungi that causes the induction.

The Structure and Regulation of Opiate Metabolite Genes

The biosynthesis of opiates and its derivatives are controlled by a number of genes required to synthesize intermediate compounds. Possibly the most important genes in the pathway, and the ones that may be the most highly regulated are the genes that code for enzymes that catalyze non reversible reactions. The genes in the opiate biosynthesis pathway that have been studied the most are the TYDC gene family and the BBE encoding gene. Tyrosine/dopa decarboxylase represents the entry point to benzy-lisoquinoline biosynthesis, and the BBE represents a key branch-point that occurs in the biosynthesis of sanguinarine.

Studies conducted on the TYDC genes of *P. somniferum* led to the discovery of 5 genes that code for the TYDC enzyme.

MORPHINE

Morphine (INN) is a highly potent opiate analgesic drug, is the principal active agent in opium, and is considered to be the prototypical opioid. Morphine was in 1803 the first alkaloid isolated from a plant source[citation needed]. Like other opioids, e.g. oxycodone, hydromorphone, and diacetylmorphine (heroin), morphine acts directly on the central nervous system (CNS) to relieve pain, particularly at the synapses of the nucleus accumbens. Morphine has a high potential for addiction; tolerance and both physical and psychological dependence develop rapidly.

History

Morphine was first isolated, which was the first active principle chemically isolated from any plant, in the autumn of 1803 in Paderborn, Germany by the German pharmacist Friedrich Wilhelm Adam Sertürner, who named it morphium after Morpheus, the Greek god of dreams. But it was not until the development of the hypodermic needle in 1853 that its use spread It was used for pain relief, and as a "cure" for opium and alcohol addiction. Later it was found out that morphine was even more addictive than either alcohol or opium, and its extensive use during the American Civil War allegedly resulted in over 400,000 sufferers from the "soldier's disease" of morphine addiction This idea has been a subject of controversy, as there have been suggestions that such a disease was in fact a hoax.

Diacetylmorphine (better known as heroin) was synthesized from morphine in 1874 and brought to market by Bayer in 1898. Heroin is approximately 1.5–2 times more potent than morphine on a milligram-for-milligram basis. Using a variety of subjective and objective measures, one study estimated the relative potency of heroin to morphine administered intravenously to post-addicts to be 1.80-2.66 mg of morphine sulfate to 1 mg of diamorphine hydrochloride (heroin).

Morphine became controlled substances in the U.S. under the Harrison Narcotics Tax Act of 1914, and possession without a prescription in the U.S. is a criminal offense.

The structural formula of morphine was determined by 1925. At least three methods of total synthesis of morphine from starting materials such as coal tar and petroleum distillates have been patented, the first of which was announced in 1952, by Dr. Marshall D. Gates, Jr at the University of Rochester. Still, the vast majority of morphine is derived from the opium poppy by either the traditional method of gathering latex from the scored unripe pods of the poppy, or processes using poppy straw, the dried pods and stems of the plant, the most widespread of which was invented in Hungary in 1925 and announced in 1930 by chemist János Kábay.

Morphine was the most commonly abused narcotic analgesic in the world up until heroin was synthesized and came into use. Until the synthesis of dihydromorphine (c.a.

1900), the dihydromorphinone class of opioids (1920s), and oxycodone (1916) and similar drugs, there generally were no other drugs in the same efficacy range as opium, morphine and heroin, with synthetics still several years away (pethidine was invented in Germany in 1937) and opioid agonists amongst the semi-synthetics were analogues and derivatives of codeine such as dihydrocodeine (Paracodin), ethylmorphine (Dionine), and benzylmorphine (Peronine). Even today, morphine is the most sought after prescription narcotic by heroin addicts when heroin is scarce, all other things being equal; local conditions and user preference may cause hydromorphone, oxymorphone, high-dose oxycodone, or methadone as well as dextromoramide in specific instances such as 1970s Australia, to top that particular list. The stop-gap drugs used by the largest absolute number of heroin addicts is probably codeine, with significant use also of dihydrocodeine, poppy straw derivatives like poppy pod and poppy seed tea, propoxyphene, and tramadol

Morphine can be used:

- as an analgesic in hospital settings to relieve;
- pain in myocardial infarction;
- pain in sickle cell crisis;
- pain associated with surgical conditions, pre- and postoperatively;
- pain associated with trauma;
- in the relief of severe chronic pain, e.g., cancer;
- pain from kidney stones (renal colic, ureterolithiasis) severe back pain;
- as an adjunct to general anesthesia;
- in epidural anesthesia or intrathecal analgesia;
- for palliative care (i.e., to alleviate pain without curing the underlying reason for it, usually because the latter is found impossible);

- as an antitussive for severe cough;
- in nebulized form, for treatment of dyspnea, although the evidence for efficacy is slim Evidence is better for other routes;
- as an anti-diarrheal in chronic conditions (e.g., for diarrhea associated with AIDS, although loperamide (a non-absorbed opioid acting only on the gut) is the most commonly used opioid for diarrhea).

Constipation

Like loperamide and other opioids, morphine acts on the myenteric plexus in the intestinal tract, reducing gut motility, causing constipation. The gastrointestinal effects of morphine are mediated primarily by μ-opioid receptors in the bowel. By inhibiting gastric emptying and reducing propulsive peristalsis of the intestine, morphine decreases the rate of intestinal transit. Reduction in gut secretion and increases in intestinal fluid absorption also contribute to the constipating effect. Opioids also may act on the gut indirectly through tonic gut spasms after inhibition of nitric oxide generation. This effect was shown in animals when a nitric oxide precursor reversed morphine-induced changes in gut motility.

Addiction

Morphine is a potentially highly addictive substance, as it can cause psychological dependence and physical dependence as well as tolerance, with an addiction potential identical to that of heroin. When used illicitly, a very serious narcotic habit can develop in a matter of weeks whereas iatrogenic morphine addiction rates have, according to a number of studies, remained nearly constant at one case in 150 to 200 for at least two centuries. In the presence of pain and the other disorders for which morphine is indicated for use, a combination of psychological and physiological factors tend to prevent true addiction from developing, although physical dependence and tolerance will develop with protracted opioid therapy, and these two factors do not add up to addiction without psychological dependence which manifests primarily as a morbid seek orientation for the drug.

In controlled studies comparing the physiological and subjective effects of injected heroin and morphine in individuals formerly addicted to opiates, subjects showed no preference for one drug over the other. Equipotent, injected doses had comparable action courses, with no difference in subjects' self-rated feelings of euphoria, ambition, nervousness, relaxation, drowsiness, or sleepiness Short-term addiction studies by the same researchers demonstrated that tolerance developed at a similar rate to both heroin and morphine. When compared to the opioids hydromorphone, fentanyl, oxycodone, and pethidine/meperidine, former addicts showed a strong preference for heroin and morphine, suggesting that heroin and morphine are particularly susceptible to abuse and addiction. Morphine and heroin were also much more likely to produce euphoria and other positive subjective effects when compared to these other opioids.

Other studies such as the Rat Park experiments suggest that morphine is less physically addictive than others suggest, and most studies on morphine addiction merely show that "severely distressed animals, like severely distressed people, will relieve their distress pharmacologically if they can." In these studies rats with a morphine "addiction" overcome their addiction themselves when placed in decent living environments with enough space, good food, companionship, areas for exercise, areas for privacy. More recent research has shown that an enriched environment may decrease morphine addiction in mice.

Withdrawal Symptoms

The withdrawal symptoms associated with morphine addiction are usually experienced shortly before the time of the next scheduled dose, sometimes within as early as a few hours (usually between 6–12 hours) after the last administration. Early symptoms include watery eyes, insomnia, diarrhea, runny nose, yawning, dysphoria, and sweating and in some cases a strong drug craving. Severe headache, restlessness, irritability, loss of appetite, body aches, severe abdominal pain, nausea and vomiting, tremors, and even stronger and more intense drug craving appear as the syndrome progresses. Severe depression and vomiting are very common. The heart rate and blood pressure are elevated and can lead to a heart attack, blood clot or stroke Chills or cold flashes with goose bumps ("cold turkey") alternating with flushing (hot flashes), kicking movements of the legs ("kicking the habit" and excessive sweating are also characteristic symptoms. Severe pains in the bones and muscles of the back and extremities occur, as do muscle spasms. At any point during this process, a suitable narcotic can be administered that will dramatically reverse the withdrawal symptoms. Major withdrawal symptoms peak between 48 and 96 hours after the last dose and subside after about 8 to 12 days. Sudden withdrawal by heavily dependent users who are in poor health is very rarely fatal. Morphine withdrawal is considered less dangerous than alcohol, barbiturate, or benzodiazepine withdrawal.

The psychological dependence associated with morphine addiction is complex and protracted. Long after the physical need for morphine has passed, the addict will usually continue to think and talk about the use of morphine (or other drugs) and feel strange or overwhelmed coping with daily activities without being under the influence of morphine. Psychological withdrawal from morphine is a very long and painful process. Addicts often suffer severe depression, anxiety, insomnia, mood swings, amnesia (forgetfulness), low self-esteem, confusion, paranoia, and other psychological disorders. The psychological dependence on morphine can, and usually does, last a lifetime. There is a high probability that relapse will occur after morphine withdrawal when neither the physical environment nor the behavioral motivators that contributed to the abuse have been altered. Testimony to morphine's addictive and reinforcing nature is its relapse rate. Abusers of morphine (and heroin), have one of the highest relapse rates among all drug users.

Hepatitis C and Morphine Withdrawal

Researchers at the University of Pennsylvania have demonstrated that morphine withdrawal complicates hepatitis C by suppressing IFN-alpha-mediated immunity and enhancing virus replication. Hepatitis C virus (HCV) is common among intravenous drug users. This high association has piqued interest in determining the effects of drug abuse, specifically morphine and heroin, on progression of the disease. The discovery of such an association would impact treatment of both HCV infection and drug abuse.

Contraindications

The following conditions are relative contraindications for morphine:

- acute respiratory depression
- renal failure (due to accumulation of the metabolite morphine-6-glucuronide)
- chemical toxicity (potentially lethal in low tolerance subjects)
- raised intracranial pressure, including head injury (exacerbation due pCO_2 increases from respiratory depression)

Older literature, based upon studies of animals with acute pancreatitis, claimed that morphine caused significant spasm of the sphincter of Oddi and could therefore worsen the pain of the disease.

Pharmacology

Morphine is the prototype narcotic drug and is the standard against which all other opioids are tested. It interacts predominantly with the μ-opioid receptor. These μ-binding sites are discretely distributed in the human brain, with high densities in the posterior amygdala, hypothalamus, thalamus, nucleus caudatus, putamen, and certain cortical areas. They are also found on the terminal axons of primary afferents within laminae I and II (substantia gelatinosa) of the spinal cord and in the spinal nucleus of the trigeminal nerve.

Morphine is a phenanthrene opioid receptor agonist – its main effect is binding to and activating the μ-opioid receptors in the central nervous system. In clinical settings, morphine exerts its principal pharmacological effect on the central nervous system and gastrointestinal tract. Its primary actions of therapeutic value are analgesia and sedation. Activation of the μ-opioid receptors is associated with analgesia, sedation, euphoria, physical dependence, and respiratory depression. Morphine is a rapid-acting narcotic, and it is known to bind very strongly to the μ-opioid receptors, and for this reason, it often has a higher incidence of euphoria/dysphoria, respiratory depression, sedation, pruritus, tolerance, and physical and psychological dependence when compared to other opioids at equianalgesic doses.

The effects of morphine can be countered with opioid antagonists such as naloxone and naltrexone; the development of tolerance to morphine may be inhibited by NMDA antagonists such as ketamine or dextromethorphan The rotation of morphine with chemically dissimilar opioids in the long-term treatment of pain will slow down the growth of tolerance in the longer run, particularly agents known to have significantly incomplete cross-tolerance with morphine such as levorphanol, ketobemidone, piritramide, and methadone and its derivatives; all of these drugs also have NMDA antagonist properties. It is believed that the strong opioid with the most incomplete cross-tolerance with morphine is either methadone or dextromoramide.

Gene Expression

Studies have shown that morphine can alter the expression of a number of genes. A single injection of morphine has been shown to alter the expression of two major groups of genes, for proteins involved in mitochondrial respiration and for cytoskeleton-related proteins.

Effects on the Immune System

Morphine has long been known to act on receptors expressed on cells of the central nervous system resulting in pain relief and analgesia. In the 1970s and '80s, evidence suggesting that opiate drug addicts show increased risk of infection (such as increased pneumonia, tuberculosis, and HIV) led scientists to believe that morphine may also affect the immune system. This possibility increased interest in the effect of chronic morphine use on the immune system.

The first step of determining that morphine may affect the immune system was to establish that the opiate receptors known to be expressed on cells of the central nervous system are also expressed on cells of the immune system. One study successfully showed that dendritic cells, part of the innate immune system, display opiate receptors. Dendritic cells are responsible for producing cytokines, which are the tools for communication in the immune system. This same study showed that dendritic cells chronically treated with morphine during their differentiation produce more interleukin-12 (IL-12), a cytokine responsible for promoting the proliferation, growth, and differentiation of T-cells (another cell of the adaptive immune system) and less interleukin-10 (IL-10), a cytokine responsible for promoting a B-cell immune response (B cells produce antibodies to fight off infection).

This regulation of cytokines appear to occur via the p38 MAPKs (mitogen activated protein kinase) dependent pathway. Usually, the p38 within the dendritic cell expresses TLR 4 (toll-like receptor 4), which is activated through the ligand LPS (lipopolysaccharide). This causes the p38 MAPK to be phosphorylated. This phosphorylation activates the p38 MAPK to begin producing IL-10 and IL-12. When the dendritic cell is chronically exposed to morphine during their differentiation process then treated with LPS, the production of cytokines is different. Once treated with morphine, the p38 MAPK does not produce IL-10, instead favoring production of IL-12. The exact mechanism through which the production of one cytokine is increased in favor over another is not known. Most likely, the morphine causes increased phosphorylation of the p38 MAPK. Transcriptional level interactions between IL-10 and IL-12 may further increase the production of IL-12 once IL-10 is not being produced. Future research may target the exact mechanism that increases the production of IL-12 in morphine treated dendritic cells. This increased production of IL-12 causes increased T-cell immune response. This response is due to the ability of IL-12 to cause T helper cells to differentiate into the Th1 cell, causing a T cell immune response.

Pharmacokinetics

Morphine is primarily metabolized into morphine-3-glucuronide (M3G) and morphine-6-glucuronide (M6G via glucuronidation by phase II metabolism enzyme UDP-glucuronosyl transferase-2B7 (UGT2B7). The cytochrome P450 (CYP) family of enzymes involved in phase I metabolism plays a lesser role. Not only does the metabolism occur in the liver but it may also take place in the brain and the kidneys. M6G has been found to be a far more potent analgesic than morphine when dosed to rodents, but crosses the blood-brain barrier with difficulty. M6G has been shown to be relatively more selective for mu-receptors than for delta- and kappa-receptors, whereas M3G does not appear to compete for opioid receptor binding. The significance of M6G formation on the observed effect of a dose of morphine is the subject of extensive debate among pharmacologists.

Chemistry

Most of the licit morphine produced is used to make codeine by methylation. It is also a precursor for many drugs including heroin (diacetylmorphine), hydromorphone, and oxymorphone. Replacement of the N-methyl group of morphine with an N-phenylethyl group results in a product that is 18 times more powerful than morphine in its opiate agonist potency. Combining this modification with the replacement of the 6-hydroxyl with a 6-methylene produces a compound some 1,443 times more potent than morphine, stronger than the Bentley compounds such as etorphine.

The structure-activity relationship of morphine has been extensively studied. As a result, more than 100 morphine derivatives (also counting codeine and related drugs) have been developed since the last quarter of the 19th Century. These drugs range from 25 per cent the strength of codeine or a little over 2 per cent of the strength of morphine, to several hundred times the strength of morphine to several powerful opioid antagoinsts including naloxone (Narcan®), naltrexone (Trexan®), and nalorphine (Nalline®) for human use and also the amongst strongest antagonists known, such as diprenorphine (M5050), the reversing agent in the Immobilon® large animal tranquilliser dart kit; the tranquilliser is another ultra-potent morphine derivative/ structural analogue, viz., etorphine (M99). Morphine-derived agonist-antagonist drugs have also been developed.

Most semi-synthetic opioids, both of the morphine and codeine subgroups, are created by modifying one or more of the following:

- Saturating, opening, or other changes to the bond betwixt positions 7 and 8 on the morphine carbon skeleton, as well as adding, removing, or modifying functional groups to these positions; saturating, reducing, eliminating, or otherwise modifying the 7-8 bond and attaching a functional group at 14 yields hydromorphinol; the oxidation of the hydroxyl group to a carbonyl and changing the 7-8 bond to single from double changes codeine into oxycodone.

- Attachment, removal or modification of functional groups to positions 3 and/or 6 (dihydrocodeine and related, hydrocodone, nicomorphine); in the case of moving the methyl functional group from position 3 to 6, codeine becomes heterocodeine which is 72 times stronger, and therefore six times stronger than morphine.
- Attachment of functional groups or other modification at position 14 (oxymorphone, oxycodone, naloxone).

Modifications at positions 2, 4, 5 or 17, usually along with other changes to the molecule elsewhere on the morphine skeleton.

Both morphine and its hydrated form, $C_{17}H_{19}NO_3H_2O$, are sparingly soluble in water. In five liters of water, only one gram of the hydrate will dissolve. For this reason, pharmaceutical companies produce sulfate and hydrochloride salts of the drug, both of which are over 300 times more water-soluble than their parent molecule. Whereas the pH of a saturated morphine hydrate solution is 8.5, the salts are acidic. Since they derive from a strong acid but weak base, they are both at about pH = 5; as a consequence, the morphine salts are mixed with small amounts of NaOH to make them suitable for injection.

A number of salts of morphine are used, and the opioids Morphine-N-Oxide (Genomorphine) which is a pharmaceutical which is no longer in common use; and Pseudomorphine, an alkaloid which exists in opium, form as degradation products of morphine.

Production

A Hungarian chemist, János Kabay, found and internationally patented a method to extract morphine from "poppy straw": dried poppy pods and stem, and other parts of the dry plant, except for seeds and root. In natural form, in poppy plant, the alkaloids are bound to meconic acid. The method is to extract from the crushed plant with diluted sulfuric acid, which is a stronger acid than meconic acid, but not so strong to react with alkaloid molecules. The extraction is performed in many steps (one amount of crushed plant is at least six to ten times extracted, so practically every alkaloid goes into the solution). From the solution obtained at the last extraction step, the alkaloids are precipitated by either ammonium hydroxide or sodium carbonate. The last step is purifying and separating morphine from other opium alkaloids (opium poppy contains at least 15–20 different alkaloids, but most of them are of very low concentration). In the 1950s and 1960s, Hungary supplied nearly 60% of Europe's total medication-purpose morphine production. To this day, poppy farming is legal in Hungary, but poppy farms are limited by law to 2 acres (8,100 m2). It is also legal to sell dried poppy in flower shops for use in floral arrangements.

It was announced in 1973 that a team at the National Institutes of Health in the United States had developed a method for total synthesis of morphine, codeine, and thebaine using coal tar as a starting material. A shortage in codeine-hydrocodone class cough suppressants (all of which can be made from morphine in one or more steps, as well as from codeine or thebaine) was the initial reason for the research.

The UN Office On Drugs & Crime Bulletin On Narcotics, issue II of 1952, describes the process which led to the final determination of the structural formula of morphine in 1925 and the invention of two methods of total synthesis of morphine.

Most morphine produced for pharmaceutical use around the world is actually converted into codeine as the concentration of the latter in both raw opium and poppy straw is much lower than that of morphine; in most countries the usage of codeine (both as end-product and precursor) is at least an order of magnitude greater than that of morphine on a weight basis and codeine is by far the most commonly-used opioid in the world. Whilst strains of poppies have been engineered to produce much higher yields of the other useful opioid pharmaceutical precursors thebaine and oripavine, no known strain of P. somniferum will produce more codeine than morphine under most or all possible conditions.

Illicit Use

The euphoria, comprehensive alleviation of distress and therefore all aspects of suffering, promotion of sociability and empathy, "body high", and anxiolysis provided by narcotic drugs including the opioids can cause the use of high doses in the absence of pain for a protracted period, which can impart a morbid craving for the drug in the user. Being the prototype of the entire opioid class of drugs means that morphine has properties that may lend it to misuse. Morphine addiction is the model upon which the current perception of addiction is based.

Animal and human studies and clinical experience back up the contention that morphine is one of the most euphoric of drugs, and via all but the IV route heroin and morphine cannot be distinguished according to studies. More significant chemical changes or the synthesis of totally new drugs yield other powerful euphorigenics such as hydromorphone (Dilaudid®, Hydal®) and oxymorphone (Numorphan®, Opana®) as well as the methylated equivalents hydrocodone and oxycodone respectively, dextromoramide (Palfium®), and piritramide (Dipidolor®), and other members of the 3,6 morphine diester category like nicomorphine.

Misuse of morphine generally entails taking more than prescribed or outside of medical supevision, injecting oral formulations, mixing it with unapproved potentiators such as alcohol, cocaine, and the like, and/or defeating the extended-release mechanism by chewing the tablets or turning into a powder for snorting or preparing injectables. The latter method can be every bit as time-consuming and involved as traditional methods of smoking opium. This and the fact that the liver destroys a large percentage of the drug on the first pass impacts the demand side of the equation for clandestine re-sellers, as many customers are not needle users and may have been disappointed with ingesting the drug orally. As morphine is generally as hard or harder to divert than oxycodone in a lot of cases, morphine in any form is uncommon on the street, although ampoules and phials of morphine injection, pure pharmaceutical morphine powder, and soluble multi-purpose tablets are very popular where available.

Morphine is a precursor in the manufacture in a large number of opioids such as dihydromorphine, hydromorphone, nicomorphine, and heroin as well as codeine, which itself has a large family of semi-synthetic derivatives.Morphine is commonly treated with acetic anhydride and ignited to yield heroin. The pharmacology of heroin and morphine is identical except the two acetyl groups increase the lipid solubility of the heroin molecule, causing it to cross the blood-brain barrier and enter the brain more rapidly. Once in the brain, these acetyl groups are removed to yield morphine, which causes the subjective effects of heroin. Thus, heroin may be thought of as a more rapidly acting form of morphine.

Precursor to other Opioids, Underground and Illicit

Illicit morphine is often produced from codeine found in over the counter cough and pain medicines. This demythlation reaction is often performed using Pyridine and hydrochloric acid.

Another source of illicit morphine comes from the extraction of morphine from extended release morphine products, such as MS-Contin. Morphine can be extracted from these products with simple extraction techniques to yield a morphine solution that can be injected Alternatively, the tablets can be crushed and snorted, injected or swallowed, although this provides much less euphoria although retaining some of the extended-release effect and the extended-release property is why MS-Contin is used in some countries alongside methadone, dihydrocodeine, buprenorphine, dihydroetorphine, piritramide, levo-alpha-acetylmethadol (LAAM) and special 24-hour formulations of hydromorphone for maintenance and detoxification of those physically dependent on opioids.

Another means of using or misusing morphine is to use chemical reactions to turn it into heroin or another stronger opioid. Morphine can, using a technique common in New Zealand (where the initial precursor is codeine) and elsewhere known as home-bake, be turned into what is usually a mixture of morphine, heroin, 3-monoacetyl-morphine, 6-monoacetylmorphine, and codeine derivatives like acetylcodeine if the process is using morphine made from demethylating codeine by mixing acetic anhydride with the morphine and cooking it in an oven between 80 and 85□C for several hours. Since heroin is one of a series of 3,6 diesters of morphine, it is possible to convert morphine to nicomorphine (Vilan®) using nicotinic anhydride, dipropanoylmorphine with propionic anhydride. Acetic acid can be used to obtain a mixture high in 3-mono-acetylmorphine, nicotinic acid (Vitamin B_3) in some form would be precursor to 3-nicotinylmorphine, and so on.

The clandestine conversion of morphine to ketones of the hydromorphone class or other derivatives like dihydromorphine (Paramorfan®), desomorphine (Permonid®), metopon &c. and codeine to hydrocodone (Dicodid®), dihydrocodeine (Paracodin®) &c. is more involved, time consuming, requires lab equipment of various types, and usually requires expensive catalysts and large amounts of morphine at the outset and is less common but still has been discovered by authorities in various ways during the last 20 years or so. Dihydromorphine can be acetylated into another 3,6 morphine diester, namely diacetyldihydromorphine (Paralaudin), and hydrocodone into thebacon.

Legal Classification

- In the United Kingdom, morphine is listed as a Class A drug under the Misuse of Drugs Act 1971 and a Schedule 2 Controlled Drug under The Misuse of Drugs Regulations 2001.
- In the United States, morphine is classified as a Schedule II drug under the Controlled Substances Act.
- In Canada, morphine is classified as a Schedule I drug under the Controlled Drugs and Substances Act.
- In Australia, morphine is classified as a Schedule 8 drug under the variously titled State and Territory Poisons Acts.
- In the Netherlands, morphine is classified as a List 1 drug under the Opium Law.
- Internationally, morphine is a Schedule I drug under the Single Convention on Narcotic Drugs.

Access to Morphine in Poor Countries

Although morphine is cheap, people in poorer countries often do not have access to it. According to a 2005 estimate by the International Narcotics Control Board, six countries (Australia, Britain, Canada, France, Germany, and the United States) consume 79 percent of the world's morphine. The less affluent countries, accounting for 80 percent of the world's population, consumed only about 6 percent of the global morphine supply. Some countries import virtually no morphine, and in others the drug is rarely available even for relieving severe pain while dying. Experts in pain management attribute the under-distribution of morphine to an unwarranted fear of the drug's potential for addiction and abuse. While morphine is clearly addictive, western doctors believe it is worthwhile to use the drug and then wean the patient off when the treatment is over.

4

PLANT HORMONE

Plant hormones (also known as phytohormones) are chemicals that regulate plant growth. Plant hormones are signal molecules produced within the plant, and occur in extremely low concentrations. Hormones regulate cellular processes in targeted cells locally and when moved to other locations, in other locations of the plant. Plants, unlike animals, lack glands that produce and secrete hormones. Plant hormones shape the plant, affecting seed growth, time of flowering, the sex of flowers, senescence of leaves and fruits. They affect which tissues grow upward and which grow downward, leaf formation and stem growth, fruit development and ripening, plant longevity and even plant death. Hormones are vital to plant growth and lacking them, plants would be mostly a mass of undifferentiated cells.

Characteristics

The word hormone is derived from Greek and means 'set in motion.' Plant hormones affect gene expression and transcription levels, cellular division and growth. They are naturally produced within plants, though very similar chemicals are produced by fungi and bacteria that can also effect plant growth A large number of related chemical compounds are synthesized by humans, they are used to regulate the growth of cultivated plants, weeds, and in vitro grown plants and plant cells; these man made compounds are called *Plant Growth Regulators* or PGRs for short. Early in the study of plant hormones, "phytohormone" was the commonly-used term, but its use is less widely applied now.

Plant hormones are not nutrients, but chemicals that in small amounts promote and influence the growth development, and differentiation of cells and tissues. The biosynthesis of plant hormones within plant tissues is often diffuse and not always localized. Plants lack glands to produce and store hormones, because, unlike animals, which have two circulatory systems (lymphatic and cardiovascular) powered by a heart that moves fluids around the body, plants use more passive means to move chemicals around the plant. Plants utilize simple chemicals as hormones, which move more easily through the plant's tissues. They are often produced and used on a local basis within the plant body, plant cells even produce hormones that affect different regions of the cell producing the hormone.

Hormones are transported within the plant by utilizing four types of movements. For localized movement, cytoplasmic streaming within cells and slow diffusion of ions and molecules between cells are utilized. Vascular tissues are used to move hormones from one part of the plant to another; these include sieve tubes that move sugars from the leaves to the roots and flowers, and xylem that moves water and mineral solutes from the roots to the foliage.

Not all plant cells respond to hormones, but those cells that do, are programmed to respond at specific points in their growth cycle. The greatest effects occur at specific stages during the cell's life, with diminished effects occurring before or after this period. Plants need hormones at very specific times during plant growth and at specific locations. They also need to disengage the effects that hormones have when they are no longer needed. The production of hormones occurs very often at sites of active growth within the meristems, before cells have fully differentiated. After production they are sometimes moved to other parts of the plant where they cause an immediate effect or they can be stored in cells to be released later. Plants use different pathways to regulate internal hormone quantities and moderate their effects; they can regulate the amount of chemicals used to biosynthesize hormones. They can store them in cells, inactivate them, or cannibalise already-formed hormones by conjugating them with carbohydrates, amino acids or peptides. Plants can also break down hormones chemically, effectively destroying them. Plants also move hormones around the plant diluting their concentrations.

The concentration of hormones required for plant responses are very low (10-6 to 10-5 mol/L). Because of these low concentrations it has been very difficult to study plant hormones and only since the late 1970s have scientists been able to start piecing together their effects and relationships to plant physiology. Much of the early work on plant hormones involved studying plants that were genetically deficient in one or involved the use of tissue cultured plants grown *in vitro* that were subjected to differing ratios of hormones and the resultant growth compared. The earliest scientific observation and study dates to the 1880s; the determination and observation of plant hormones and their identification was spread-out over the next 70 years.

Classes of Plant Hormones

It is generally accepted that there are five major classes of plant hormones, some of which are made up of many different chemicals that can vary in structure from one plant to the next. The chemicals are each grouped together into one of these classes based on their structural similarities and on their effects on plant physiology. Other plant hormones and growth regulators are not easily grouped into these classes, they exist naturally or are synthesized by humans or other organisms, including chemicals that inhibit plant growth or interrupt the physiological processes within plants. Each class has positive as well as inhibitory functions, and most often work in tandem with each other, with varying ratios of one or more interplaying to affect growth regulation.

Abscisic Acid

Abscisic acid also called ABA, was discovered and researched under two different names before its chemical properties were fully known, it was called dormin and abscicin II. Once it was determined that the two latter named compounds were the same, it was named abscisic acid. The name "abscisic acid" was given because it was found in high concentrations in newly-abscissed or freshly-fallen leaves.

This class of PGR is composed of one chemical compound normally produced in the leaves of plants, originating from chloroplasts, especially when plants are under stress. In general, it acts as an inhibitory chemical compound that affects bud growth, seed and bud dormancy. It mediates changes within the apical meristem causing bud dormancy and the alteration of the last set of leaves into protective bud covers. Since it was found in freshly-adscissed leaves, it was thought to play a role in the processes of natural leaf drop but further research has disproven this. In plant species from temperate parts of the world it plays a role in leaf and seed dormancy by inhibiting growth, but, as it is dissipated from seeds or buds, growth begins. In other plants, as ABA levels decrease, growth then commences as gibberellin levels increase. Without ABA, buds and seeds would start to grow during warm periods in winter and be killed when it froze again. Since ABA dissipates slowly from the tissues and its effects take time to be offset by other plant hormones, there is a delay in physiological pathways that provide some protection from premature growth. It accumulates within seeds during fruit maturation, preventing seed germination within the fruit, or seed germination before winter. Abscisic acid's effects are degraded within plant tissues during cold temperatures or by its removal by water washing in out of the tissues, releasing the seeds and buds from dormancy.

In plants under water stress ABA plays a role in closing the stomata. Soon after plants are water stressed and the roots are deficient in water, a signal moves up to the leaves causing the formation of ABA precursors there which then move to the roots. The roots then release ABA which is translocated to the foliage through the vascular system and modulates the potassium and sodium uptake within the guard cells, which then lose turgidity, closing the stomata. ABA exists in all parts of the plant and its concentration within any tissue seems to mediate its effects and function as a hormone, its degradation or more properly catabolism within the plant affects metabolic reactions and cellular growth and production of other hormones. Plants start life as a seed with high ABA levels, just before the seed germinates ABA levels decrease; during germination and early growth of the seedling, ABA levels decrease even more. As plants begin to produce shoots with fully functional leaves - ABA levels begin to increase, slowing down cellular growth in more "mature" areas of the plant. Stress from water or predation effects ABA production and catabolism rates which mediate another cascade of effects triggering specific responses from targeted cells. Scientists are still piecing together the complex interactions and effects of this and other phytohormones.

Cytokinins

Cytokinins or CKs are a group of chemicals that influence cell division and shoot formation. They were called kinins in the past when the first cytokinins were isolated from yeast cells. They also help delay senescence or the aging of tissues, are responsible for mediating auxin transport throughout the plant, and affect internodal length and leaf growth. They have a highly-synergistic effect in concert with auxins and the ratios of these two groups of plant hormones affect most major growth periods during a plant's lifetime. Cytokinins counter the apical dominance induced by auxins; they in conjunction with ethylene promote abscission of leaves, flower parts and fruits.

Gibberellins

Gibberellin A1Gibberellins or GAs include a large range of chemicals that are produced naturally within plants and by fungi. They were first discovered when Japanese researchers noticed a chemical produced by a fungus called Gibberella fujikuroi that produced abnormal growth in rice plants. Gibberellins play a major role in seed germination, affecting enzyme production that mobilizes food production that new cells need for growth. This is done by modulating chromosomal transcription. In seedlings a layer of cells called the aleurone layer wraps around the endosperm tissue: During seed germination, the seedling produces GA that is transported to the aleurone layer, which responds by producing enzymes that break down stored food reserves within the endosperm, which are utilized by the growing seedling. GAs produce bolting of rosette-forming plants, increasing internodal length. They promote flowering, cellular division, and in seeds growth after germination. Gibberellins also reverse the inhibition of shoot growth and dormancy induced by ABA.

Other Known Hormones

- **Brassinolides** - plant steroids that are chemically similar to animal steroid hormones. First isolated from pollen of the mustard family and extensively studied in Arabidopsis. They promote cell elongation and cell division, differentiation of xylem tissues, and inhibit leaf abscission. Plants that are deficient in brassinolides suffer from dwarfism.

- **Salicylic acid** - activates genes in some plants that produce chemicals that aid in the defense against pathogenic invaders.
- **Jasmonates** - are produced from fatty acids and seem to promote the production of defense proteins that are used to fend off invading organisms. They are believed to also have a role in seed germination, and affect the storage of protein in seeds, and seem to affect root growth.
- **Plant peptide hormones** - encompass all small secreted peptides that are involved in cell-to-cell signaling. These small peptide hormones play crucial roles in plant growth and development, including defense mechanisms, the control of cell division and expansion, and pollen self-incompatibility.
- **Polyamines** - are strongly basic molecules with low molecular weight that have been found in all organisms studied thus far. They are essential for plant growth and development and affect the process of mitosis and meiosis.
- **Nitric oxide (NO)** - serves as signal in hormonal and defense responses.
- Strigolactones, implicated in the inhibition of shoot branching.

Potential Medical Applications

Plant stress hormones activate cellular responses, including cell death, to diverse stress situations in plants. Researchers have found that some plant stress hormones share the ability to adversely affect human cancer cells For example, sodium salicylate has been found to suppress proliferation of lymphoblastic leukemia, prostate, breast, and melanoma human cancer cells. Jasmonic acid, a plant stress hormone that belongs to the jasmonate family, induced death in lymphoblastic leukemia cells. Methyl jasmonate has been found to induce cell death in a number of cancer cell lines.

Hormones and Plant Propagation

Synthetic plant hormones or PGRs are commonly used in a number of different techniques involving plant propagation from cuttings, grafting, micropropagation, and tissue culture.

The propagation of plants by cuttings of fully-developed leaves, stems, or roots is performed by gardeners utilizing auxin as a rooting compound applied to the cut surface; the auxins are taken into the plant and promote root initiation. In grafting, auxin promotes callus tissue formation, which joins the surfaces of the graft together. In micropropagation, different PGRs are used to promote multiplication and then rooting of new plantlets. In the tissue-culturing of plant cells, PGRs are used to produce callus growth, multiplication, and rooting.

Seed Dormancy

Plant hormones affect seed germination and dormancy by affecting different parts of the seed.

Embryo dormancy is characterized by a high ABA/GA ratio, whereas the seed has a high ABA sensitivity and low GA sensitivity. To release the seed from this type of dormancy and initiate seed germination, an alteration in hormone biosynthesis and degradation towards a low ABA/GA ratio, along with a decrease in ABA sensitivity and an increase in GA sensitivity needs to occur.

ABA controls embryo dormancy, and GA embryo germination. Seed coat dormancy involves the mechanical restriction of the seed coat, this along with a low embryo growth potential, effectively produces seed dormancy. GA releases this dormancy by increasing the embryo growth potential, and/or weakening the seed coat so the radical of the seedling can break through the seed coat. Different types of seed coats can be made up of living or dead cells and both types can be influenced by hormones; those composed of living cells are acted upon after seed formation while the sead coats composed of dead cells can be influenced by hormones during the formation of the seed coat. ABA affects testa or seed coat growth characteristics, including thickness, and effects the GA-mediated embryo growth potential. These conditions and effects occur during the formation of the seed, often in response to environmental conditions. Hormones also mediate endosperm dormancy: Endosperm in most seeds is composed of living tissue that can actively respond to hormones generated by the embryo. The endosperm often acts as a barrier to seed germination, playing a part in seed coat dormancy or in the germination process. Living cells respond to and also affect the ABA/GA ratio, and mediate cellular sensitivity; GA thus increases the embryo growth potential and can promote endosperm weakening. GA also affects both ABA-independent and ABA-inhibiting processes within the endosperm.

AUXIN

Auxins are a class of plant growth substance (often called phytohormone or plant hormone). Auxins play an essential role in coordination of many growth and behavioral processes in the plant life cycle, they and the behavior they played in plant growth was first revealed by a Dutch scientist named Fritz Went.

Overview

Auxins derive their name from the Greek word "auxano" means "I grow increase". They were the first of the major plant hormones to be discovered and are a major coordinating signal in plant development. Their pattern of active transport through the plant is complex. They typically act in concert with (or opposition to) other plant hormones.

For example, the ratio of auxin to cytokinin in certain plant tissues determines initiation of root versus shoot buds. Thus a plant can (as a whole) react on external conditions and adjust to them, without requiring a nervous system. On a molecular level, auxins have an aromatic ring and a carboxylic acid group.

The most important member of the auxin family is indole-3-acetic acid (IAA). It generates the majority of auxin effects in intact plants, and is the most potent native auxin. However, molecules of IAA are chemically labile in aqueous solution, so IAA is not used commercially as a plant growth regulator.

- Naturally-occurring auxins include 4-chloro-indoleacetic acid, phenylacetic acid (PAA) and indole-3-butyric acid (IBA).
- Synthetic auxin analogs include 1-naphthaleneacetic acid (NAA), 2,4-dichlorophenoxyacetic acid (2,4-D), and others.

Auxins are often used to promote initiation of adventitious roots and are the active ingredient of the commercial preparations used in horticulture to root stem cuttings. They can also be used to promote uniform flowering, to promote fruit set, and to prevent premature fruit drop.

Used in high doses, auxin stimulates the production of ethylene. Excess ethylene can inhibit elongation growth, cause leaves to fall (leaf abscission), and even kill the plant. Some synthetic auxins such as 2, 4-D and 2, 4, 5-trichlorophenoxyacetic acid (2, 4, 5-T) have been used as herbicides. Broad-leaf plants (dicots) such as dandelions are much more susceptible to auxins than narrow-leaf plants (monocots) like grass and cereal crops. These synthetic auxins were the active agents in Agent Orange, a defoliant used extensively by American forces in the Vietnam War.

Hormonal Activity

Auxins coordinate development at all levels in plants, from the cellular level to organs and ultimately the whole plant.

Molecular Mechanisms

Auxins directly stimulate or inhibit the expression of specific genes. Auxin induces transcription by targeting for degradation members of the Aux/IAA family of transcriptional repressor proteins, The degradation of the Aux/IAAs leads to the derepression of Auxin Respose Factors (ARF) - mediated transcription. Aux/IAAs are targeted for degradation by ubiquitination, catalysed by an SCF-type ubiquitin-protein ligase.

In 2005, it was demonstrated that the F-box protein TIR1, which is part of the ubiquitin ligase complex SCFTIR1, is an auxin receptor. Upon binding of auxin, TIR1 recruits specific transcriptional repressors (the Aux/IAA repressors) for ubiquitination by the SCF complex. This marking process leads to the degradation of the repressors by the proteasome, alleviating repression and leading to expression of specific genes in response to auxins.

Another protein called ABP1 (Auxin Binding Protein 1) is a putative receptor, but its role is unclear. Electrophysiological experiments with protoplasts and anti-ABP1 antibodies suggest that ABP1 may have a function at the plasma membrane.

On a Cellular Level

On the cellular level, auxin is essential for cell growth, affecting both cell division and cellular expansion. Depending on the specific tissue, auxin may promote axial elongation (as in shoots), lateral expansion (as in root swelling), or isodiametric expansion (as in fruit growth). In some cases (coleoptile growth) auxin-promoted cellular expansion occurs in the absence of cell division. In other cases, auxin-promoted cell division and cell expansion may be closely sequenced within the same tissue (root initiation, fruit growth). In a living plant it appears that auxins and other plant hormones nearly always interact to determine patterns of plant development.

According to the acid growth hypothesis for auxin action, auxins may directly stimulate the early phases of cell elongation by causing responsive cells to actively transport hydrogen ions out of the cell, thus lowering the pH around cells. This acidification of the cell wall region activates wall-loosening proteins known as expansins, which allow slippage of cellulose microfibrils in the cell wall, making the cell wall less rigid. When the cell wall is loosened by the action of auxins, this now-less-rigid wall is expanded by cell turgor pressure, which presses against the cell wall.

However, the acid growth hypothesis does not by itself account for the increased synthesis and transport of cell wall precursors and secretory activity in the Golgi system that accompany and sustain auxin-promoted cell expansion.

Organ Patterns

Growth and division of plant cells together result in growth of tissue, and specific tissue growth contributes to the development of plant organs. Growth of cells contributes to the plant's size, but uneven localized growth produces bending, turning and directionalization of organs- for example, stems turning toward light sources (phototropism), roots growing in response to gravity (gravitropism), and other tropisms.

Organization of the Plant

As auxins contribute to organ shaping, they are also fundamentally required for proper development of the plant itself. Without hormonal regulation and organization, plants would be merely proliferating heaps of similar cells. Auxin employment begins in the embryo of the plant, where directional distribution of auxin ushers in subsequent growth and development of primary growth poles, then forms buds of future organs. Throughout the plant's life, auxin helps the plant maintain the polarity of growth and recognize where it has its branches (or any organ) connected.

An important principle of plant organization based upon auxin distribution is apical dominance, which means that the auxin produced by the apical bud (or growing tip) diffuses downwards and inhibits the development of ulterior lateral bud growth, which would otherwise compete with the apical tip for light and nutrients. Removing the apical tip and its suppressive hormone allows the lower dormant lateral buds to develop, and the buds between the leaf stalk and stem produce new shoots which compete to become the lead growth. This behavior is used in pruning by horticulturists.

Uneven distribution of auxin: To cause growth in the required domains, it is necessary that auxins be active preferentially in them. Auxins are not synthesized everywhere, but each cell retains the potential ability to do so, and only under specific conditions will auxin synthesis be activated. For that purpose, not only do auxins have to be translocated toward those sites where they are needed but there has to be an established mechanism to detect those sites. Translocation is driven throughout the plant body primarily from peaks of shoots to peaks of roots. For long distances, relocation occurs via the stream of fluid in phloem vessels, but, for short-distance transport, a unique system of coordinated polar transport directly from cell to cell is exploited. This process of polar auxin transport is directional and very strictly regulated. It is based in uneven distribution of auxin efflux carriers on the plasma membrane, which send auxins in the proper direction.

A 2006 study showed plant-specific pin-formed (PIN) proteins are vital in transporting auxin. PINs also regulate auxin efflux from mammalian and yeast cells

Locations

- In shoot (and root) meristematic tissue
- In young leaves
- In mature leaves in very tiny amounts
- In mature root cells in even smaller amounts
- Transported throughout the plant more prominently downward from the shoot apices.

Effects

The plant hormone stimulates cell elongation. It stimulates the Wall Loosening Factors, for example, elastins, to loosen the cell walls. If gibberellins are also present, the effect is stronger. It also stimulates cell division if cytokinins are present. When auxin and cytokinin are applied to callus, rooting can be generated if the auxin concentration is higher than cytokinin concentration while xylem tissues can be generated when the auxin concentration is equal to the cytokinins.

It participates in phototropism, geotropism, hydrotropism and other developmental changes. The uneven distribution of auxin, due to environmental cues (for example, unidirectional light and gravity force), results in uneven plant tissue growth.

It also induces sugar and mineral accumulation at the site of application.

Wounding Response

It induces formation and organization of phloem and xylem. When the plant is wounded, the auxin may induce the Cell differentiation and regeneration of the vascular tissues.

Root Growth and Development

Auxin induces new root formation by breaking root apical dominance induced by cytokinins. In horticulture, auxins, especially NAA and IBA, are commonly applied to stimulate root growth when taking cuttings of plants. However, high concentrations of auxin inhibit root elongation and instead enhance adventitious root formation. Removal of the root tip can lead to inhibition of secondary root formation.

Apical Dominance

It induces shoot apical dominance; the axillary buds are inhibited by auxin. When the apex of the plant is removed, the inhibitory effect is removed and the growth of lateral buds is enhanced as a high concentration of auxin directly stimulates ethylene synthesis in lateral buds causes inhibition of its growth and potentiation of apical dominance.

Ethylene Biosynthesis

In low concentrations, auxin can inhibit ethylene formation and transport of precursor in plants; however, high concentrations of flowering.

Auxin plays a minor role in the initiation of flowering. It can delay the senescence of flowers in low concentrations.

Herbicide Manufacture

The defoliant Agent Orange was a mix of 2, 4-D and 2, 4, 5-T. The compound 2, 4-D is still in use and is thought to be safe, but 2, 4, 5-T was more or less banned by the EPA in 1979. The dioxin TCDD is an unavoidable contaminant produced in the manufacture of 2, 4, 5-T. As a result of the integral dioxin contamination, 2, 4, 5-T has been implicated in leukaemia, miscarriages birth defects, liver damage, and other diseases. Agent Orange was sprayed in Vietnam as a defoliant to deny ground cover to the Vietnamese army.

Ethylene

Ethylene (or IUPAC name ethene) is the chemical compound wit the formula C_2H4. It is the simplest alkene.

Because it contains a carbon-carbon double bond, ethylene is called an unsaturated hydrocarbon or an olefin. It is extremely important in industry and also has a role in biology as a hormone Ethylene is the most produced organic compound in the world; global production of ethylene exceeded 75 million metric tonnes per year in 2005 To meet the ever increasing demand for ethylene, sharp increases in production facilities have been added globally, particularly in the Gulf countries.

Structure

This hydrocarbon has four hydrogen atoms bound to a pair of carbon atoms that are connected by a double bond. All six atoms that comprise ethylene are coplanar. The H-C-H angle is 117°, close to the 120° for ideal sp^2 hybridized carbon. The molecule is also relatively rigid: rotation about the C-C bond is a high energy process that requires breaking the p-bond, while retaining the s-bond between the carbon atoms.

The double bond is a region of high electron density, and most reactions occur at this double bond position.

History

From 1795 on, ethylene was referred to as the olefiant gas (oil-making gas), because it combined with chlorine to produce the oil of the Dutch (1, 2-dichloroethane). Ethylene was first synthesized in 1795 by a collaboration of four Dutch chemists.

In the mid-19th century, the suffix -ene (an Ancient Greek root added to the end of female names meaning "daughter of") was widely used to refer to a molecule or part thereof that contained one fewer hydrogen atoms than the molecule being modified. Thus, ethylene (C_2H_4) was the "daughter of ethyl" (C_2H_5). The name ethylene was used in this sense as early as 1852.

In 1866, the German chemist August Wilhelm von Hofmann proposed a system of hydrocarbon nomenclature in which the suffixes -ane, -ene, -ine, -one, and -une were used to denote the hydrocarbons with 0, 2, 4, 6, and 8 fewer hydrogens than their parent alkane. In this system, ethylene became ethene. Hofmann's system eventually became the basis for the Geneva nomenclature approved by the International Congress of Chemists in 1892, which remains at the core of the IUPAC nomenclature. However, by that time, the name ethylene was deeply entrenched, and it remains in wide use today, especially in the chemical industry.

Nomenclature

The 1979 IUPAC nomenclature rules made an exception for retaining the non-systematic name ethylene however, this decision was reversed in the 1993 rules so the correct name is now ethene.

Uses

• Approximately 80% of ethylene used in the United States and Europe is used to create ethylene oxide, ethylene dichloride, and polyethylene. In smaller quantities, ethylene is used as an anesthetic agent (in an 85% ethylene/15% oxygen ratio), to hasten fruit ripening, as well as a welding gas.

- Polyethylenes of various density and melt flow account for more than 50% of world ethylene demand. The primary use of polyethylene is in film applications for packaging, carrier bags and trash liners. Other applications include injection moulding, pipe extrusion, wire and cable sheathing and insulation, as well as extrusion coating of paper and cardboard.
- Ethylene derivatives include: ethylene oxide, styrene monomer (via ethyl benzene) and linear higher olefins.
- Ethylene oxide is a key raw material in the production of surfactants and detergents. It is also used to

manufacture ethylene glycols, which are in turn used in packaging and textiles, and to make glycol ether solvents.

- Styrene monomer is used principally in polystyrene for packaging and insulation, as well as in styrene butadiene rubber for tires and footwear.
- Linear higher olefins are used as base materials for the manufacture of detergents, plasticisers, synthetic lubricants and additives, but also as co-monomers in the production of polyethylenes.
- Ethylene is a key component in Levinstein sulfur mustard, a chemical weapon agent.

Production

Ethylene is produced in the petrochemical industry by steam cracking. In this process, gaseous or light liquid hydrocarbons are heated to 750-950 °C, inducing numerous free radical reactions followed by immediate quench to freeze the reactions. This process converts large hydrocarbons into smaller ones and introduces unsaturation. Ethylene is separated from the resulting complex mixture by repeated compression and distillation. In a related process used in oil refineries, high molecular weight hydrocarbons are cracked over zeolite catalysts. Heavier feedstocks, such as naphtha and gas oils require at least two "quench towers" downstream of the cracking furnaces to recirculate pyrolysis-derived gasoline and process water. When cracking a mixture of ethane and propane, only one water quench tower is required.

The areas of an ethylene plant are:

- steam cracking furnaces;
- primary and secondary heat recovery with quench;
- a dilution steam recycle system between the furnaces and the quench system;

- primary compression of the cracked gas (3 stages of compression);
- hydrogen sulfide and carbon dioxide removal (acid gas removal);
- secondary compression (1 or 2 stages);
- drying of the cracked gas;
- cryogenic treatment.

All of the cold cracked gas stream goes to the demethanizer tower. The overhead stream from the demethanizer tower consists of all the hydrogen and methane that was in the cracked gas stream. Different methods of cryogenically treating this overhead stream results in the separation of the hydrogen and the methane. This usually involves liquid methane at a temperature around -250 ºF (-156.7 ºC). Complete recovery of all the methane is critical to the economical operation of an ethylene plant. Often one or two Turboexpanders are used for Methane recovery from the demethanizer overhead stream.

The bottom stream from the demethanizer tower goes to the deethanizer tower. The overhead stream from the deethanizer tower consists of all the C_2,'s that were in the cracked gas stream. The C_2's then go to a C_2 splitter. The product ethylene is taken from the overhead of the tower and the ethane coming from the bottom of the splitter is recycled to the furnaces to be cracked again.

The bottom stream from the deethanizer tower goes to the depropanizer tower. The overhead stream from the depropanizer tower consists of all the C3's that were in the cracked gas stream. Prior to sending the C3's to the C3 splitter this stream is hydrogenated in order to react out the methylacetylene and propadiene. Then this stream is sent to the C3 splitter. The overhead stream from the C3 splitter is product propylene and the bottom stream from the C3 splitter is propane which can be sent back to the furnaces for cracking or used as fuel.

The bottom stream from the depropanizer tower is fed to the debutanizer tower. The overhead stream from the debutanizer is all of the C4's that was in the cracked gas stream. The bottom stream from the debutanizer consists of everything in the cracked gas stream that is C5 or heavier. This could be called a light pyrolysis gasoline.

Since the production of ethylene is energy intensive, much effort has been dedicated recovering heat from the gas leaving the furnaces. Most of the energy recovered from the cracked gas is used to make high pressure (1200 psig) steam. This steam is in turn used to drive the turbines for compressing cracked gas, the propylene refrigeration compressor, and the ethylene refrigeration compressor. An ethylene plant, once running, does not need to import any steam to drive its steam turbines. A typical world scale ethylene plant (about 1.5 billion pounds of ethylene per year) uses a 45,000 horsepower (34,000 kW) cracked gas compressor, a 30,000 horsepower (22,000 kW) propylene compressor, and a 15,000 horsepower (11,000 kW) ethylene compressor.

When starting an ethylene plant it is important to start the cooling systems in the proper order. The cooling systems consist of Cooling Tower Water (CTW); propylene refrigeration with four or five different levels or stages. Each level corresponds to a particular pressure and temperature; and three or four stages of ethylene regfrigeration. The CTW must be started first because the propylene system needs it to condense propylene and the ethylene refrigeration systems needs it to desuperheat high pressure ethylene. The propylene system must start next because the ethylene system needs high pressure propylene for desuperheating the high pressure ethylene stage and the low pressure propylene stage for condensing the high pressure ethylene. While the ethylene plant is running, the plant can continue to run for a time if the ethylene refrigeration compressor shuts down. However, if the propylene compressor shuts down the whole plant must be shut down immediately.

Manufacturers

World largest ethylene complex is located in Iran. The complex will produce over 1,320 million metric tons of ethylene a year, it could also produce 306,000 tons of propylene, 600,000 tons of a variety of linear light and heavy polyethylene, 300,000 tons of polypropylene, 443,000 tons of ethylene glycol, and 245,000 tons of different 4C compounds annually.

Laboratory Preparation

Ethylene can be conveniently produced in the laboratory by distilling absolute ethanol with an excess of concentrated sulfuric acid and washing the distillate vapor stream in an aqueous solution of sodium hydroxide to remove the sulfur dioxide contaminant.

Peculiarity of Spectrum

Although ethylene is a relatively simple molecule, its spectrum is considered to be one of the most difficult to explain adequately from both a theoretical and practical perspective. For this reason, it is often used as a test case in computational chemistry. Of particular note is the difficulty in characterizing the ultraviolet absorption of the molecule. Interest in the subtleties and details of the ethylene spectrum can be dated back to at least the 1950s.

Chemical Reactions

Ethylene is an extremely important building block in the petrochemical industry. It can undergo many types of reactions which leads to a plethora of major chemical products. A list of some major types of reactions includes:

1. Polymerization;
2. Oxidation;
3. Halogenation and Hydrohalogenation;
4. Alkylation;
5. Hydration;

6. Oligomerization;
7. Oxo-reaction; and
8. a ripening agent for fruits and vegetables.

Additions to Double Bond

Like most alkenes, ethylene reacts with halogens to produce halogenated hydrocarbons1, 2-C_2H_4X2. It can also react with water to produce ethanol, but the rate at which this happens is very slow unless a suitable catalyst, such as phosphoric or sulfuric acid, is used. Under high pressure, and, in the presence of a catalytic metal (platinum, rhodium, nickel), hydrogen will react with ethylene to form ethane.

Ethylene is used primarily as an intermediate in the manufacture of other chemicals in the synthesis of monomers. Ethylene can be chlorinated to produce 1, 2-dichloroethane (ethylene dichloride). This can be converted to vinyl chloride, the monomer precursor to plastic polyvinyl chloride, or combined with benzene to produce ethylbenzene, which is used in the manufacture of polystyrene, another important plastic.

Ethylene is more reactive than alkanes because of two reasons:

1. It has a double bond, one called the p-bond(pi) and one called the s-bond (sigma), where the p-bond is weak and the s-bond is strong. The presence of the p-bond makes it a high energy molecule. Thus bromine water decolourises readily when it is added to ethylene.
2. High electron density at the double bond makes it react readily. It is broken in an addition reaction to produce many useful products.

Polymerization

Ethylene polymerizes to produce polyethylene, also called polyethene or polythene, the world's most widely-used plastic.

Major polyethylene product groups are low density polyethylene, high density polyethylene, polyethylene copolymers, as well as ethylene-propylene co- & terpolymers.

Oxidation

Ethylene is oxidized to produce ethylene oxide, which is hydrolysed to ethylene glycol. It is also a precursor to vinyl acetate.

Ethylene undergoes oxidation by palladium to give acetaldehyde. This conversion was at one time a major industrial process. The process proceeds via the initial complexation of ethylene to a Pd(II) center.

Major intermediates of the oxidation of Ethylene are ethylene oxide, acetaldehyde, vinyl acetate and ethylene glycol. The list of products made from these intermediates is long. Some of them are: polyesters, polyurethane, morpholine, ethanolamines, aspirin and glycol ethers

Halogenation and Hydrohalogenation

Major intermediates from the halogenation and hydrohalogenation of ethylene include: ethylene dichloride, ethyl chloride and ethylene dibromide. Some products in this group are: polyvinyl chloride, trichloroethylene, perchloroethylene, methyl chloroform, polyvinylidiene chloride and copolymers, and ethyl bromide.

Alkylation

Major chemical intermediates from the alkylation of ethylene include: ethylbenzene, ethyl toluene, ethyl anilines, 1, 4-hexadiene and aluminium alkyls. Products of these intermediates include polystyrene, unsaturated polyesters and ethylene-propylene terpolymers

Hydration

Ethanol is the primary intermediate of the hydration of ethylene. Important products from ethanol are:

- ethylamines;
- acetaldehyde; and
- ethyl acetate.

Oligomerization

The primary products of the Oligomerization of ethylene are alpha-olefins and linear primary.

Oxo-reaction

The Oxo-reaction of ethylene results in propionaldehyde with its primary products of propionic acid and n-propyl alcohol.

In the synthesis of fine chemicals.

Ethylene is useful in organic synthesis Representative reactions include Diels-Alder additions, ene reaction, and arene alkylation.

Miscellaneous

Ethylene is found in many lip gloss products.

Production of ethylene in mineral oil-filled transformers is a key indicator of severe localized overheating (>750 °C).

Ethylene as a Plant Hormone

Ethylene acts physiologically as a hormone in plant It exists as a gas and acts at trace levels throughout the life of the plant by stimulating or regulating the ripening of fruit, the opening of flowers, and the abscission (or shedding) of leaves. Its biosynthesis starts from methionine with 1-aminocyclopropane-1-carboxylic acid (ACC) as a key intermediate.

History of Ethylene in Plant Biology

Ethylene has been used in practice since the ancient Egyptians, who would gash figs in order to stimulate ripening (wounding stimulates ethylene production by plant tissues). The ancient Chinese would burn incense in closed rooms to enhance the ripening of pears. In 1864, it was discovered that gas leaks from street lights led to stunting of growth, twisting of plants, and abnormal thickening of stems. In 1901, a Russian scientist named Dimitry Neljubow showed that the active component was ethylene. Doubt discovered that ethylene stimulated abscission in 1917 It wasn't until 1934 that Gane reported that plants synthesize ethylene. In 1935, Crocker proposed that ethylene was the plant hormone responsible for fruit ripening as well as senescence of vegetative tissues.

Ethylene Biosynthesis in Plants

It has been shown that ethylene is produced from essentially all parts of higher plants, including leaves, stems, roots, flowers, fruits, tubers, and seedlings.

> "Ethylene production is regulated by a variety of developmental and environmental factors. During the life of the plant, ethylene production is induced during certain stages of growth such as germination, ripening of fruits, abscission of leaves, and senescence of flowers. Ethylene production can also be induced by a variety of external aspects such as mechanical wounding, environmental stresses, and certain chemicals including auxin and other regulators".

The biosynsthesis of the hormone starts with conversion of the amino acid methionine to S-adenosyl-L-methionine (SAM, also called Adomet) by the enzyme Met Adenosyltransferase. SAM is then converted to 1-aminocyclopropane-1-carboxylic-acid (ACC) by the enzyme ACC synthase (ACS); the activity of ACS is the rate-limiting step in ethylene production, therefore regulation of this enzyme is key for the ethylene biosynthesis. The final step requires oxygen and involves the action of the enzyme ACC-oxidase (ACO), formerly known as the Ethylene Forming Enzyme (EFE). Ethylene biosynthesis can be induced by endogenous or exogenous ethylene. ACC synthesis increases with high levels of auxins, specially Indole Acetic Acid (IAA), and cytokinins. ACC synthase is inhibited by abscisic acid.

Ethylene Perception in Plants

Ethylene could be perceived by a transmembrane protein dimer complex. The first gene encoding an ethylene receptor was first cloned from Arabidopsis thaliana by Caren Chang, Elliot Meyerowitz and colleagues at the California Institute of Technology and then in tomato by Jack Wilkinson, Harry Klee and colleagues at the Monsanto Company. Ethylene receptors are encoded by multiple genes in the Arabidopsis and tomato genomes. The gene family is comprised of five receptors in Arabidopsis and at least six in tomato, most of which have been shown to bind ethylene. DNA sequences for ethylene receptors have also been identified in many other plant species and an ethylene binding protein has even been identified in Cyanobacteria.

Environmental and Biological Triggers of Ethylene

Environmental cues can induce the biosynthesis of the plant hormone. Flooding, drought, chilling, wounding, and pathogen attack can induce ethylene formation in the plant.

In flooding, root suffers from lack of oxygen, or anoxia, which leads to the synthesis of 1-Aminocyclopropane-1-carboxylic acid (ACC). The ACC is transported upwards in the plant and then oxidized in leaves. The product, the ethylene causes epinasty of the leaves.

One speculation recently put forth for epinasty is the downard pointing leaves may act as pump handles in the wind. The ethylene may or may not additionally induce the growth of a valve in the xylem, but the idea would be that the plant would harness the power of the wind to pump out more water from the roots of the plants than would normally happen with transpiration.

Physiological Responses of Plants

Like the other plant hormones, ethylene is considered to have pleiotropic effects. This essentially means that it is thought that at least some of the effects of the hormone are unrelated. What is actually caused by the gas may depend on the tissue affected as well as environmental conditions. In the evolution of plants, ethylene would simply be a message that was coopted for unrelated uses by plants during different periods of the evolutionary development.

List of Plant Responses to Ethylene

- Seedling triple response, thickening and shortening of hypocotyl with pronounced apical hook. This is thought to be a seedling's reaction to an obstacle in the soil such a stone, allowing it to push past the obstruction.
- In pollination, when the pollen reaches the stigma, the precursor of the ethylene, ACC, is secreted to the petal, the ACC releases ethylene with ACC oxidase.
- Stimulates leaf and flower senescence.
- Stimulates senescence of mature xylem cells in preparation for plant use.
- Inhibits shoot growth except in some habitually flooded plants like rice.
- Induces leaf abscission.
- Induces seed germination.
- Induces root hair growth – increasing the efficiency of water and mineral absorption.
- Induces the growth of adventitious roots during flooding
- Stimulates epinasty – leaf petiole grows out, leaf hangs down and curls into itself.
- Stimulates fruit ripening.

- Induces a climacteric rise in respiration in some fruit which causes a release of additional ethylene. This can be the one bad apple in a barrel spoiling the rest phenomenon.
- Affects neighboring individuals.
- Disease/wounding resistance.
- Inhibits stem growth outside of seedling stage.
- Stimulates stem and cell broadening and lateral branch growth also outside of seedling stage.
- Synthesis is stimulated by auxin and maybe cytokinin as well.
- Ethylene levels are decreased by light.
- The flooding of roots stimulates the production of ACC which travels through the xylem to the stem and leaves where it is converted to the gas.
- Interference with auxin transport (with high auxin concentrations).
- Inhibits stomatal closing except in some water plants or habitually flooded ones such as some rice varieties, where the opposite occurs (conserving CO_2 and O_2).
- Where ethylene induces stomatal closing, it also induces stem elongation.
- Induces flowering in pineapples.

Commercial Issues

Ethylene shortens the shelf life of many fruits by hastening fruit ripening and floral senescence. Tomatoes, bananas and apples will ripen faster in the presence of ethylene. Bananas placed next to other fruits will produce enough ethylene to cause accelerated fruit ripening. Ethylene will shorten the shelf life of cut flowers and potted plants by accelerating floral senescence and floral abscission.

Flowers and plants which are subjected to stress during shipping, handling, or storage produce ethylene causing a significant reduction in floral display. Flowers affected by ethylene include carnation, geranium, petunia, rose, and many others.

Ethylene can cause significant economic losses for florists, markets, suppliers, and growers. Researchers have come up with several ways to inhibit ethylene, including inhibiting ethylene synthesis and inhibiting ethylene perception. Inhibiting ethylene synthesis is less effective for reducing post-harvest losses since ethylene from other sources can still have an effect. By inhibiting ethylene perception, fruits, plants and flowers don't respond to ethylene produced endogenously or from exogenous sources. Inhibitors of ethylene perception include compounds that have a similar shape to ethylene, but do not elicit the ethylene response. An example of an ethylene perception inhibitor is 1-methylcyclopropene (1-MCP).

Commercial growers of bromeliads, including pineapple plants, use ethylene to induce flowering. Plants can be induced to flower either by treatment with the gas in a chamber, or by placing a banana peel next to the plant in an enclosed area.

Effects Upon Humans

Depending on the concentration, ethylene gas can cause a pleasant odor, euphoria, nausea, hyperglycemia, a variety of psychological effects, blood pressure changes, hypoxia, loss of consciousness, or death.

Symptoms

Ethylene has a pleasant sweet faint odor, and has a slightly sweet taste, and as it enhances fruit ripening, assists in the development of odour-active aroma volatiles (especially esters), which are responsible for the specific smell of each kind of flower or fruit.

In mild doses, ethylene produces states of euphoria, associated with stimulus to the pleasure centers of the human brain.

Exposure at 37.5% for 15 minutes may result in marked memory disturbances. Humans exposed to as much as 50% ethylene in air, whereby the oxygen availability is decreased to 10%, experience a complete loss of consciousness and may subsequently die due to hypoxia.

Symptoms of ethylene exposure include the following:

- Mild exposure in air
- Percent of O_2 saturation at 90%
- Night vision decreased
- Mild euphoria reported
- Moderate exposure in air
- Percent of O_2 saturation at 82 to 90%
- Respiratory rate has compensatory increase
- Pulse, also a compensatory increase
- Night vision is decreased further, focus is simplified
- Performance ability is somewhat reduced, mild distortion to speech, utterances increasingly ambiguous.
- General alertness level is somewhat reduced to anything but central concerns.
- Symptoms may begin in those patients with pre-existing significant cardiac, pulmonary, or hematologic diseases.
- Euphoria.
- High concentration in air.
- Percent of O_2 saturation at 64 to 82%.
- Compensatory mechanisms increasingly become inadequate.
- Air hunger, gasping for breath.

- Fatigue, lassitude, inability to maintain balance.
- Tunnel vision, out-of-body experiences.
- Dizziness.
- Mild to persistent headache.
- Belligerence, certainty of truth.
- Extreme euphoria, belief in capacities of the self enhanced.
- Visual acuity is reduced, dreamlike seeing of visions.
- Numbness and tingling of extremities.
- Hyperventilation.
- Distortions of judgment, abnormal or illogical inferences drawn.
- Memory loss after event.
- Increased cyanosis.
- Decreased ability for escape from toxic environment.
- Very high concentration in air
- Percent of O_2 saturation at 60 to 70% or less.
- Further deterioration in judgment and coordination may occur in 3 to 5 minutes or less.
- Severe oxygen deprivation.
- Loss of consciousness results when the air contains about 11% of oxygen.
- Death occurs quickly when the oxygen content falls to 8% or less.
- Very high concentrations in oxygen.
- Prolonged inhalation of about 85% in oxygen is slightly toxic, resulting in a slow fall in blood pressure.
- At about 94% in oxygen, ethylene is acutely fatal.

Medical Use

Ethylene has long been in use as an inhalatory anaesthetic. When used as a surgical anaesthetic, it is always administered with oxygen with an increased risk of fire. In such cases, however, it acts as a simple, rapid anaesthetic having a quick recovery.

Historical Significance

Many geologists and scholars believe that the famous Greek Oracle at Delphi (the Pythia) went into her trance-like state as an effect of ethylene rising from ground faults.

Safety

There is no evidence to indicate that prolonged exposure to low concentrations of ethylene can result in chronic effects. Prolonged exposure to high concentrations may cause permanent effects because of oxygen deprivation. Prolonged inhalation of about 85% in oxygen (a relatively high concentration) is also slightly toxic, resulting in a slow fall in blood pressure. At about 94% in oxygen, ethylene is acutely fatal.

It shows little or no carcinogenic or mutagenic properties. Although there may be moderate hyperglycemia, post operative nausea - while higher than nitrous oxide - is less than in the use of cyclopropane. During the induction and early phases, blood pressure may rise a little, but this effect may be due to patient anxiety, as blood pressure quickly returns to normal. Cardiac arrythmias are infrequent and cardio-vascular effects are benign.

5

PHEROMONE

A pheromone is a chemical that triggers a natural behavioral response in another member of the same species. There are alarm pheromones, food trail pheromones, sex pheromones, and many others that affect behavior or physiology. Their use among insects has been particularly well documented. In addition, some vertebrates and plants communicate by using pheromones.

Background

The term "pheromone" was introduced by Peter Karlson and Martin Lüscher in 1959, based on the Greek word *pherein* (to transport) and *hormone* (to stimulate). They are also classified as ecto-hormones. These chemical messengers are transported outside of the body and result in a direct developmental effect on hormone levels or behavioral change. They proposed the term to describe chemical signals from conspecifics which elicit innate behaviours soon after Butenandt characterized the first such chemical, Bombykol (a chemically well-characterized pheromone released by the female silkworm to attract mates).

Types of Pheromones

Aggregation Pheromones

Aggregation pheromones function in defense against predators, mate selection, and overcoming host resistance by mass attack. A group of individuals at one location are referred as aggregation, whether consisting of one sex or both sexes. Male-produced sex attractant have been called aggregation pheromones, because they usually result in the arrival of both sexes at a calling site and increase in density of conspecifics surrounding of the pheromone source. Most sex pheromones produced by the females and small percentage of sex attractants are produced by males. Aggregation pheromones have been found in members of the Coleoptera, Hemiptera, Homoptera, Dictyoptera and Orthoptera. In the past decades, the importance of applying aggregation pheromones in the management of the boll weevil (*Anthonomus grandis*), stored product weevils (*Sitophilus zeamais*), *Sitophilus granarius*, *Sitophilus oryzae* and pea and bean weevil (*Sitona lineatus*) has been demonstrated. Aggregation pheromones are among the most ecologically selective pest suppression methods. They are not toxic and they are effective at very low concentrations.

Alarm Pheromones

Some species release a volatile substance when attacked by a predator that can trigger flight (in aphids) or aggression (in ants, bees, termites) in members of the same species. Pheromones also exist in plants: certain plants emit alarm pheromones when grazed upon, resulting in tannin production in neighboring plants. These tannins make the plants less appetizing for the herbivore.

Epideictic Pheromones

Epideictic pheromones are different from territory pheromones, when it comes to insects. Fabre observed and noted how "females who lay their eggs in these fruits deposit these mysterious substances in the vicinity of their clutch to signal to other females of the same species they should clutch elsewhere."

Releaser Pheromones

Releaser pheromones are powerful attractant molecules that some organisms may use to attract mates from a distance of two miles or more. This type of pheromone generally elicits a rapid response but is quickly degraded. In contrast, a primer pheromone has a slower onset and a longer duration. Ex. Rabbit (mothers) release mammary pheromones that trigger immediate nursing behavior by their babies.

Signal Pheromones

Signal pheromones cause short term changes; such as, the neurotransmitter release which activates a response. For instance, GnRH molecule functions as a neurotransmitter in rats to elicit lordosis, which is a behavioral effect.

Primer Pheromones

Primer pheromones trigger a change of developmental events (in which they differ from all the other pheromones, which trigger a change in behavior).

Territorial Pheromones

Laid down in the environment, territorial pheromones mark the boundaries of an organism's territory. In dogs, these hormones are present in the urine, which they deposit on landmarks serving to mark the perimeter of the claimed territory.

Trail Pheromones

Trail pheromones are common in social insects. For example, ants mark their paths with these pheromones, which are non-volatile hydrocarbons.

Certain ants y renewed because it evaporates quickly. When the supply begins to dwindle, the trail making ceases. In at least one species of ant, trails that no longer lead to food are also marked with a repellent pheromone.

Information Pheromones

Information pheromones are indicative of an animal's identity or territory. For example, dogs and cats deposit chemicals in and around their territory, which then serve as an indicator for other members of the species about the presence of the occupant in that territory.

Sex Pheromones

In animals, sex pheromones indicate the availability of the female for breeding. Male animals may also emit pheromones that convey information about their species and genotype. Many insect species release sex pheromones to attract a mate, and many lepidopterans (moths and butterflies) can detect a potential mate from as far away as 10 kilometers (6.25 mi). Traps containing pheromones are used by farmers to detect and monitor insect population in orchards (apple, pear, peach, walnut...). At the microscopic level, a gamete pheromone may provide a trail leading the opposite sex's gametes towards it to accomplish fertilization. Pheromones are also used in the detection of oestrus in sows. Boar pheromones are sprayed into the sty, and those sows which exhibit sexual arousal are known to be currently available for breeding. Sea urchins release pheromones into the surrounding water, sending a chemical message that triggers other urchins in the colony to eject their sex cells simultaneously.

Other Pheromones

This classification, based on the effects on behavior, remains artificial. Pheromones fill many additional functions.

- Nasonov pheromones (worker bees)
- Royal pheromones (bees)
- Calming (appeasement) pheromones (mammals).

Animals

Pheromones of the pest insect species, such as the Japanese beetle and the gypsy moth, can be used to induce many behaviors. As a result, the pheromones can be used to trap pests for monitoring purposes, to control the population by creating confusion, to disrupt mating, as well as to prevent further egg laying.

In mammals and reptiles, pheromones may be detected by the vomeronasal organ (VNO), or Jacobson's organ, which lies between the nose and mouth and is the first stage of the accessory olfactory system. Some pheromones in these animals are detected by regular olfactory membranes.

Humans

The best known case involves the reported synchronization of menstrual cycles among women based on unconscious odour cues (the McClintock effect, named after the primary investigator, Martha McClintock, of the University of Chicago). This study exposed a group of women to a whiff of perspiration from other women. It was found that it caused their menstrual cycles to speed up or slow down depending on the time in the month the sweat was collected; before, during, or after ovulation. Therefore, this study proposed that there are two types of pheromone involved: "One, produced prior to ovulation, shortens the ovarian cycle; and the second, produced just at ovulation, lengthens the cycle". However recent studies and reviews of the McClintock methodology have called into question the validity of her results.

Other studies have suggested that people might be using odor cues associated with the immune system to select mates who are not closely related to themselves. Using a brain imaging technique, Swedish researchers have shown that homosexual and heterosexual males' brains respond differently to two odours that may be involved in sexual arousal, and that the homosexual men respond in the same way as heterosexual women, though it could not be determined whether this was cause or effect. The study was expanded to include homosexual women; the results were consistent with previous findings meaning that homosexual women were not as responsive to male identified odours, while their response to female cues was similar to heterosexual males. According to the researchers, this research suggests a possible role for human pheromones in the biological basis of sexual orientation.

Another study demonstrated that the smell of androstadienone, a chemical component of male sweat, maintains higher levels of cortisol in females. The scientists suggest that the ability of this compound to influence the endocrine balance of the opposite sex makes it a human pheromonal chemosignal In 2002, a study published in the quarterly journal Physiology and Behavior showed an unnamed synthetic chemical in women's perfume appeared to increase intimate contact with men. The authors hypothesize, but do not demonstrate, that the observed behavioural differences are olfactory mediated.

In 2006, it was shown that a second mouse receptor sub-class is found in the olfactory epithelium. Called the trace amine-associated receptors (TAAR), some are activated by volatile amines found in mouse urine, including one putative mouse pheromone. Orthologous receptors exist in humans providing, the authors propose, evidence for a mechanism of human pheromone detection.

Some body spray advertisers claim that their products contain human sexual pheromones which act as an aphrodisiac. In the 1970's, "copulins" were patented as products which release human pheromones, based on research on rhesus monkeys. Subsequently, androstenone, axillary sweat, and "vomodors" have been claimed to act as human pheromones Despite these claims, no pheromonal substance has ever been demonstrated to directly influence human behavior in a peer reviewed study.

HONEYBEE PHEROMONES

Honey bee pheromones are mixtures of chemical substances released by individual bees into the hive or environment that cause changes in the physiology and behaviour of other bees.

Introduction

Honeybees have one of the most complex pheromonal communication systems found in nature, possessing 15 known glands that produce an array of compounds. Pheromones are produced as a liquid and transmitted by direct contact as a liquid or as a vapor. Pheromones may be volatile or non-volatile.

The pheromones are chemical messengers secreted by a queen, drone, worker bee or laying worker bee that elicit a response in other bees. The chemical messages are received by the bee's antenna and other body parts. Honey bee (Apis mellifera) pheromones can be grouped into releaser pheromones with short term effects and primer pheromones with long term effects.

Primer pheromones change the physiology of the recipient. Releaser pheromones change the behavior of the recipient. Releaser pheromones have a short term effect and they trigger an almost immediate behavioral response from the receiving bee. Under certain conditions a pheromone can act as both a releaser and primer pheromone.

Pheromones are not single chemicals, but rather a complex mixture of numerous chemicals in different percentages.

Types of Honeybee Pheromone

Alarm Pheromone

Two main alarm pheromones have been identified in honeybee workers. One is released by the Koschevnikov gland, near the sting shaft, and consists of more than 40 chemical compounds, including isopentyl acetate (IPA), butyl acetate, 1-hexanol, n-butanol, 1-octanol, hexyl acetate, octyl acetate, n-pentyl acetate and 2-nonanol. These chemical compounds have low molecular weights, are highly volatile, and appear to be the least specific of all pheromones. Alarm pheromones are released when a bee stings another animal, and attract other bees to the location and causes the other bees to behave defensively, i.e. sting or charge. Smoke can mask the bees' alarm pheromone. The other alarm pheromone is released by the mandibular glands and consists of 2-heptanone, which is also a highly volatile substance. This compound has a repellent effect and it was proposed that it is used to deter potential enemies and robber bees. Interestingly, the amounts of 2-heptanone increase with the age of bees and becomes higher in the case of foragers. It was therefore suggested that 2-heptanone is used by foragers to scent-mark recently visited and depleted foragers, which indeed are avoided by foraging bees.

Brood Recognition Pheromone

Another pheromone is responsible for preventing worker bees from bearing offspring in a colony that still has developing young. Both larvae and pupae emit a "brood recognition" pheromone. This inhibits ovarian development in worker bees and helps nurse bees distinguish worker larvae from drone larvae and pupae. This pheromone is a ten-component blend of fatty-acid esters, which also modulates adult caste ratios and foraging ontogeny dependent on its concentration. The components of brood pheromone have been shown to vary with the age of the developing bee. An artificial brood pheromone was invented by Yves Le Conte, Leam Sreng, Jérome Trouiller, and Serge Henri Poitou and patented in 1996.

Drone Pheromone

Drones produce a pheromone that attracts other flying drones to promote drone aggregations at sites suitable for mating with virgin queens.

Dufour's Gland Pheromone

The Dufour's gland opens into the dorsal vaginal wall. Dufour's gland and its secretion have been somewhat of a mystery. The gland secretes its alkaline products in to the vaginal cavity, and it has been assumed to be deposited on the eggs as they are laid. Indeed, Dufour's secretions allow worker bees to distinguish between eggs laid by the queen, which are attractive, and those laid by workers. The complex of as many as 24 chemicals differs between workers in "queenright" colonies and workers of queenless colonies. In the latter, the workers' Dufour secretions are similar to those of a healthy queen. The secretions of workers in queenright colonies are long-chain alkanes with odd numbers of carbon atoms, but those of egg-laying queens and egg-laying workers of queenless colonies also include long chain esters.

Egg marking Pheromone

This pheromone, similar to that described above, helps nurse bees distinguish between eggs laid by the queen bee and eggs laid by a laying worker.

Footprint Pheromone

This pheromone is left by bees when they walk and is useful in enhancing Nasonov pheromones in searching for nectar.

In the queen, it is an oily secretion of the queen's tarsal glands that is deposited on the comb as she walks across it. This inhibits queen cell construction (thereby inhibiting swarming), and it production diminishes as the queen ages.

Forager Pheromone

Ethyl oleate is released by older forager bees to slow the maturing of nurse bees. This primer pheromone acts as a distributed regulator to keep the ratio of nurse bees to forager bees in the balance that is most beneficial to the hive.

Nasonov Pheromone

This pheromone is emitted by the worker bees and used for orientation.

Other Pheromones

Other pheromones produced by most honeybees include rectal gland pheromone, tarsal pheromone, wax gland and comb pheromone, and tergite gland pheromone.

Types of Queen Honeybee Pheromone

Queen Mandibular Pheromone (QMP)

The QMP, emitted by the queen, is one of the most important sets of pheromones in the bee hive. It affects social behaviour, maintenance of the hive, swarming, mating behaviour, and inhibition of ovary development in worker bees. The effects can be short and/or long term. Some of the chemicals found in QMP are carboxylic acids and aromatic compounds. The following compounds have been shown to be important in retinue attraction of workers to their queen and other effects.

- (E)-9-oxodec-2-enoic acid (9-ODA) - inhibits queen rearing as well as ovarian development in worker bees; strong sexual attractant for drones when on a nuptial flight; critical to worker recognition of the presence of a queen in the hive.
- (R, E)-(-)-9-hydroxy-2-enoic acid (9-HDA) promotes stability of a swarm, or a "calming" influence.
- (S,E)-(+)-9-HDA
- Methyl-p-hydroxybenzoate (HOB)
- 4-hydroxy-3-methoxy phenylethanol (HVA)

Early work on synthetic pheromones was done by Keith N. Slessor, Lori-ann Kaminski, Gaylord G. S. King, John H. Borden, and Mark L. Winston; their work was patented in

1991. Synthetic queen mandibular pheromone (QMP) is a mixture of five components 9-ODA , (-) isomer (9-HDA), (+) isomer of (9-HDA), HOB and HVA in a ratio of 118:50:22:10:1.

Queen Retinue Pheromone (QRP)

The following compounds have also been identified, of which only coniferyl alcohol is found in the mandibular glands. The combination of the 5 QMP compounds and the 4 compounds below is called the Queen Retinue Pheromone (QRP). These compounds are important for the retinue attraction of worker bees around their queen.

- methyl (Z)-octadec-9-enoate (methyl oleate)
- (E)-3-(4-hydroxy-3-methoxyphenyl)-prop-2-en-1-ol (coniferyl alcohol)
- hexadecan-1-ol
- (Z9, Z12, Z15)-octadeca-9, 12, 15-trienoic acid (linolenic acid).

6
SUGAR

Sugar is a class of edible crystalline substances, mainly sucrose, lactose, and fructose. Human taste buds interpret its flavor as sweet. Sugar as a basic food carbohydrate primarily comes from sugar cane and from sugar beet, but also appears in fruit, honey, sorghum, sugar maple (in maple syrup), and in many other sources. It forms the main ingredient in much candy. Excessive consumption of sugar has been associated with increased incidences of type 2 diabetes, obesity and tooth decay.

TERMINOLOGY

Popular

In non-scientific use, the term sugar refers to sucrose (also called "table sugar" or "saccharose") — a white crystalline solid disaccharide. In this informal sense, the word "sugar" principally refers to crystalline sugars.

Humans most commonly use sucrose as their sugar of choice for altering the flavor and properties (such as mouthfeel, preservation, and texture) of beverages and food. Commercially produced table sugar comes either from sugar cane or from sugar beet. Manufacturing and preparing food may involve other sugars, including palm sugar and fructose, generally obtained from corn (maize) or from fruit.

Sugar may dissolve in water to form a syrup. A great many foods exist which principally contain dissolved sugar. Generically known as "syrups", they may also have other more specific names such as "honey" or "molasses".

Scientific

Scientifically, sugar refers to any monosaccharide or disaccharide. Monosaccharides (also called "simple sugars"), such as glucose, store chemical energy which biological cells convert to other types of energy.

In a list of ingredients, any word that ends with "-ose" (such as "glucose", "dextrose", "fructose", etc.) will likely denote a sugar. Sometimes such words may also refer to any types of carbohydrates soluble in water.

Glucose (a type of sugar found in human blood plasma) has the molecular formula $C_6 H_{12} O_6$.

Culinary/Nutritional

In culinary terms, the foodstuff known as sugar delivers a primary taste sensation of sweetness. Apart from the many forms of sugar and of sugar-containing foodstuffs, alternative non-sugar-based sweeteners exist, and these particularly attract interest from people who have problems with their blood sugar level (such as diabetics) and people who wish to limit their calorie-intake while still enjoying sweet foods. Both natural and synthetic substitutes exist with no significant carbohydrate (and thus low-calorie) content: for instance stevia (a herb), and saccharin (produced from naturally occurring but not necessarily naturally edible substances by inducing appropriate chemical reactions).

History

A sugarloaf was a traditional form for sugar in the 17th to 19th centuries, which required a sugar nip to break off pieces.

Originally, people chewed the cane raw to extract its sweetness. Indians discovered how to crystallize sugar during the Gupta dynasty.

Sugarcane was originally from tropical South Asia and Southeast Asia. Different species likely originated in different locations with S. barberi originating in India and S. edule and S. officinarum coming from New Guinea.

During the Muslim Agricultural Revolution, Arab entrepreneurs adopted the techniques of sugar production from India and then refined and transformed them into a large-scale industry. Arabs set up the first large scale sugar mills, refineries, factories and plantations.

The 1390s saw the development of a better press, which doubled the juice obtained from the cane. This permitted economic expansion of sugar plantations to Andalucia and to the Algarve. The 1420s saw sugar production extended to the Canary Islands, Madeira and the Azores.

The Portuguese took sugar to Brazil. Hans Staden, published in 1555, writes that by 1540 Santa Catarina Island had 800 sugar mills and that the north coast of Brazil, Demarara and Surinam had another 2,000. Approximately 3,000 small mills built before 1550 in the New World created an unprecedented demand for cast iron gears, levers, axles and other implements. Specialist trades in mold-making and iron-casting developed in Europe due to the expansion of sugar production. Sugar mill construction developed technological skills needed for a nascent industrial revolution in the early 17th century.

After 1625 the Dutch carried sugarcane from South America to the Caribbean islands — where it became grown from Barbados to the Virgin Islands. The years 1625 to 1750 saw sugar become worth its weight in gold With the European colonization of the Americas, the Caribbean became the world's largest source of sugar. These islands could supply sugarcane using slave labor and produce sugar at prices vastly lower than those of cane sugar imported from the East.

During the eighteenth century, sugar became enormously popular and the sugar market went through a series of booms. As Europeans established sugar plantations on the larger Caribbean islands, prices fell, especially in Britain. By the eighteenth century all levels of society had become common consumers of the former luxury product. At first most sugar in Britain went into tea, but later confectionery and chocolates became extremely popular. Suppliers commonly sold sugar in solid cones and consumers required a sugar nip, a pliers-like tool, to break off pieces.

Beginning in the late 18th century, the production of sugar became increasingly mechanized. The steam engine first powered a sugar mill in Jamaica in 1768, and soon after, steam replaced direct firing as the source of process heat. During the same century, Europeans began experimenting with sugar production from other crops. Andreas Marggraf identified sucrose in beet root and his student Franz Achard built a sugar beet processing factory in Silesia. However the beet-sugar industry really took off during the Napoleonic Wars, when France and the continent were cut off from caribbean sugar. Today 30% of the world's sugar is produced from beets.

Today, a large beet refinery producing around 1,500 tonnes of sugar a day needs a permanent workforce of about 150 for 24-hour production.

Etymology

In the case of sugar, the etymology reflects the spread of the commodity. The English word, "sugar" originates from the Arabic and Persian word *'shakar'*, itself derived from Sanskrit *'Sharkara'*. It came to English by way of French, Spanish and/or Italian, which derived their word for sugar from the Arabic and Persian *shakar,* (whence the Portuguese word açúcar, the Spanish word *'azúcar'*, the Italian word *'zucchero'*, the Old French word *'zuchre'* and the contemporary French word *sucre*). (Compare the OED.) The Greek word for "sugar", *'zahari'*, means "pebble". Note that the English word jaggery (meaning "coarse brown Indian sugar") has similar ultimate etymological origins (presumably in Sanskrit).

As a Food

Originally a luxury sugar eventually became sufficiently cheap and common to influence standard cuisine. Britain and the Caribbean islands have cuisines where the use of sugar became particularly prominent. Sugar forms a major element in confectionery and in desserts. Cooks use it as a food preservative as well as for sweetening.

Human Health

Studies have indicated potential links between processed sugar consumption and health hazards, including obesity and tooth decay. John Yudkin showed that the consumption of sugar and refined sweeteners is closely associated with coronary heart disease. It is also considered as a source of endogenous glycation processes.

Tooth Decay

Tooth decay has arguably become the most prominent health hazard associated with the consumption of sugar. Oral bacteria such as *Streptococcus mutans* live in dental plaque and metabolize sugars into lactic acid. High concentrations of acid may result on the surface of a tooth, leading to tooth demineralization.

The American Dental Association sees tooth decay as caused "mostly" by starchy foods like breadsticks, cereals and potato chips that linger on teeth and prolong acid production, not by simple sugars that dissolve rapidly in the mouth.

Diabetes

Diabetes, a disease that causes the body to metabolize sugar poorly, occurs when either:

- the body attacks the cells producing insulin, the chemical that allows the metabolizing of sugar in the body's cells (Type 1 diabetes)
- the body's cells ignore insulin (Type 2 diabetes)

When glucose builds up in the bloodstream, it can cause two problems:

1. in the short term, cells become starved for energy because they do not have access to the glucose.
2. in the long term, frequent glucose build-up increases the acidity of the blood, damaging many of the body's organs, including the eyes, kidneys, nerves and/or heart.

Authorities advise diabetics to avoid sugar-rich foods to prevent adverse reactions.

Obesity

In the United States of America, a scientific/health debate has started over the causes of a steep rise in obesity in the general population — and one view posits increased consumption of carbohydrates in recent decades as a major factor.

Obesity can result from a number of factors including:

- an increased intake of energy-dense foods — high in fat and sugars but low in vitamins, minerals and other micronutrients (see United Nations advice below); and
- decreased physical activity.

The National Health and Nutrition Examination Survey indicates that the population in the United States has increased its proportion of energy consumption from carbohydrates and decreased its proportion from total fat while obesity has increased. This implies, along with the United Nations report cited below, that obesity may correlate better with sugar consumption than with fat consumption, and that reducing fat consumption while increasing sugar consumption actually increases the level of obesity. The following table summarizes this study (based on the proportion of energy intake from different food sources for US Adults 20-74 years old, as carried out by the U.S. Department of Health and Human Services, Centers for Disease Control and Prevention, National Center for Health Statistics, Hyattsville, MD.

Year	Sex	Carbohydrate	Fat	Protein	Obesity
1971	Male	42.4%	36.9%	16.5%	12.1%
1971	Female	45.4%	36.1%	16.9%	16.6%
2000	Male	49.0%	32.8%	15.5%	27.7%
2000	Female	51.6%	32.8%	15.1%	34.0%

Another study published in 2002 and conducted by the National Academy of Sciences over a 3-year period concluded: "There is no clear and consistent association between increased intakes of added sugars and BMI." (BMI or "Body mass index" measures body-weight and height.)

Gout

Researchers have implicated sugary drinks high in fructose in a surge in cases of the painful joint disease gout.

Cancer

A link between sugar and cancer has been conjectured for some time but this remains a controversial topic. Some recent studies lend support to this theory However no major medical or nutritional organization currently recommends reducing sugar consumption to prevent cancer.

United Nations Nutritional Advice

In 2003, four United Nations agencies, (including the World Health Organization (WHO) and the Food and Agriculture Organization (FAO)) commissioned a report compiled by a panel of 30 international experts. The panel stated that the total of free sugars (all monosaccharides and disaccharides added to foods by manufacturers, cooks or consumers, plus sugars naturally present in honey, syrups and fruit juices) should not account for more than 10% of the energy intake of a healthy diet, while carbohydrates in total should represent between 55% and 75% of the energy intake.

Debate on Extrinsic Sugar

Argument continues as to the value of extrinsic sugar (sugar added to food) compared to that of intrinsic sugar (naturally present in food). Adding sugar to food particularly enhances taste, but does increase the total number of calories, among other negative effects on health and physiology.

In the United States of America, sugar has become increasingly evident in food products, as more food manufacturers add sugar or high fructose corn syrup to a wide variety of consumables. Candy bars, soft drinks, chips, snacks, fruit juice, peanut butter, soups, ice cream, jams, jellies, yogurt, and many breads have added sugars.

Concerns of Vegetarians and Vegans

The sugar refining industry often uses bone char (calcinated animal bones) for decolorizing This may concern some vegans and vegetarians; about a quarter of the sugar in the U.S. is processed using bone char as a filter and the rest is processed with activated carbon. As bone char does not get into the sugar, the relevant authorities consider sugar processed this way as parve/kosher.

Vegetarians and vegans may also object to the impact that the burning of the cane fields (a common part of the harvesting practice) has on insects, rats, snakes, and other life residing in the fields.

Production

Harvested sugarcane from India ready for processing. Table sugar (sucrose) comes from plant sources. Two important sugar crops predominate: sugarcane (*Saccharum spp.*) and sugar beets (Beta vulgaris), in which sugar can account for 12% to 20% of the plant's dry weight. Some minor commercial sugar crops include the date palm (Phoenix dactylifera), sorghum (*Sorghum vulgare*), and the sugar maple (*Acer saccharum*). In the financial year 2001-2002, worldwide production of sugar amounted to 134.1 million tonnes.

The first production of sugar from sugarcane took place in India. Alexander the Great's companions reported seeing "honey produced without the intervention of bees" and it remained exotic in Europe until the Arabs started cultivating it in Sicily and Spain. Only after the Crusades did it begin to rival honey as a sweetener in Europe. The Spanish began cultivating sugarcane in the West Indies in 1506. The Portuguese first cultivated sugarcane in Brazil in 1532.

Most cane sugar comes from countries with warm climates, such as Brazil, India, China, Thailand, Mexico and Australia, the top sugar-producing countries in the world. Brazil overshadows most countries, with roughly 30 million tonnes of cane sugar produced in 2006, while India produced 21 million, China 11 million, and Thailand and Mexico roughly 5 million each. Viewed by region, Asia predominates in cane sugar production, with large contributions from China, India and Thailand and other countries combining to account for 40% of global production in 2006. South America comes in second place with 32% of global production; Africa and Central America each produce 8% and Australia 5%. The United States, the Caribbean and Europe make up the remainder, with roughly 3% each.

Beet sugar comes from regions with cooler climates: northwest and eastern Europe, northern Japan, plus some areas in the United States (including California). In the northern hemisphere, the beet-growing season ends with the start of harvesting around September. Harvesting and processing continues until March in some cases. The availability of processing plant capacity, and the weather both influence the duration of harvesting and processing - the industry can lay up harvested beet until processed, but a frost-damaged beet becomes effectively unprocessable.

The European Union (EU) has become the world's second-largest sugar exporter. The Common Agricultural Policy of the EU sets maximum quotas for members' production to match supply and demand, and a price. Europe exports excess production quota (approximately 5 million tonnes in 2003). Part of this, "quota" sugar, gets subsidised from industry levies, the remainder (approximately half) sells as "C quota" sugar at market prices without subsidy. These subsidies and a high import tariff make it difficult for other countries to export to the EU states, or to compete with the Europeans on world markets.

The United States sets high sugar prices to support its producers, with the effect that many former consumers of sugar have switched to corn syrup (beverage manufacturers) or moved out of the country (candymakers).

The cheap prices of glucose syrups produced from wheat and corn (maize) threaten the traditional sugar market. Used in combination with artificial sweeteners, they can allow drink manufacturers to produce very low-cost goods.

Cane

Since the 6th century BC cane sugar producers have crushed the harvested vegetable material from sugarcane in order to collect and filter the juice. They then treat the liquid [often with lime (calcium oxide)] to remove impurities and then neutralize it. Boiling the juice then allows the sediment to settle to the bottom for dredging out, while the scum rises to the surface for skimming off. In cooling, the liquid crystallizes, usually in the process of stirring, to produce sugar crystals. Centrifuges usually remove the uncrystallized syrup. The producers can then either sell the resultant sugar, as is, for use; or process it further to produce lighter grades. This processing may take place in another factory in another country. Sugar cane appears fourth in the list for agriculture in China.

Sugar Beet

Beet sugar producers slice the washed beets, then extract the sugar with hot water in a "diffuser". An alkaline solution ("milk of lime" and carbon dioxide from the lime kiln) then serves to precipitate impurities. After filtration, evaporation concentrates the juice to a content of about 70% solids, and controlled crystallisation extracts the sugar. A centrifuge removes the sugar crystals from the liquid, which gets recycled in the crystalliser stages. When economic constraints prevent the removal of more sugar, the manufacturer discards the remaining liquid, now known as molasses.

Cane Versus Beet

Little perceptible difference exists between sugar produced from beet and that from cane. Chemical tests can distinguish the two, and some tests aim to detect fraudulent abuse of European Union subsidies or to aid in the detection of adulterated fruit juice.

The production of sugarcane needs approximately four times as much water as the production of sugar beet, therefore some countries that traditionally produced cane sugar (such as Egypt) have seen the building of new beet sugar factories recently. On the other hand, sugar cane tolerates hot climates better. Some sugar factories process both sugar cane and sugar beets and extend their processing period in that way.

The production of sugar results in residues which differ substantially depending on the raw materials used and on the place of production. While cooks often use cane molasses in food preparation, humans find molasses from sugar beet unpalatable, and it therefore ends up mostly as industrial fermentation feedstock (for example in alcohol distilleries), or as animal feed. Once dried, either type of molasses can serve as fuel for burning.

Culinary Sugars

So-called raw sugars comprise yellow to brown sugars made by clarifying the source syrup by boiling and drying with heat, until it becomes a crystalline solid, with minimal chemical processing. Raw beet sugars result from the processing of sugar beet juice, but only as intermediates en route to white sugar. Types of raw sugar include demerara, muscovado, and turbinado. Mauritius and Malawi export significant quantities of such specialty sugars. Manufacturers sometimes prepare raw sugar as loaves rather than as a crystalline powder, by pouring sugar and molasses together into molds and allowing the mixture to dry. This results in sugar-cakes or loaves, called jaggery or gur in India, pingbian tang in China, and panela, panocha, pile, piloncillo and pão-de-açúcar in various parts of Latin America. In South America, truly raw sugar, unheated and made from sugarcane grown on farms, does not have a large market-share.

Mill white sugar, also called plantation white, crystal sugar, or superior sugar, consists of raw sugar where the production process does not remove colored impurities, but rather bleaches them white by exposure to sulfur dioxide. Though the most common form of sugar in sugarcane-growing areas, this product does not store or ship well; after a few weeks, its impurities tend to promote discoloration and clumping.

Blanco directo, a white sugar common in India and other south Asian countries, comes from precipitating many impurities out of the cane juice by using phosphatation — a treatment with phosphoric acid and calcium hydroxide similar to the carbonatation technique used in beet sugar refining. In terms of sucrose purity, blanco directo is more pure than mill white, but less pure than white refined sugar.

White refined sugar has become the most common form of sugar in North America as well as in Europe. Refined sugar can be made by dissolving raw sugar and purifying it with a phosphoric acid method similar to that used for blanco directo, a carbonatation process involving calcium hydroxide and carbon dioxide, or by various filtration strategies. It is then further purified by filtration through a bed of activated carbon or bone char depending on where the processing takes place. Beet sugar refineries produce refined white sugar directly without an intermediate raw stage. White refined sugar is typically sold as granulated sugar, which has been dried to prevent clumping.

Granulated sugar comes in various crystal sizes — for home and industrial use — depending on the application:

Coarse-grained sugars, such as sanding sugar (also called "pearl sugar", "decorating sugar", nibbed sugar or sugar nibs) adds "sparkle" and flavor for decorating to baked goods, candies, cookies/biscuits and other desserts. The sparkling effect occurs because the sugar forms large crystals which reflect light. Sanding sugar, a large-crystal sugar, serves for making edible decorations. It has larger granules that sparkle when sprinkled on baked goods and candies and will not dissolve when subjected to heat.

Normal granulated sugars for table use: typically they have a grain size about 0.5 mm across.

Finer grades result from selectively sieving the granulated sugar caste (0.35 mm), commonly used in baking superfine sugar, also called baker's sugar, berry sugar, or bar sugar — favored for sweetening drinks or for preparing meringue.

Finest Grades

Powdered sugar, 10X sugar, confectioner's sugar (0.060 mm), or icing sugar (0.024 mm), produced by grinding sugar to a fine powder. The manufacturer may add a small amount of anticaking agent to prevent clumping — either cornstarch (1% to 3%) or tri-calcium phosphate.

Sugar Cubes

Retailers also sell sugar cubes or lumps for convenient consumption of a standardized amount. Suppliers of sugarcubes make them by mixing sugar crystals with sugar syrup.

Brown Sugar Crystals

Brown sugars come from the late stages of sugar refining, when sugar forms fine crystals with significant molasses content, or from coating white refined sugar with a cane molasses syrup. Their color and taste become stronger with increasing molasses content, as do their moisture-retaining properties. Brown sugars also tend to harden if exposed to the atmosphere, although proper handling can reverse this.

The World Health Organisation and the Food and Agriculture Organization of the United Nations expert report (WHO Technical Report Series 916 Diet, Nutrition and the Prevention of Chronic Diseases) defines free sugars as all monosaccharides and disaccharides added to foods by the manufacturer, cook or consumer, plus sugars naturally present in honey, syrups and fruit juices. This includes all the sugars referred to above. The term distinguishes these forms from all other culinary sugars added in their natural form with no refining at all.

Natural sugars comprise all completely unrefined sugars: effectively all sugars not defined as free sugars. The WHO Technical Report Series 916 Diet, Nutrition and the

Prevention of Chronic Diseases approves only natural sugars as carbohydrates for unrestricted consumption. Natural sugars come in fruit, grains and vegetables in their natural or cooked form.

Chemistry

Sucrose: a disaccharide of glucose and fructose important molecules in the body. Biochemists regard sugars as relatively simple carbohydrates. Sugars include monosaccharides, disaccharides, trisaccharides and the oligo-saccharides - containing 1, 2, 3, and 4 or more mono-saccharide units respectively. Sugars contain either aldehyde groups (-CHO) or ketone groups (C=O), where there are carbon-oxygen double bonds, making the sugars reactive. Most simple sugars (monosaccharides) conform to $(CH_2O)n$ where n is between 3 and 7. A notable exception, deoxyribose, as its name suggests, has a "missing" oxygen atom. All saccharides with more than one ring in their structure result from two or more monosaccharides joined by glycosidic bonds with the resultant loss of a molecule of water (H_2O) per bond.

As well as using classifications based on their reactive group, chemists may also subdivide sugars according to the number of carbons they contain. Derivatives of trioses ($C_3H_6O_3$) are intermediates in glycolysis. Pentoses (5-carbon sugars) include ribose and deoxyribose, which form part of nucleic acids. Ribose also forms a component of several chemicals that have importance in the metabolic process, including NADH and ATP. Hexoses (6-carbon sugars) include glucose, a universal substrate for the production of energy in the form of ATP. Through photosynthesis plants produce glucose, which has the formula $C_6H_{12}O_6$, and then convert it for storage as an energy reserve in the form of other carbohydrates such as starch, or (as in cane and beet) as sucrose (table sugar). Sucrose has the chemical formula $C_{12}H_{22}O_{11}$.

Many pentoses and hexoses can form ring structures. In these closed-chain forms, the aldehyde or ketone group remains unfree, so many of the reactions typical of these groups cannot occur. Glucose in solution exists mostly in the ring form at equilibrium, with less than 0.1% of the molecules in the open-chain form.

Monosaccharides in a closed-chain form can form glycosidic bonds with other monosaccharides, creating disaccharides (such as sucrose) and polysaccharides (such as starch). Enzymes must hydrolyse or otherwise break these glycosidic bonds before such compounds become metabolised. After digestion and absorption. The principal monosaccharides present in the blood and internal tissues include glucose, fructose, and galactose.

The prefix "glyco-" indicates the presence of a sugar in an otherwise non-carbohydrate substance. Note for example glycoproteins, proteins connected to one or more sugars.

Monosaccharides include fructose, glucose, galactose and mannose. Disaccharides occur most commonly as sucrose (cane or beet sugar - made from one glucose and one fructose), lactose (milk sugar - made from one glucose and one galactose) and maltose (made of two glucoses). These disaccharides have the formula $C_{12}H_{22}O_{11}$.

Hydrolysis can convert sucrose into a syrup of fructose and glucose, producing invert sugar. This resulting syrup, sweeter than the original sucrose, has uses in making confections because it does not crystallize as easily and thus produces a smoother finished product.

If combined with fine ash, sugar will burn with a blue flame.

Dissolved Sugar Content

Scientists and the sugar industry use degrees Brix (symbol °Bx), introduced by Antoine Brix, as units of measurement of the mass ratio of dissolved substance to water in a liquid. A 25 °Bx sucrose solution has 25 grams of sucrose per 100 grams of liquid; or, to put it another way, 25 grams of sucrose sugar and 75 grams of water exist in the 100 grams of solution.

An infrared Brix sensor measures the vibrational frequency of the sugar molecules, giving a Brix degrees measurement. This does not equate to Brix degrees from a density or refractive index measurement because it will specifically measure dissolved sugar concentration instead of all dissolved solids. When using a refractometer, one should report the result as "refractometric dried substance" (RDS). One might speak of a liquid as having 20 °Bx RDS. This refers to a measure of percent by weight of total dried solids and, although not technically the same as Brix degrees determined through an infrared method, renders an accurate measurement of sucrose content, since sucrose in fact forms the majority of dried solids. The advent of in-line infrared Brix measurement sensors has made measuring the amount of dissolved sugar in products economical using a direct measurement.

Purity

Technicians usually measure the purity (sucrose content) of sugar by polarimetry — the measurement of the rotation of plane-polarized light by a solution of sugar.

Baking Weight/Mass Volume Relationship

Different culinary sugars have different densities due to differences in particle size and inclusion of moisture.

The Domino Sugar Company has established the following volume to weight conversions:

- Brown sugar 1 cup = 195g = 6.88 oz
- Granular sugar 1 cup = 200g = 7.06 oz
- Powdered sugar 1 cup = 120g = 4.23 oz

7

TERPENE

Terpenes are a large and varied class of hydrocarbons, produced primarily by a wide variety of plants, particularly conifers though also by some insects such as termites or swallowtail butterflies, which emit terpenes from their osmeterium.

They are the major components of resin, and of turpentine produced from resin. The name "terpene" is derived from the word "turpentine". In addition to their roles as end-products in many organisms, terpenes are major biosynthetic building blocks within nearly every living creature. Steroids, for example, are derivatives of the triterpene squalene.

When terpenes are modified chemically, such as by oxidation or rearrangement of the carbon skeleton, the resulting compounds are generally referred to as terpenoids. Some authors will use the term terpene to include all terpenoids. Terpenoids are also known as Isoprenoids.

Terpenes and terpenoids are the primary constituents of the essential oils of many types of plants and flowers. Essential oils are used widely as natural flavour additives for food, as fragrances in perfumery, and in traditional and alternative medicines such as aromatherapy. Synthetic variations and derivatives of natural terpenes and terpenoids also greatly expand the variety of aromas used in perfumery and flavors used in food additives. Vitamin A is an example of a terpene.

Structure and Biosynthesis

Terpenes are derived biosynthetically from units of isoprene, which has the molecular formula C_5H_8. The basic molecular formulae of terpenes are multiples of that, $(C_5H_8)n$ where n is the number of linked isoprene units. This is called the isoprene rule or the C_5 rule. The isoprene units may be linked together "head to tail" to form linear chains or they may be arranged to form rings. One can consider the isoprene unit as one of nature's common building blocks.

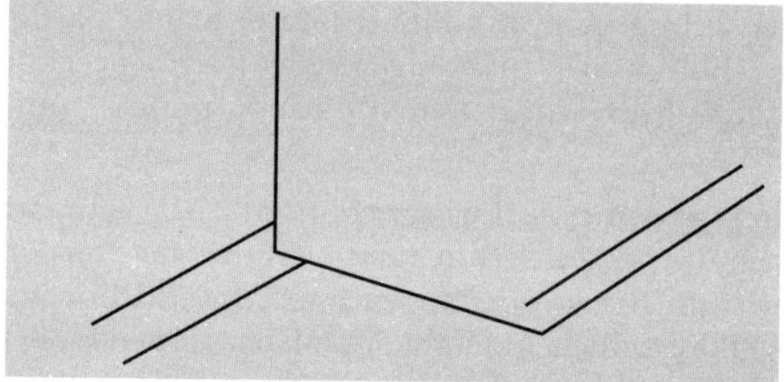

Fig. 7.1: Isoprene

Fig. 7.2: Dimethylallyl pyrophosphate

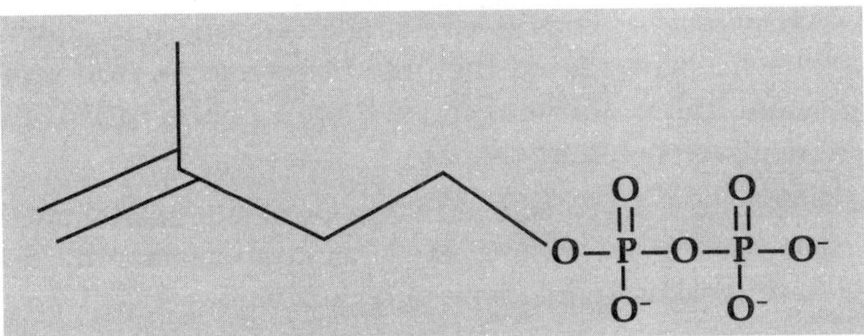

Fig. 7.3: Isopentenyl pyrophosphate

Isoprene itself does not undergo the building process, but rather activated forms, isopentenyl pyrophosphate (IPP or also isopentenyl diphosphate) and dimethylallyl pyrophosphate (DMAPP or also dimethylallyl diphosphate), are the components in the biosynthetic pathway. IPP is formed from acetyl-CoA via the intermediacy of mevalonic acid in the HMG-CoA reductase pathway. An alternative, totally unrelated biosynthesis pathway of IPP is known in some bacterial groups and the plastids of plants, the so-called MEP(2-Methyl-D-erythritol-4-phosphate)-pathway, which is initiated from C5-sugars. In both pathways, IPP is isomerized to DMAPP by the enzyme isopentenyl pyrophosphate isomerase.

As chains of isoprene units are built up, the resulting terpenes are classified sequentially by size as hemiterpenes, monoterpenes, sesquiterpenes, diterpenes, sesterterpenes, triterpenes, and tetraterpenes.

Types

Terpenes may be classified by the number of terpene units in the molecule; a prefix in the name indicates the number of terpene units needed to assemble the molecule. A single terpene unit is formed from two molecules of isoprene, so that a monoterpene consists of one terpene but two isoprene units.

- *Hemiterpenes* consist of a single isoprene unit. Isoprene itself is considered the only hemiterpene, but oxygen-containing derivatives such as prenol and isovaleric acid are hemiterpenoids.
- *Monoterpenes* consist of two isoprene units and have the molecular formula $C_{10}H_{16}$. Examples of monoterpenes are: geraniol, limonene and terpineol.
- *Sesquiterpenes* consist of three isoprene units and have the molecular formula $C_{15}H_{24}$. Examples of sesquiterpenes are: farnesenes, farnesol. The sesqui-prefix means one and a half.
- Diterpenes are composed for four isoprene units and have the molecular formula $C_{20}H_{32}$. They derive from geranylgeranyl pyrophosphate. Examples of diterpenes are cafestol, kahweol, cembrene and taxadiene (precursor of taxol). Diterpenes also form the basis for biologically important compounds such as retinol, retinal, and phytol. They are known to be antimicrobial and antiinflammatory.
- *Sesterterpenes,* terpenes having 25 carbons and five isoprene units, are rare relative to the other sizes. The sester- prefix means half to three, i.e. two and a half. Examples of sesterterpenes are geranylfarnesol.
- *Triterpenes* consist of six isoprene units and have the molecular formula $C_{30}H_{48}$. The linear triterpene squalene, the major constituent of shark liver oil, is derived from the reductive coupling of two molecules of farnesyl pyrophosphate. Squalene is then processed biosynthetically to generate either lanosterol or cycloartenol, the structural precursors to all the steroids.
- *Tetraterpenes* contain eight isoprene units and have the molecular formula $C_{40}H_{64}$. Biologically important tetraterpenes include the acyclic lycopene, the monocyclic gamma-carotene, and the bicyclic alpha- and beta-carotenes.

- Polyterpenes consist of long chains of many isoprene units. Natural rubber consists of polyisoprene in which the double bonds are cis. Some plants produce a polyisoprene with trans double bonds, known as gutta-percha.

Agri-chemical Use

Research into terpenes has found that many of them possess qualities that make them ideal active ingredients as part of natural agricultural pesticides.

Turpentine (also called spirit of turpentine, oil of turpentine, wood turpentine, gum turpentine) is a fluid obtained by the distillation of resin obtained from trees, mainly pine trees. It is composed of terpenes, mainly the monoterpenes alpha-pinene and beta-pinene. It is sometimes known colloquially as turps, but this more often refers to turpentine substitute (or mineral turpentine).

Production

One of the earliest sources was the terebinth or turpentine tree (*Pistacia terebinthus*), a Mediterranean tree related to the pistachio.

Important pines for turpentine production include: Maritime Pine (*Pinus pinaster*), Aleppo Pine (*Pinus halepensis*), Masson's Pine (*Pinus massoniana*), Sumatran Pine (*Pinus merkusii*), Longleaf Pine (Pinus palustris), Loblolly Pine (*Pinus taeda*) and Ponderosa Pine (*Pinus ponderosa*).

When producing chemical wood pulp from pines with the kraft process, turpentine is collected as a byproduct. Often it is burned at the mill for energy production.

Industrial and Other End Uses

The two primary uses of turpentine in industry are as a solvent and as a source of materials for organic synthesis.

- As a solvent, turpentine is used for thinning oil-based paints, for producing varnishes, and as a raw material for the chemical industry. Its industrial use as a solvent in industrialized nations has largely been replaced by the much cheaper turpentine substitutes distilled from crude oil.

- *Canada balsam,* also called *Canada turpentine* or balsam of fir, is a turpentine which is made from the resin of the balsam fir.
- *Venice turpentine* is produced from the Western Larch Larix occidentalis.
- Turpentine is also used as a source of raw materials in the synthesis of *fragrant chemical compounds.* Commercially used camphor, linalool, alpha-terpineol, and geraniol are all usually produced from alpha-pinene and beta-pinene, which are two of the chief chemical components of turpentine. These pinenes are separated and purified by distillation. The mixture of diterpenes and triterpenes that is left as residue after turpentine distillation is sold as rosin.
- Turpentine is also added to many *cleaning and sanitary products* due to its antiseptic properties and its "clean scent".
- In early 19th Century America, turpentine was sometimes *burned in lamps* as a cheap alternative to whale oil. It was most commonly used for outdoor lighting, due to its strong odor.
- Turpentine has long been used as a *solvent, mixed with beeswax* or with *carnauba wax,* to make fine *furniture wax* for use as a protective coating over oiled wood finishes (e.g., lemon oil).

Hazards

Turpentine is an organic solvent, and thus poses many of the same hazards as do other such substances. Its vapour can irritate the skin and eyes, damage the lungs and respiratory system, as well as the central nervous system when inhaled, and cause renal failure when ingested, among other things. It is extremely flammable.

Medicinal Elixir

Turpentine and petroleum distillates such as coal oil and kerosene have been used medicinally since ancient times, as topical and sometimes internal home remedies. Topically it has been used for abrasions and wounds, as a treatment for lice, and when mixed with animal fat it has been used as a chest rub, or inhaler for nasal and throat ailments. Many modern chest rubs, such as the Vicks variety, still contain turpentine in their formulations.

Though internal administration of these toxic products is no longer common today, it was once administered by masking the taste by dosing sugar cubes, molasses, or honey, or when unavailable, straight. It was touted as treatment for intestinal parasites due to its alleged antiseptic and diuretic properties, and a general cure-all.

Terpenoids

The terpenoids, sometimes referred to as isoprenoids, are a large and diverse class of naturally-occurring organic chemicals similar to terpenes, derived from five-carbon isoprene units assembled and modified in thousands of ways. Most are multicyclic structures that differ from one another not only in functional groups but also in their basic carbon skeletons. These lipids can be found in all classes of living things, and are the largest group of natural products.

Plant terpenoids are used extensively for their aromatic qualities. They play a role in traditional herbal remedies and are under investigation for antibacterial, antineoplastic, and other pharmaceutical functions. Terpenoids contribute to the scent of eucalyptus, the flavors of cinnamon, cloves, and ginger, and the color of yellow flowers. Well-known terpenoids include citral, menthol, camphor, Salvinorin A in the plant Salvia divinorum, and the cannabinoids found in Cannabis.

The steroids and sterols in animals are biologically produced from terpenoid precursors. Sometimes terpenoids are added to proteins, e.g., to enhance their attachment to the cell membrane; this is known as isoprenylation.

Many of these are substrates for plant Cytochrome P_{450}.

Structure and Classification

Terpenes are hydrocarbons resulting from the combination of several isoprene units. Terpenoids can be thought of as modified terpenes, wherein methyl groups have been moved or removed, or oxygen atoms added. (Some authors use the term "terpene" more broadly, to include the terpenoids.) Just like terpenes, the terpenoids can be classified according to the number of isoprene units used:

- Monoterpenoids, 2 isoprene units
- Sesquiterpenoids, 3 isoprene units
- Diterpenoids, 4 isoprene units
- Sesterterpenoids, 5 isoprene units
- Triterpenoids, 6 isoprene units
- Tetraterpenoids, 8 isoprene units
- Polyterpenoids with a larger number of isoprene units.

Terpenoids can also be classified according to the number of cyclic structures they contain.

Mevalonic Acid Pathway

Many organisms manufacture terpenoids through the HMG-CoA reductase pathway, the pathway that also produces cholesterol. The reactions take place in the cytosol. The pathway was discovered in the 1950s.

MEP/DOXP Pathway

The 2-C-methyl-D-erythritol 4-phosphate/1-deoxy-D-xylulose 5-phosphate pathway (MEP/DOXP pathway), also known as non-mevalonate pathway or mevalonic acid-independent pathway, takes place in the plastids of plants and apicomplexan protozoa, as well as in many bacteria. It was discovered in the late 1980s.

Pyruvate and *glyceraldehyde 3-phosphate* are converted by DOXP synthase (Dxs) to 1-deoxy-D-xylulose 5-phosphate, and by DOXP reductase (Dxr, IspC) to 2-C-methyl-D-erythritol 4-phosphate (MEP). The subsequent three reaction steps catalyzed by 4-diphosphocytidyl-2-C-methyl-D-erythritol synthase (YgbP, IspD), 4-diphosphocytidyl-2-C-methyl-D-erythritol kinase (YchB, IspE), and 2-C-methyl-D-erythritol 2,4-cyclodiphosphate synthase (YgbB, IspF) mediate the formation of 2-C-methyl-D-erythritol 2,4-cyclopyrophosphate (MEcPP). Finally, MEcPP is converted to (E)-4-hydroxy-3-methyl-but-2-enyl pyrophosphate (HMB-PP) by HMB-PP synthase (GcpE, IspG), and HMB-PP is converted to isopentenyl pyrophosphate (IPP) and dimethylallyl pyrophosphate (DMAPP) by HMB-PP reductase (LytB, IspH).

IPP and DMAPP are the end-products in either pathway, and are the precursors of isoprene, monoterpenoids (10-carbon), diterpenoids (20-carbon), carotenoids (40-carbon), chlorophylls, and plastoquinone-9 (45-carbon). Synthesis of all higher terpenoids proceeds via formation of geranyl pyrophosphate (GPP), farnesyl pyrophosphate (FPP), and geranylgeranyl pyrophosphate (GGPP).

Although both pathways, MVA and MEP, are mutually exclusive in most organisms, interactions between them have been reported in plants and few bacteria species.

8

OIL

An oil is a substance that is in a viscous liquid state ("oily") at ambient temperatures or slightly warmer, and is both hydrophobic (immiscible with water) and lipophilic (miscible with other oils, literally). This general definition includes compound classes with otherwise unrelated chemical structures, properties, and uses, including vegetable oils, petrochemical oils, and volatile essential oils. Oil is a nonpolar substance.

The term oil is often used colloquially to refer to petroleum.

Types of Oils

All oils, with their high carbon and hydrogen content, can be traced back to organic sources.

Mineral Oils

Mineral oils, found in porous rocks underground, are no exception, as they were originally the organic material, such as dead plankton, accumulated on the seafloor in geologically ancient times. Through various geochemical processes this material was converted to mineral oil, or petroleum, and its components, such as kerosene, paraffin waxes, gasoline, diesel and such. These are classified as mineral oils as they do not have an organic origin on human timescales, and are instead derived from underground geologic locations, ranging from rocks, to underground traps, to sands.

Other oily substances can also be found in the environment, the most well-known being asphalt, occurring naturally underground or, where there are leaks, in tar pits.

Petroleum and other mineral oils, (specifically labelled as petrochemicals), have become such a crucial resource to human civilization in modern times they are often referred to by the ubiquitous term of "oil" itself.

Organic Oil

Oils are also produced by plants, animals and other organisms through organic processes, and these oils are remarkable in their diversity. Oil is a somewhat vague term to use chemically, and the scientific term for oils, fats, waxes, cholesterol and other oily substances found in living things and their secretions, is lipids.

Lipids, ranging from waxes to steroids, are somewhat hard to characterize, and are united in a group almost solely based on the fact that they all repel, or refuse to dissolve, in water, and are however comfortably miscible in other liquid lipids. They also have a high carbon and hydrogen content, and are considerably lacking in oxygen compared to other organic compounds and minerals.

Synthetic Oils

Synthetic oil is a lubricant, consisting of chemical compounds which are artificially made (synthesized) from compounds other than crude oil (petroleum). Synthetic oil is used as a substitute for lubricant refined from petroleum, because it generally provides superior mechanical and chemical properties than those found in traditional mineral oils.

APPLICATIONS

Health advantages are claimed for a number of specific oils such as omega 3 oils (fish oil, flaxseed oil, etc), evening primrose oil and olive oil. The term, "oily hair" is actually a misconception. Trans fats, often produced by hydrogenating vegetable oils, are known to be harmful to health.

Food Oils

Many edible vegetable and animal oils, and also fats, are used in cooking and food preparation. In particular, many foods are fried in oil much hotter than boiling water. Oils are also used for flavouring and for modifying the texture of foods.

Fuel

Almost all oils burn in air generating heat, which can be used directly, or converted into other forms of fuels by various means. For example, heating water into steam which is funneled into a turbine which turns a generator, which then produces electricity. Oils are used as fuels for heating, lighting (e.g. kerosene lamp), powering combustion engines, and other purposes. Oils used for this purpose nowadays are usually derived from petroleum, (fuel oil, diesel oil, gasoline (petrol), etc), though biological oils such as biodiesel are gaining market share.

Heat Transport

Many oils have higher boiling points than water and are electrical insulators, making them useful for liquid cooling systems, especially where electricity is used.

Lubrication

Due to their non-polarity, oils do not easily adhere to other substances. This makes oils useful as lubricants for various engineering purposes. Mineral oils are more suitable than biological oils, which degrade rapidly in most environmental conditions.

Painting

Color pigments can be easily suspended in oil, making it suitable as supporting medium for paints. The slow drying process and miscibility of oil facilitates a realistic style. This method has been used since the 15th century.

Petrochemicals

Crude oil can be processed into petroleum, plastics, and other substances.

Hair

Oil is used on hair to give it a lustrous look. It helps to avoid tangles and roughness to the hair. It also helps the hair to be stabilized and grow faster.

Electricity Generation

Oil and any of its more refined products have been used to create electricity. This can be done by means of a steam engine, or by means of a turbine driven by exhaust gases. A steam engine turns the thermal energy into rotary motion, which can then be transformed into electricity, by means of a generator. In an exhaust gas turbine, the combustion products from burning the fuel expand, thereby turning a turbine. The turbine is coupled to an electrical generator.

Other Usages

Sulfuric acid has been called oil of vitriol in pre-scientific times, due to its syrupy consistency. Even in modern times, sulfuric acid is sometimes called vitriolic acid, and caustic personalities are called "vitriolic." Sulfuric acid is not a petrochemical, and in modern parlance, is not an oil.

Religion

Oils have been used throughout history as a fragrant or religious medium. Oil is often seen as a spiritually purifying agent. It is used in religious ceremonies, such as the chrism used in baptism, and has traditionally been used to anoint kings and queens. Oil that is associated with one or more saints is known as "oil of saints" and believed by some to have beneficial properties, as is "oil of martyrs.

ESSENTIAL OIL

An essential oil is a concentrated, hydrophobic liquid containing volatile aroma compounds from plants. They are also known as volatile or ethereal oils, or simply as the "oil of" the plant material from which they were extracted, such as oil of clove. An oil is "essential" in the sense that it carries a distinctive scent, or essence, of the plant. Essential oils do not as a group need to have any specific chemical properties in common, beyond conveying characteristic fragrances. They are not to be confused with essential fatty acids.

Essential oils are generally extracted by distillation. Other processes include expression, or solvent extraction. They are used in perfumes, cosmetics and bath products, for flavoring food and drink, and for scenting incense and household cleaning products.

Various essential oils have been used medicinally at different periods in history. Medical applications proposed by those who sell medicinal oils range from skin treatments to remedies for cancer, and are often based on historical use of these oils for these purposes. Such claims are now subject to regulation in most countries, and have grown correspondingly more vague, to stay within these regulations.

Interest in essential oils has revived in recent decades, with the popularity of aromatherapy, a branch of alternative medicine which claims that the specific aromas carried by essential oils have curative effects. Oils are volatilized or diluted in a carrier oil and used in massage, diffused in the air by a nebulizer or by heating over a candle flame, or burned as incense, for example.

Production

Distillation

Today, most common essential oils, such as lavender, peppermint, and eucalyptus, are distilled. Raw plant material, consisting of the flowers, leaves, wood, bark, roots, seeds, or peel, is put into an alembic (distillation apparatus) over water. As the water is heated the steam passes through the plant material, vaporizing the volatile compounds. The vapors flow through a coil where they condense back to liquid, which is then collected in the receiving vessel.

Most oils are distilled in a single process. One exception is Ylang-ylang (Cananga odorata), which takes 22 hours to complete through a Fractional distillation.

The recondensed water is referred to as a hydrosol, hydrolat, herbal distillate or plant water essence, which may be sold as another fragrant product. Popular hydrosols are rose water, lavender water, lemon balm, clary sage and orange blossom water. The use of herbal distillates in cosmetics is increasing. Some plant hydrosols have unpleasant smells and are therefore not sold.

Expression

Most citrus peel oils are expressed mechanically, or cold-pressed. Due to the large quantities of oil in citrus peel and the relatively low cost to grow and harvest the raw materials, citrus-fruit oils are cheaper than most other essential oils. Lemon or sweet orange oils that are obtained as by-products of the citrus industry are even cheaper.

Prior to the discovery of distillation, all essential oils were extracted by pressing.

Solvent Extraction

Most flowers contain too little volatile oil to undergo expression and their chemical components are too delicate and easily denatured by the high heat used in steam distillation. Instead, a solvent such as hexane or supercritical carbon dioxide is used to extract the oils. Extracts from hexane and other hydrophobic solvent are called concretes, which is a mixture of essential oil, waxes, resins, and other lipophilic (oil soluble) plant material.

Although highly fragrant, concretes contain large quantities of non-fragrant waxes and resins. As such another solvent, often ethyl alcohol, which only dissolves the fragrant low-molecular weight compounds, is used to extract the fragrant oil from the concrete. The alcohol is removed by a second distillation, leaving behind the absolute.

Supercritical carbon dioxide is used as a solvent in supercritical fluid extraction. This method has many benefits, including avoiding petrochemical residues in the product and the loss of some "top notes" when steam distillation is used. It does not yield an absolute directly. The supercritical carbon dioxide will extract both the waxes and the essential oils that make up the concrete. Subsequent processing with liquid carbon dioxide, achieved in the same extractor by merely lowering the extraction temperature, will separate the waxes from the essential oils. This lower temperature process prevents the decomposition and denaturing of compounds. When the extraction is complete, the pressure is reduced to ambient and the carbon dioxide reverts back to a gas, leaving no residue. An animated presentation describing the process is available for viewing.

Supercritical carbon dioxide is also used for making decaffeinated coffee. However, although it uses the same basic principals it is a different process because of the difference in scale.

Production Quantities

Estimates of total production of essential oils are difficult to obtain. One estimate, compiled from data in 1989, 1990 and 1994 from various sources gives the following total production, in tonnes, of essential oils for which more than 1,000 tonnes were produced.

Oil	Tonnes
Sweet orange	12,000
Mentha arvensis	4,800
Peppermint	3,200
Cedarwood	2,600
Lemon	2,300
Eucalyptus globulus	2,070
Litsea cubeba	2,000
Clove (leaf)	2,000
Spearmint	1,300

Use in Aromatherapy

Aromatherapy is a form of alternative medicine, in which healing effects are ascribed to the aromatic compounds in essential oils and other plant extracts. Many common essential oils have medicinal properties that have been applied in folk medicine since ancient times and are still widely used today. For example, many essential oils have antiseptic properties Many are also claimed to have an uplifting effect on the mind. The claims are supported in some studies and unconfirmed in others.

Dilution

Essential oils are usually lipophilic (literally: "oil-loving") compounds that usually are not miscible with water. Instead, they can be diluted in solvents like pure ethanol (alcohol), polyethylene glycol, or oils.

Raw Materials

Rose Oil

The most well-known essential oil is probably rose oil, produced from the petals of Rosa damascena and Rosa centifolia. Steam-distilled rose oil is known as "rose otto" while the solvent extracted product is known as "rose absolute".

Dangers

Because of their concentrated nature, essential oils generally should not be applied directly to the skin in their undiluted or "neat" form. Some can cause severe irritation, or provoke an allergic reaction. Instead, essential oils should be blended with a vegetable-based "carrier" oil (a.k.a., a base, or "fixed" oil) before being applied. Common carrier oils include olive, almond, hazelnut and grapeseed. Only neutral oils should be used. Common ratio of essential oil disbursed in a carrier oil is 0.5-3% (most under 10%), and depends on its intended purpose. Some essential oils, including many of the citrus peel oils, are photosensitizers (i.e., increasing the skin's vulnerability to sunlight, making it more likely to burn). Industrial users of essential oils should consult the material safety data sheets (MSDS) to determine the hazards and handling requirements of particular oils.

Gynecomastia

Estrogenic and antiandrogenic activity have been reported by in vitro study of tea tree oil and lavender essential oils. Case reports suggest that the oils may be implicated in some cases of gynecomastia, an abnormal breast tissue growth, in prepubescent boys.

Pesticide Residues

There is some concern about pesticide residues in essential oils, particularly those used therapeutically. For this reason, many practitioners of aromatherapy buy organically produced oils.

Ingestion

While some advocate the ingestion of essential oils for therapeutic purposes, this should never be done except under the supervision of someone licensed to prescribe such treatment. Some common essential oils such as Eucalyptus are toxic internally. Pharmacopoeia standards for medicinal oils should be heeded. Some oils can be toxic to some domestic animals, cats in particular The internal use of essential oils can pose hazards to pregnant women, as some can be abortifacients in dose 0.5–10 ml.

Smoke

The smoke from burning essential oils may contain carcinogens, such as polycyclic aromatic hydrocarbons (PAHs). Essential oils are naturally high in volatile organic compounds (VOCs).

Flammable Liquid

The flash point of each essential oil is different. Many of the common essential oils such as tea tree, lavender, and citrus oils are classed as a Class 3 Flammable Liquid as they have a flash point of 50-60 °C.

Toxicology

LD_{50} of most essential oils or their main components are 0.5-10 g/kg (orally or skin test).

RESIN

Resin is a hydrocarbon secretion of many plants, particularly coniferous trees. It is valued for its chemical constituents and uses, such as varnishes and adhesives, as an important source of raw materials for organic synthesis, or for incense and perfume. Fossilized resins are the source of amber. Resins are also a material in nail polish.

The term is also used for synthetic substances of similar properties. Resins have a very long history and are mentioned by both ancient Greek Theophrastus and ancient Roman Pliny the Elder, especially as the forms known as frankincense and myrrh. They were highly prized substances used for many purposes, especially perfumery and as incense in religious rites.

Chemistry

The resin produced by most plants is a viscous liquid, composed mainly of volatile fluid terpenes, with lesser components of dissolved non-volatile solids which make resin thick and sticky. The most common terpenes in resin are the bicyclic terpenes alpha-pinene, beta-pinene, delta-3 carene and sabinene, the monocyclic terpenes limonene and terpinolene, and smaller amounts of the tricyclic sesquiterpenes, longifolene, caryophyllene and delta-cadinene. Some resins also contain a high proportion of resin acids. The individual components of resin can be separated by fractional distillation.

A few plants produce resins with different compositions, most notably Jeffrey Pine and Gray Pine, the volatile components of which are largely pure n-heptane with little or no terpenes. The exceptional purity of the n-heptane distilled from Jeffrey Pine resin, unmixed with other isomers of heptane, led to its being used as the defining zero point on the octane rating scale of petrol quality. Because heptane is highly flammable, distillation of resins containing it is very dangerous. Some resin distilleries in California exploded because they mistook Jeffrey Pine for the similar but terpene-producing Ponderosa Pine. At the time the two pines were considered to be the same species of pine; they were only classified as separate species in 1853.

Some resins when soft are known as 'oleo-resins', and when containing benzoic acid or cinnamic acid they are called balsams. Other resinous products in their natural condition are a mix with gum or mucilaginous substances and known as gum resins. Many compound resins have distinct and characteristic odors, from their admixture with essential oils.

Certain resins are obtained in a fossilized condition, amber being the most notable instance of this class; African copal and the kauri gum of New Zealand are also procured in a semi-fossil condition.

Derivatives

Solidified resin from which the volatile terpene components have been removed by distillation is known as rosin. Typical rosin is a transparent or translucent mass, with a vitreous fracture and a faintly yellow or brown colour, non-odorous or having only a slight turpentine odour and taste.

It is insoluble in water, mostly soluble in alcohol, essential oils, ether and hot fatty oils, and softens and melts under the influence of heat, is not capable of sublimation, and burns with a bright but smoky flame.

This comprises a complex mixture of different substances including organic acids named the resin acids. These are closely related to the terpenes, and derive from them through partial oxidation. Resin acids can be dissolved in alkalis to form resin soaps, from which the purified resin acids are regenerated by treatment with acids. Examples of resin acids are abietic acid (sylvic acid), $C_{20}H_{30}O_2$, plicatic acid contained in cedar, and pimaric acid, $C_{20}H_{35}O_2$, a constituent of gallipot resin. Abietic acid can also be extracted from rosin by means of hot alcohol; it crystallizes in leaflets, and on oxidation yields trimellitic acid, isophthalic acid and terebic acid. Pimaric acid closely resembles abietic acid into which it passes when distilled in a vacuum; it has been supposed to consist of three isomers.

Synthetic Resins

Synthetic resins are materials with similar properties to natural resins—viscous liquids capable of hardening. They are typically manufactured by esterification or soaping of organic compounds. The classic variety is epoxy resin, manufactured through polymerization-polyaddition or polycondensation reactions, used as a thermoset polymer for adhesives and composites. Epoxy resin is two times stronger than concrete, seamless and waterproof. Accordingly, it has been mainly in use for industrial flooring purposes since the 1960s. Since 2000, however, epoxy and polyurethane resins are used in interiors as well, mainly in Western Europe.

One more category, which constitutes 75% of resins used, is unsaturated polyester resin. Ion exchange resin is another important class with application in water purification and catalysis of organic reactions. See also AT-10 resin, melamine resin. Another synthetic polymer is also sometimes called by the same suffix, acetal resin. By contrast with the other synthetics, however, it has a simple chain structure with the repeat unit of form -[CH_2O]-.

The hard transparent resins, such as the copals, dammars, mastic and sandarac, are principally used for varnishes and cement, while the softer odoriferous oleo-resins (frankincense, elemi, turpentine, copaiba) and gum resins containing essential oils (ammoniacum, asafoetida, gamboge, myrrh, and scammony) are more largely used for therapeutic purposes and incense.

Resin in the form of rosin is used for the upkeep of bows for stringed instruments (i.e. violin, viola, cello, double bass), because of its quality for adding friction to the hair. Ballet dancers may apply crushed rosin to their shoes to increase grip on a slippery floor.

Resin has also been used as a medium for sculpture by artists such as Eva Hesse, and in other types of artwork.

Also, resin is used in some skateboard decks. It makes the skateboard more durable, making it less likely to get pressure-related cracks, chipping, or breaking in half.

Conservators use resins to consolidate fragile items such as bone found on archaeological sites. The resin acts to bind the fragile material inside its molecular structure. In Pompeii, resin is now used instead of plaster to recreate the bodies of Mount Vesuvius' victims, because it is more durable.

9
HERBALISM

Herbalism is a traditional medicinal or folk medicine practice based on the use of plants and plant extracts. Herbalism is also known as botanical medicine, medical herbalism, herbal medicine, herbology, and phytotherapy. Sometimes the scope of herbal medicine is extended to include fungi and bee products, as well as minerals, shells and certain animal part.

Many plants synthesize substances that are useful to the maintenance of health in humans and other animals. These include aromatic substances, most of which are phenols or their oxygen-substituted derivatives such as tannins. Many are secondary metabolites, of which at least 12,000 have been isolated—a number estimated to be less than 10% of the total. In many cases, these substances (particularly the alkaloids) serve as plant defense mechanisms against predation by microorganisms, insects, and herbivores. Many of the herbs and spices used by humans to season food yield useful medicinal compounds.

Anthropology of Herbalism

People on all continents have used hundreds to thousands of indigenous plants for treatment of ailments since prehistoric times. The first generally accepted use of plants as healing agents was depicted in the cave paintings discovered in the Lascaux caves in France, which have been radiocarbon-dated to between 13,000-25,000 BC. Medicinal herbs were found in the personal effects of an Ice man, whose body was frozen in the Swiss Alps for more than 5,300 years, which appear to have been used to treat the parasites found in his intestines. Anthropology or Anthropologists theorize that animals evolved a tendency to seek out bitter plant parts in response to illness.

Indigenous healers often claim to have learned by observing that sick animals change their food preferences to nibble at bitter herbs they would normally reject Field biologists have provided corroborating evidence based on observation of diverse species, such as chimpanzees, chickens, sheep and butterflies. Lowland gorillas take 90% of their diet from the fruits of Aframomum melegueta, a relative of the ginger plant, that is a potent antimicrobial and apparently keeps shigellosis and similar infections at bay.

Researchers from Ohio Wesleyan University found that some birds select nesting material rich in antimicrobial agents which protect their young from harmful bacteria.

Sick animals tend to forage plants rich in secondary metabolites, such as tannins and alkaloids Since these phytochemicals often have antiviral, antibacterial, antifungal and antihelminthic properties, a plausible case can be made for self-medication by animals in the wild.

Some animals have digestive systems especially adapted to cope with certain plant toxins. For example, the koala can live on the leaves and shoots of the eucalyptus, a plant that is dangerous to most animals A plant that is harmless to a particular animal may not be safe for humans to ingest A reasonable conjecture is that these discoveries were traditionally collected by the medicine people of indigenous tribes, who then passed on safety information and cautions.

The use of herbs and spices in cuisine developed in part as a response to the threat of food-born pathogens. Studies show that in tropical climates where pathogens are the most abundant recipes are the most highly spiced. Further, the spices with the most potent antimicrobial activity tend to be selected In all cultures vegetables are spiced less than meat, presumably because they are more resistant to spoilage.

Herbs in History

In the written record, the study of herbs dates back over 5000 years to the Sumerians, who described well-established medicinal uses for such plants as laurel, caraway, and thyme. Ancient Egyptian medicine of 1000 B.C. are known to have used garlic, opium, castor oil, coriander, mint, indigo, and other herbs for medicine and the Old Testament also mentions herb use and cultivation, including mandrake, vetch, caraway, wheat, barley, and rye.

Indian Ayurveda medicine has been using herbs such as turmeric and curcumin possibly as early as 1900 B.C Many other herbs and minerals used in Ayurveda were later described by ancient Indian herbalists such as Charaka and Sushruta during the 1st millenium BC. The *Sushruta Samhita* attributed to Sushruta in the 6th century BC describes 700 medicinal plants, 64 preparations from mineral sources, and 57 preparations based on animal sources.

The first Chinese herbal book, the Shennong Bencao Jing, compiled during the Han Dynasty but dating back to a much earlier date, possibly 2700 B.C., lists 365 medicinal plants and their uses - including ma-Huang, the shrub that introduced the drug ephedrine to modern medicine. Succeeding generations augmented on the *Shennong Bencao Jing*, as in the *Yaoxing Lun* (*Treatise on the Nature of Medicinal Herbs*), a 7th century Tang Dynasty treatise on herbal medicine.

The ancient Greeks and Romans made medicinal use of plants. Greek and Roman medicinal practices, as preserved in the writings of Hippocrates and - especially - Galen, provided the patterns for later western medicine. Hippocrates advocated the use of a few simple herbal drugs - along with fresh air, rest, and proper diet. Galen, on the other had, recommended large doses of drug mixtures - including plant, animal, and mineral ingredients. The Greek physician compiled the first European treatise on the properties and uses of medicinal plants, *De Materia Medica*. In the first century AD, Dioscorides wrote a compendium of more than 500 plants that remained an authoritative reference into the 17th century. Similarly important for herbalists and botanists of later centuries was the Greek book that founded the science of botany, Theophrastus' *Historia Plantarum*, written in the fourth century B.C.

Middle Ages

The uses of plants for medicine and other purposes changed little in early medieval Europe. Many Greek and Roman writings on medicine, as on other subjects, were preserved by hand copying of manuscripts in monasteries. The monasteries thus tended to become local centers of medical knowledge, and their herb gardens provided the raw materials for simple treatment of common disorders. At the same time, folk medicine in the home and village continues uninterrupted, supporting numerous wandering and settled herbalists. Among these were the "wise-women," who prescribed herbal remedies often along with spells and enchantments. It was not until the late Middle Ages that women who were knowledgeable in herb lore became the targets of the witch hysteria. One of the most famous women in the herbal tradition was Hildegard of Bingen. A twelfth century Benedictine nun, she wrote a medical text called *Causes and Cures*.

Medical schools known as, Bimaristan began to appear from the 9th century in the medieval Islamic world, which was generally more advanced than medieval Europe at the time. The Arabs venerated Greco-Roman culture and learning, and translated tens of thousands of texts into Arabic for further study As a trading culture, the Arab travellers had access to plant material from distant places such as China and India. Herbals, medical texts and translations of the classics of antiquity filtered in from east and west Muslim botanists and Muslim physicians significantly expanded on the earlier knowledge of materia medica. For example, al-Dinawari described more than 637 plant drugs in the 9th century, and Ibn al-Baitar described more than 1,400 different plants, foods and drugs, over 300 of which were his own original discoveries, in the 13th century The experimental scientific method was introduced into the field of materia medica in the 13th century by the Andalusian-Arab botanist Abu al-Abbas al-Nabati, the teacher of Ibn al-Baitar. Al-Nabati introduced empirical techniques in the testing, description and identification of numerous materia medica, and he separated unverified reports from those supported by actual tests and observations. This allowed the study of materia medica to evolve into the science of pharmacology.

Avicenna's *The Canon of Medicine* (1025) is considered the first pharmacopoeia and lists 800 tested drugs, plants and minerals Book Two is devoted to a discussion of the healing properties of herbs, including nutmeg, senna, sandalwood, rhubarb, myrrh, cinammon, and rosewater Baghdad was an important centre for Arab herbalism, as was Al-Andalus between 800 and 1400. Abulcasis (936-1013) of Cordoba authored *The Book of Simples*, an important source for later European herbals, while Ibn al-Baitar (1197-1248) of Malaga authored the *Corpus of Simples*, the most complete Arab herbal which introduced 200 new healing herbs, including tamarind, aconite, and *Nux vomica*. Other pharmacopoeia books include that written by Abu-Rayhan Biruni in the 11th century and Ibn Zuhr (Avenzoar) in the 12th century (and printed in 1491). The origins of clinical pharmacology also date back to the Middle Ages in Avicenna's *The Canon of Medicine*, Peter of Spain's *Commentary on Isaac*, and John of St Amand's *Commentary on the Antedotary of Nicholas*. In particular, the Canon introduced clinical trials randomized controlled trials and efficacy tests.

Alongside the university system, folk medicine continued to thrive. The continuing importance of herbs for the centuries following the Middle Ages is indicated by the hundreds of herbals published after the invention of printing in the fifteenth century. Theophrastus' *Historia Plantarum* was one of the first books to be printed, but Dioscorides' *De Materia Medica*, Avicenna's *Canon of Medicine* and Avenzoar's *Pharmacopoeia* were not far behind.

Modern Era

The fifteenth, sixteenth, and seventeenth centuries were the great age of herbals, many of them available for the first time in English and other languages rather than Latin or Greek. The first herbal to be published in English was the anonymous Grete Herball of 1526. The two best-known herbals in English were *The Herball or General History of Plants* (1597) by John Gerard and *The English Physician Enlarged* (1653) by Nicholas Culpeper. Gerard's text was basically a pirated translation of a book by the Belgian herbalist Dodoens and his illustrations came from a German botanical work. The original edition contained many errors due to faulty matching of the two parts. Culpeper's blend of traditional medicine with astrology, magic, and folklore was ridiculed by the physicians of his day yet his book - like Gerard's and other herbals - enjoyed phenomenal popularity. *The Age of Exploration* and the *Columbian Exchange* introduced new medicinal plants to Europe. The Badianus Manuscript was an illustrated Aztec herbal translated into Latin in the 16th century.

The second millennium, however, also saw the beginning of a slow erosion of the pre-eminent position held by plants as sources of therapeutic effects. This began with the introduction of the physician, the introduction of active chemical drugs (like arsenic, copper sulfate, iron, mercury, and sulfur), followed by the rapid development of chemistry and the other physical sciences, led increasingly to the dominance of chemotherapy - chemical medicine - as the orthodox system of the twentieth century.

Role of Herbal Medicine in Modern Human Society

The use of herbs to treat disease is almost universal among non-industrialized societies a number of traditions came to dominate the practice of herbal medicine at the end of the twentieth century:

- The herbal medicine system, based on Greek and Roman sources
- The Siddha and Ayurvedic medicine systems from various South Asian Countries.
- Chinese herbal medicine (Chinese herbology).
- Unani-Tibb medicine.
- Shamanic Herbalism.

Many of the pharmaceuticals currently available to physicians have a long history of use as herbal remedies, including opium, aspirin, digitalis, and quinine. The World Health Organization (WHO) estimates that 80 percent of the world's population presently uses herbal medicine for some aspect of primary health care Pharmaceuticals are prohibitively expensive for most of the world's population, half of which lives on less than $2 U.S. per day In comparison, herbal medicines can be grown from seed or gathered from nature for little or no cost. Herbal medicine is a major component in all traditional medicine systems, and a common element in Siddha, Ayurvedic, homeopathic, naturopathic, traditional Chinese medicine, and Native American medicine.

The use of, and search for, drugs and dietary supplements derived from plants have accelerated in recent years. Pharmacologists, microbiologists, botanists, and natural-products chemists are combing the Earth for phytochemicals and leads that could be developed for treatment of various diseases. In fact, according to the World Health Organisation, approximately 25% of modern drugs used in the United States have been derived from plants.

Three quarters of plants that provide active ingredients for prescription drugs came to the attention of researchers because of their use in traditional medicine.

- Among the 120 active compounds currently isolated from the higher plants and widely used in modern medicine today, 80 percent show a positive correlation between their modern therapeutic use and the traditional use of the plants from which they are derived.
- More than two thirds of the world's plant species - at least 35,000 of which are estimated to have medicinal value - come from the developing countries.
- At least 7000 medical compounds in the modern pharmacopoeia are derived from plants.

Biological Background

All plants produce chemical compounds as part of their normal metabolic activities. These include primary metabolites, such as sugars and fats, found in all plants, and secondary metabolites found in a smaller range of plants, some useful ones found only in a particular genus or species. Pigments harvest light, protect the organism from radiation and display colors to attract pollinators. Many common weeds have medicinal properties.

The functions of secondary metabolites are varied. For example, some secondary metabolites are toxins used to deter predation, and others are pheromones used to attract insects for pollination. Phytoalexins protect against bacterial and fungal attacks. Allelochemicals inhibit rival plants that are competing for soil and light.

Plants upregulate and downregulate their biochemical paths in response to the local mix of herbivores, pollinators and microorganisms The chemical profile of a single plant may vary over time as it reacts to changing conditions. It is the secondary metabolites and pigments that can have therapeutic actions in humans and which can be refined to produce drugs.

Plants synthesize a bewildering variety of phytochemicals but most are derivatives of a few biochemical motifs.

- Alkaloids contain a ring with nitrogen. Many alkaloids have dramatic effects on the central nervous system. Caffeine is an alkaloid that provides a mild lift but the alkaloids in datura cause severe intoxication and even death.
- Phenolics contain phenol rings. The anthocyanins that give grapes their purple color, the isoflavones, the phytoestrogens from soy and the tannins that give tea its astringency are phenolics.
- Turpenoids are built up from terpene building blocks. Each terpene consists of two paired isoprenes. The names monoterpenes, sesquiterpenes, diterpenes and triterpenes are based on the number of isoprene units. The fragrance of rose and lavender is due to monoterpenes. The carotenoids produce the reds, yellows and oranges of pumpkin, corn and tomatoes.
- Glycosides consist of a glucose moiety attached to an aglycone. The aglycone is a molecule that is bioactive in its free form but inert until the glycoside bond is broken by water or enzymes. This mechanism allows the plant to defer the availability of the molecule to an

appropriate time, similar to a safety lock on a gun. An example is the cyanoglycosides in cherry pits that release toxins only when bitten by a herbivore.

The word drug itself comes from the Dutch word *"drug"* (via the French word *Drogue*), which means 'dried plant'. Some examples are inulin from the roots of dahlias, quinine from the cinchona, morphine and codeine from the poppy, and digoxin from the foxglove.

The active ingredient in willow bark, once prescribed by Hippocrates, is salicin, which is converted in the body into salicylic acid. The discovery of salicylic acid would eventually lead to the development of the acetylated form acetylsalicylic acid, also known as "aspirin", when it was isolated from a plant known as meadowsweet. The word aspirin comes from an abbreviation of meadowsweet's Latin genus Spiraea, with an additional "A" at the beginning to acknowledge acetylation, and "in" was added at the end for easier pronunciation Aspirin" was originally a brand name, and is still a protected trademark in some countries. This medication was patented by Bayer AG.

Herbal Philosophy

Since herbalism is such a diverse field few generalizations apply universally. Nevertheless a rough consensus can be inferred.

Most herbalists concede that pharmaceuticals are more effective in emergency situations where time is of the essence. An example would be where a patient had elevated blood pressure that posed imminent danger. However they claim that over the long term herbs can help the patient resist disease and in addition provide nutritional and immunological support that pharmaceuticals lack. They view their goal as prevention as well as cure.

Herbalists tend to use extracts from parts of plants, such as the roots or leaves but not isolate particular phytochemicals. Pharmaceutical medicine prefers single ingredients on the grounds that dosage can be more easily quantified. Herbalists reject the notion of a single active ingredient. They argue that the different phytochemicals present in many herbs will interact to enhance the therapeutic effects of the herb and dilute toxicity. Furthermore, they argue that a single ingredient may contribute to multiple effects. Herbalists deny that herbal synergism can be duplicated with synthetic chemicals. They argue that phytochemical interactions and trace components may alter the drug response in ways that cannot currently be replicated with a combination of a few putative active ingredients. Pharmaceutical researchers recognize the concept of drug synergism but note that clinical trials may be used to investigate the efficacy of a particular herbal preparation, provided the formulation of that herb is consistent.

In specific cases the claims of synergy and multi-functionality have been supported by science. The open question is how widely both can be generalized. Herbalists would argue that cases of synergy can be widely generalized, on the basis of their interpretation of evolutionary history, not necessarily shared by the pharmaceutical community. Plants are subject to similar selection pressures as humans and therefore they must develop resistance to threats such as radiation, reactive oxygen species and microbial attack in order to survive. Optimal chemical defenses have been selected for and have thus developed over millions of years. Human diseases are multifactorial and may be treated by consuming the chemical defences that they believe to be present in herbs. Bacteria, inflammation, nutrition and ROS (reactive oxygen species) may all play a role in arterial disease. Herbalists claim a single herb may simultaneously address several of these factors. Likewise a factor such as ROS may underly more than one condition. In short herbalists view their field as the study of a web of relationships rather than a quest for single cause and a single cure for a single condition.

In selecting herbal treatments herbalists may use forms of information that are not applicable to pharmacists. Because herbs can moonlight as vegetables, teas or spices they have a huge consumer base and large-scale epidemiological studies become feasible. Ethnobotanical studies are another source of information. For example, when indigenous peoples from geographically dispersed areas use closely related herbs for the same purpose that is taken as supporting evidence for its efficacy. Herbalists contend that historical medical records and herbals are underutilized resources They favor the use of convergent information in assessing the medical value of plants. An example would be when in-vitro activity is consistent with traditional use.

In strains of herbalism rely on sources that would be widely considered unreliable and would not be accepted in a scientifically oriented herbal journal. These include astrology, the Bible, intuition, dreams, "plant spirits", etc.

Popularity

A survey released in May 2004 by the National Center for Complementary and Alternative Medicine focused on who used complementary and alternative medicines (CAM), what was used, and why it was used. The survey was limited to adults, aged 18 years and over during 2002, living in the United States.

According to this survey, herbal therapy, or use of natural products other than vitamins and minerals, was the most commonly used CAM therapy (18.9%) when all use of prayer was excluded.

Herbal remedies are very common in Europe. In Germany, herbal medications are dispensed by apothecaries (e.g., Apotheke). Prescription drugs are sold alongside essential oils, herbal extracts, or herbal teas. Herbal remedies are seen by some as a treatment to be preferred to chemical medications which have been industrially produced.

In the United Kingdom, the training of medical herbalists is done by state funded Universities. For example, Bachelor of Science degrees in herbal medicine are offered at Universities such as University of East London, Middlesex University, of Central Lancashire, University of Westminster, University of Lincoln and Napier University in Edinburgh at the present.

Types of Herbal Medicine Systems

Use of medicinal plants can be as informal as, for example, culinary use or consumption of an herbal tea or supplement, although the sale of some herbs considered dangerous is often restricted to the public. Sometimes such herbs are provided to professional herbalists by specialist companies. Many herbalists, both professional and amateur, often grow or "wildcraft" their own herbs.

Some researchers trained in both western and traditional Chinese medicine have attempted to deconstruct ancient medical texts in the light of modern science. One idea is that the yin-yang balance, at least with regard to herbs, corresponds to the pro-oxidant and anti-oxidant balance. This interpretation is supported by several investigations of the ORAC ratings of various yin and yang herbs.

Eclectic medicine came out of the vitalist tradition, similar to physiomedicalism and bridged the European and Native American traditions Cherokee medicine tends to divide herbs into foods, medicines and toxins and to use seven plants in the treatment of disease, which is defined with both spiritual and physiological aspects, according to Cherokee herbalist David Winston.

In India, Ayurvedic medicine has quite complex formulas with 30 or more ingredients, including a sizable number of ingredients that have undergone "alchemical processing", chosen to balance "Vata", "Pitta" or "Kapha."

In Tamil Nadu, Tamil have their own medicinal system now popularly called the *Siddha* medicinal system. The *Siddha* system is entirely in the Tamil language. It contains roughly 300,000 versus covering diverse aspects of medicine such as anatomy, sex (*"kokokam"* is the sexual treatise of par excellence), herbal, mineral and metallic compositions to cure many diseases that are relevant even today. Ayurveda is in Sanskrit, but Sanskrit was not generally used as a mother tongue and hence its medicines are mostly taken from *Siddha* and other local traditions.

In addition there are more modern theories of herbal combination like William LeSassier's triune formula which combined Pythagorean imagery with Chinese medicine ideas and resulted in 9 herb formulas which supplemented, drained or neutrally nourished the main organ systems affected and three associated systems His system has been taught to thousands of influential American herbalists through his own apprenticeship programs during his lifetime, the William LeSassier Archiveand the David Winston Center for Herbal Studies.

Many traditional African remedies have performed well in initial laboratory tests to ensure they are not toxic and in tests on animals. Gawo, a herb used in traditional treatments, has been tested in rats by researchers from Nigeria's University of Jos and the National Institute for Pharmaceutical Research and Development. According to research in the African Journal of Biotechnology, Gawo passed tests for toxicity and reduced induced fevers, diarrhoea and inflammation.

Routes of Administration

The exact composition of a herbal product is influenced by the method of extraction. A tisane will be rich in polar components because water is a polar solvent. Oil on the other hand is a non-polar solvent and it will absorb non-polar compounds. Alcohol lies somewhere in between.

- *Tinctures* (alcoholic extracts of herbs such as echinacea extract. Usually obtained by combining 100% pure ethanol (or a mixture of 100% ethanol with water) with the herb. A completed tincture has a ethanol percentage of at least 40-60% (sometimes up to 90%).

- *Herbal wine* and *elixirs*; these are alcoholic extract of herbs; usually with an ethanol percentage of 12-38% Herbal wine is a maceration of herbs in wine, while an elixir is a maceration of herbs in spirits (eg vodka, grappa, ...)
- *Tisanes* (hot-water extracts of herb, such as chamomile)
- *Decoctions* (long-term boiled extract of usually roots or bark)
- *Macerates* (cold infusion of plants with high mucilage-content as sage, thyme, ...) Plants are chopped and added to cold water. They are then left to stand for 7 to 12 hours (depending on herb used). For most macerates 10 hours is used.
- *Vinegars* (prepared at the same way as tinctures).
- Topicals.
- *Essential oils*- application of essential oil extracts, usually diluted in a carrier oil (many essential oils can burn the skin or are simply too high dose used straight – diluting in olive oil or another food grade oil can allow these to be used safely as a topica.
- *Salves, oils, balms, creams* and *lotions*- Most topical applications are oil extractions of herbs. Taking a food grade oil and soaking herbs in it for anywhere from weeks to months allows certain phytochemicals to be extracted into the oil. This oil can then be made into salves, creams, lotions, or simply used as an oil for topical application. Many massage oils, antibacterial salves and wound healing compounds are made this way.
- *Poultices and compresses*- One can also make a poultice or compress using whole herb (or the appropriate part

of the plant) usually crushed or dried and re-hydrated with a small amount of water and then applied directly in a bandage, cloth or just as is.

- Whole herb consumption. This can occur in either dried form (herbal powder, or fresh (juice, fresh leaves and other plant parts. Just as Hippocrates said "Let food be thy medicine", it has become clear that eating vegetables also easily fits within this category of getting health through consumables (besides medicinal herbs). All of the vitamins, minerals and antioxidants are phytochemicals that we are accessing through our diet. There are clearly some whole herbs consumed that are more powerful than others. Shiitake mushrooms boost the immune system and are also tasty so they are enjoyed in soups or other food preparations for the cold and flu season. Alfalfa is also considered a health food Garlic lowers cholesterol, improves blood flow, fights bacteria, viruses and yeast.

- *Syrups*- extracts of herbs made with syrup or honey. Sixty five parts of sugar are mixed with 35 parts of water and herb. The whole is then boiled and macerated for three weeks.

- *Extracts*- include liquid extracts, dry extracts and nebulisates. Liquid extracts are liquids with a lower ethanol percentage than tinctures. They can (and are usually) made by vacuum distilling tinctures. Dry extracts are extracts of plant material which are evaporated into a dry mass. They can then be further refined to a capsule or tablet. A nebulisate is a dry extract created by freeze-drying.

- *Inhalation* as in *aromatherapy* can be used as a mood changing treatment to fight a sinus infection or cough, or to cleanse the skin on a deeper level (steam rather than direct inhalation here).

Examples of Plants used as Medicine

Few herbal remedies have conclusively demonstrated any positive effect on humans, mainly because of inadequate testing. Many of the studies cited refer to animal model investigations or in-vitro assays and therefore cannot provide more than weak supportive evidence.

Risks to Health

In some cases, herbal medicines offer an inexpensive and safe alternative to pharmaceuticals. In the U.S., which has just 4% of the world's population, 106,000 patients died from and 2.2 million were seriously injured by adverse effects of pharmaceuticals in the year 1994 (Journal of the American Medical Association. Proper double-blind clinical trials are needed to determine the safety and efficacy of each plant before they can be recommended for medical use In addition, many consumers believe that herbal medicines are safe because they are natural. Herbal medicines may interact with synthetic drugs causing toxicity to the patient, herbal products may have contamination that is a safety consideration, and herbal medicines, without proven efficacy, may be used to replace medicines that have a proven efficacy.

Standardization of purity and dosage is not mandated in the United States, but even products made to the same specification may differ as a result of biochemical variations within a species of plant. Plants have chemical defense mechanisms against predators that can have adverse or lethal effects on humans. Examples of highly toxic herbs include poison hemlock and nightshade They are not marketed to the public as herbs, because the risks are well known, partly due to a long and colorful history in Europe, associated with "sorcery", "magic" and intrigue Although not frequent, adverse reactions have been reported for herbs in widespread use On occasion serious untoward outcomes have been linked to herb consumption. A case of major potassium depletion has been attributed to chronic licorice ingestion Black cohosh has been implicated in a case of liver failure Few studies are available on the safety of herbs for pregnant women.

Herb drug interactions are a concern. In consultation with a physician, usage of herbal remedies should be clarified, as some herbal remedies have the potential to cause adverse drug interactions when used in combination with various prescription and over-the-counter pharmaceuticals.

Dangerously low blood pressure may result from the combination of an herbal remedy that lowers blood pressure together with prescription medicine that has the same effect. Some herbs may amplify the effects of anticoagulants Certain herbs as well as common fruit interfere with cytochrome P450, an enzyme critical to drug metabolism.

Effectiveness

The gold standard for pharmaceutical testing is repeated, large-scale, randomized, double-blind tests. Some plant products or pharmaceutical drugs derived from them are incorporated into mainstream medicine. To recoup the considerable costs of testing to the regulatory standards, the substances are patented by pharmaceutical companies and sold at a substantial profit.

Many herbs have shown positive results in-vitro, animal model or small-scale clinical tests but many studies on herbal treatments have also found negative results he quality of the trials on herbal remedies is highly variable and many trials of herbal treatments have been found to be of poor quality, with many trials lacking an intention to treat analysis or a comment on whether blinding was successful The few randomized, double-blind tests that receive attention in mainstream medical publications are often questioned on methodological grounds or interpretation. Likewise, studies published in peer-reviewed medical journals such as *Journal of the American Medical Association* receive more consideration than those published in specialized herbal journals. This preference may be due to the possibility of location bias for such trials. One study found that non-impact factor alternative medicine journals published more studies with positive results than negative results and that trials finding positive results were of lower quality than trials finding negative results. High impact factor mainstream medical journals, on the other hand, published equal numbers of trials with positive and negative results. In high impact journals, trials finding positive results were also found to have lower quality scores than trials finding negative results. Another study found studies of phyomedicine to have superior quality to matched studies of pharmaceuticals However, this study used a matched pair design and excluded all herbal trials that were not controlled, did not use a placebo or did not use random or quasi random assignment.

Herbalists criticize mainstream studies on the grounds that they make insufficient use of historical usage. They maintain that tradition can guide the selection of factors such as optimal dose, species, time of harvesting and target population.

Dosage is in general an outstanding issue for herbal treatments: while most conventional medicines are heavily tested to determine the most effective and safest dosages (especially in relation to things like body weight, drug interactions, etc.), there are fewer varieties of dosages for various herbal treatments on the market. Furthermore, herbal medicines taken in whole form cannot generally guarantee a consistent dosage or drug quality, since certain samples may contain more or less of a given active ingredient.

Several methods of standardization may be applied to herbs. One is the ratio of raw materials to solvent. However different specimens of even the same plant species may vary in chemical content. Another method is standardization on a signal chemical.

Clinical Studies

In 2004 the U.S. National Center for Complementary and Alternative Medicine of the National Institutes of Health began funding clinical trials into the effectiveness of herbal medicine.

Name Confusion

The common names of herbs (folk taxonomy) may not reflect differences in scientific taxonomy, and the same (or a very similar) common name might group together different plant species with different effects. For example, in 1993 in Belgium, a formula created by medical doctors including some Traditional Chinese medicine (TCM) herbs for weight loss. One herb (Stephania tetrandra) was swapped for another (Aristolochia fangchi) whose name in Chinese was extremely similar but which contained higher levels of a renal toxin, aristolochic acid; this mistake resulted in 105 cases of kidney damage Note that neither herb used in a TCM context would be used for weight loss or given for long periods of time.

In Chinese medicine these herbs are used for certain forms of acute arthritis and edema.

Standards and Quality Control

The issue of regulation is an area of continuing controversy in the EU and USA. At one end of the spectrum, some herbalists maintain that traditional remedies have a long history of use, and do not require the level of safety testing as xenobiotics or single ingredients in an artificially concentrated form. On the other hand, others are in favor of legally enforced quality standards, safety testing and prescription by a qualified practitioner. Some professional herbalist organizations have made statements calling for a category of regulation for herbal products Yet others agree with the need for more quality testing but believe it can be managed through reputation without government intervention. The legal status of herbal ingredients varies by country.

In the United States, most herbal remedies are regulated as dietary supplements by the Food and Drug Administration Manufacturers of products falling into this category are not required to prove the safety or efficacy of their product, though the FDA may withdraw a product from sale should it prove harmful.

The National Nutritional Foods Association, the industry's largest trade association, has run a program since 2002, examining the products and factory conditions of member companies, giving them the right to display the GMP (Good Manufacturing Practices) seal of approval on their products.

In the UK, herbal remedies that are bought over the counter are regulated as supplements, as in the US. However, herbal remedies prescribed and dispensed by a qualified "Medical Herbalist", after a personal consultation, are regulated as medicines.

A Medical Herbalist can prescribe some herbs which are not available over the counter, covered by Schedule III of the Medicines Act. Forthcoming changes to laws regulating herbal products in the UK, are intended to ensure the quality of herbal products used.

Some herbs, such as cannabis, however, are outright banned in most countries for various reasons. Since 2004, the sales of ephedra as an dietary supplement is prohibited in the United States by the FDA.

Danger of Extinction

On January 18, 2008, the Botanic Gardens Conservation International (representing botanic gardens in 120 countries) stated that "400 medicinal plants are at risk of extinction, from over-collection and deforestation, threatening the discovery of future cures for disease." These included Yew trees (the bark is used for cancer drugs, paclitaxel); Hoodia (from Namibia, source of weight loss drugs); half of Magnolias (used as Chinese medicine for 5,000 years to fight cancer, dementia and heart disease); and Autumn crocus (for gout). The group also found that 5 billion people benefit from traditional plant-based medicine for health care.

10

FLAVONOID

The term flavonoid (or bioflavonoid) refers to a class of plant secondary metabolites. According to the IUPAC nomenclature, they can be classified into:

- flavonoids, derived from 2-phenylchromen-4-one (2-phenyl-1, 4-benzopyrone) structure;
- isoflavonoids, derived from 3-phenylchromen-4-one (3-phenyl-1, 4-benzopyrone) structure;
- neoflavonoids, derived from 4-phenylcoumarine (4-phenyl-1, 2-benzopyrone) structure.

Flavonoids are most commonly known for their antioxidant activity. However, it is now known that the health benefits they provide against cancer and heart disease are the result of other mechanisms Flavonoids are also commonly referred to as bioflavonoids in the media – the terms are largely equivalent and interchangeable, for most flavonoids are biological in origin.

Biosynthesis

Flavonoids are synthesized by the phenylpropanoid metabolic pathway in which the amino acid phenylalanine is used to produce 4-coumaroyl-CoA This can be combined with malonyl-CoA to yield the true backbone of flavonoids, a group of compounds called chalcones, which contain two phenyl rings. Conjugate ring-closure of chalcones results in the familiar form of flavonoids, the three-ringed structure of a flavone. The metabolic pathway continues through a series of enzymatic modifications to yield flavanones? dihydroflavonols? anthocyanins. Along this pathway, many products can be formed, including the flavonols, flavan-3-ols, proanthocyanidins (tannins) and a host of other polyphenolics.

Biological Effects

Flavonoids are widely distributed in plants fulfilling many functions including producing yellow or red/blue pigmentation in flowers and protection from attack by microbes and insects. The widespread distribution of flavonoids, their variety and their relatively low toxicity compared to other active plant compounds (for instance alkaloids) mean that many animals, including humans, ingest significant quantities in their diet. Flavonoids have been referred to as "nature's biological response modifiers" because of strong experimental evidence of their inherent ability to modify the body's reaction to allergens, viruses, and carcinogens. They show anti-allergic, anti-inflammatory, anti-microbial and anti-cancer activity.

Consumers and food manufacturers have become interested in flavonoids for their medicinal properties, especially their potential role in the prevention of cancers and cardiovascular disease. The beneficial effects of fruit, vegetables, and tea or even red wine have been attributed to flavonoid compounds rather than to known nutrients and vitamins.

Health Benefits Aside from Antioxidant Values

In 2007, research conducted at the Linus Pauling Institute and published in Free Radical Biology and Medicine indicates that inside the human body, flavonoids themselves are of little or no direct antioxidant value. Unlike in the controlled conditions of a test tube, flavonoids are poorly absorbed by the human body (less than 5%), and most of what is absorbed is quickly metabolized and excreted from the body.

The huge increase in antioxidant capacity of blood seen after the consumption of flavonoid-rich foods is not caused directly by the flavonoids themselves, but most likely is due to increased uric acid levels that result from expelling flavonoids from the body. According to Frei, "we can now follow the activity of flavonoids in the body, and one thing that is clear is that the body sees them as foreign compounds and is trying to get rid of them. But this process of gearing up to get rid of unwanted compounds is inducing so-called Phase II enzymes that also help eliminate mutagens and carcinogens, and therefore may be of value in cancer prevention ... Flavonoids could also induce mechanisms that help kill cancer cells and inhibit tumor invasion."

Their research also indicated that only small amounts of flavonoids are necessary to see these medical benefits. Taking large dietary supplements provides no extra benefit and may pose some risks.

Diarrhoea

A study done at Children's Hospital & Research Center Oakland, in collaboration with scientists at Heinrich Heine University in Germany, has shown that epicatechin, quercetin and luteolin can inhibit the development of fluids that result in diarrhea by targeting the intestinal cystic fibrosis transmembrane conductance regulator Cl– transport inhibiting cAMP-stimulated Cl– secretion in the intestine

Important Flavonoids

This article or section needs to be updated. Please update the article to reflect recent events or newly available information, and remove this template when finished.

Quercetin

Quercetin is a flavonoid and, to be more specific, a flavonol. It is the aglycone form of a number of other flavonoid glycosides, such as rutin and quercitrin, found in citrus fruit, buckwheat and onions. Quercetin forms the glycosides quercitrin and rutin together with rhamnose and rutinose, respectively. It may also help to prevent some types of cancer, however currently there is more research needed in this area.

Epicatechin

Epicatechin (EC) Epicatechin improves blood flow and thus seems good for cardiac health. Cocoa, the major ingredient of dark chocolate, contains relatively high amounts of epicatechin and has been found to have nearly twice the antioxidant content of red wine and up to three times that of green tea in in-vitro tests But in the test outlined above it now appears the beneficial antioxidant effects are minimal as the antioxidants are rapidly excreted from the body.

Oligomeric Proanthocyanidins

Proanthocyanidins extracts demonstrate a wide range of pharmacological activity. Their effects include increasing intracellular vitamin C levels, decreasing capillary permeability and fragility, scavenging oxidants and free radicals, and inhibiting destruction of collagen, the most abundant protein in the body.

Important Dietary Sources

Good sources of flavonoids include all citrus fruits, berries, ginkgo biloba, onions parsley pulses tea (especially white and green tea), red wine, seabuckthorn, and dark chocolate (with a cocoa content of seventy percent or greater).

Citrus

The citrus bioflavonoids include hesperidin (a glycoside of the flavanone hesperetin), quercitrin, rutin (two glycosides of the flavonol quercetin), and the flavone tangeritin. In addition to possessing antioxidant activity and an ability to increase intracellular levels of vitamin C, rutin and hesperidin exert beneficial effects on capillary permeability and blood flow. They also exhibit some of the anti-allergy and anti-inflammatory benefits of quercetin. Quercetin can also inhibit reverse transcriptase, part of the replication process of retroviruses The therapeutical relevance of this inhibition has not been established. Hydroxyethylrutosides (HER) have been used in the treatment of capillary permeability, easy bruising, hemorrhoids, and varicose veins.

Ginkgo

Leaf extract from the Ginkgo tree is widely marketed as an herbal supplement. The active ingredients are flavoglycosides.

Tea

Bai Hao Yinzhen from Fuding in Fujian Province, widely considered the best grade of white tea Green tea flavonoids are potent antioxidant compounds, thought to reduce incidence of cancer and heart disease. The major flavonoids in green tea are the kaempferol and catechins [catechin, epicatechin, epicatechin gallate, and epigallocatechin gallate (EGCG)].

In producing teas such as oolong tea and black tea, the leaves are allowed to oxidize, during which enzymes present in the tea convert some or all of the catechins to larger molecules. However, green tea is produced by steaming the fresh-cut leaf, which inactivates these enzymes, and oxidation does not significantly occur. White tea is the least processed of teas and is shown to present the highest amount of catechins known to occur in camellia sinensis.

Wine

Grape skins contain significant amounts of flavonoids as well as other polyphenols Both red and white wine contain flavonoids; however, since red wine is produced by fermentation in the presence of the grape skins, red wine has been observed to contain higher levels of flavonoids, and other polyphenolics such as resveratrol.

Dark Chocolate

Flavonoids exist naturally in cacao, but because they can be bitter, they are often removed from chocolate, even the dark variety.

Subgroups

Over 5000 naturally occurring flavonoids have been characterized from various plants. They have been classified according to their chemical structure, and are usually subdivided into the following subgroups.

Antioxidant Activities of Flavonoids

Flavonoids are compounds found in fruits, vegetables, and certain beverages that have diverse beneficial biochemical and antioxidant effects. Their dietary intake is quite high compared to other dietary antioxidants like vitamins C and E. The antioxidant activity of flavonoids depends on their molecular structure, and structural characteristics of certain flavonoids found in hops and beer confer surprisingly potent antioxidant activity exceeding that of red wine, tea, or soy.

Flavonoids are polyphenolic compounds that are ubiquitous in nature and are categorized, according to chemical structure, into flavonols, flavones, flavanones, isoflavones, catechins, anthocyanidins and chalcones. Over 4,000 flavonoids have been identified, many of which occur in fruits, vegetables and beverages (tea, coffee, beer, wine and fruit drinks). The flavonoids have aroused considerable interest recently because of their potential beneficial effects on human health-they have been reported to have antiviral, anti-allergic, antiplatelet, anti-inflammatory, antitumor and antioxidant activities.

Antioxidants are compounds that protect cells against the damaging effects of reactive oxygen species, such as singlet oxygen, superoxide, peroxyl radicals, hydroxyl radicals and peroxynitrite. An imbalance between antioxidants and reactive oxygen species results in oxidative stress, leading to cellular damage. Oxidative stress has been linked to cancer, aging, atherosclerosis, ischemic injury, inflammation and neurodegenerative diseases (Parkinson's and Alzheimer's). Flavonoids may help provide protection against these diseases by contributing, along with antioxidant vitamins and enzymes, to the total antioxidant defense system of the human body. Epidemiological studies have shown that flavonoid intake is inversely related to mortality from coronary heart disease and to the incidence of heart attacks.

The recognized dietary antioxidants are vitamin C, vitamin E, selenium, and carotenoids. However, recent studies have demonstrated that flavonoids found in fruits and vegetables may also act as antioxidants. Like alpha-tocopherol (vitamin E), flavonoids contain chemical structural elements that may be responsible for their antioxidant activities. A recent study by Dr. van Acker and his colleagues in the Netherlands suggests that flavonoids can replace vitamin E as chain-breaking anti-oxidants in liver microsomal membranes. The contribution of flavonoids to the antioxidant defense system may be substantial considering that the total daily intake of flavonoids can range from 50 to 800 mg. This intake is high compared to the average daily intake of other dietary antioxidants like vitamin C (70 mg), vitamin E (7-10 mg) or carotenoids (2-3 mg). Flavonoid intake depends upon the consumption of fruits, vegetables, and certain beverages, such as red wine, tea, and beer. The high consumption of tea and wine may be most influential on total flavonoid intake in certain groups of people.

The oxidation of low-density lipoprotein (LDL) has been recognized to play an important role in atherosclerosis.

Immune system cells called macrophages recognize and engulf oxidized LDL, a process that leads to the formation of atherosclerotic plaques in the arterial wall. LDL oxidation can be induced by macrophages and can also be catalyzed by metal ions like copper. Several studies have shown that certain flavonoids can protect LDL from being oxidized by these two mechanisms.

The capacity of flavonoids to act as antioxidants depends upon their molecular structure. The position of hydroxyl groups and other features in the chemical structure of flavonoids are important for their antioxidant and free radical scavenging activities. Quercetin, the most abundant dietary flavonol, is a potent antioxidant because it has all the right structural features for free radical scavenging activity.

Recently, chalcone and flavanone flavonoids with prenyl or geranyl side chains have been identified in hops and beer by Dr. Fred Stevens and Dr. Max Deinzer at Oregon State University. Hops are used in beer for flavor. Xanthohumol (a chalcone) and isoxanthohumol and 6-prenylnaringenin (flavanones) are the major prenyl-flavonoids found in beer. Although the antioxidant activities of these compounds have not been studied, these flavonoids may be responsible for the antioxidant activity of lager beer, which is higher than that of green tea, red wine, or grape juice as reported earlier by Dr. Joe A. Vinson from the University of Scranton in Pennsylvania. Xanthohumol is found only in beer but in small concentrations.

To assess the antioxidant activity of the prenylated flavonoids, we-in collaboration with LPI researchers-evaluated the capacity of these flavonoids to inhibit the oxidation of LDL by copper. The antioxidant properties of the prenylflavonoids were compared to those of quercetin (a flavonol), genistein (the major isoflavone in soy), chalconaringenin (a non-prenylated chalcone), naringenin (a non-prenylated flavanone), and vitamin E. The possible interaction of xanthohumol, the major prenylchalcone in beer, with vitamin E to inhibit LDL oxidation induced by copper was also examined.

Our results showed that the prenylchalcones and prenylflavones are effective in preventing LDL oxidation initiated by copper and that the prenylchalcones generally have greater antioxidant activity than the prenylflavanones. Xanthohumol, the major prenylchalcone in hops and beer, is a more powerful antioxidant than vitamin E or genistein. However, xanthohumol was less potent than quercetin. The potency of xanthohumol as an antioxidant is markedly increased when combined with an equivalent amount of vitamin E.

As reported in the Journal of Agricultural and Food Chemistry, we also found that the prenyl group plays an important role in the antioxidant activity of certain flavonoids. A flavonoid chalcone (chalconaringenin) and a flavanone (naringenin) with no prenyl groups act as pro-oxidants, i.e. they promote rather than limit the oxidation of LDL by copper. However, adding a prenyl group to these flavonoid molecules counteracted their pro-oxidant activities.

Our work reveals that there are unique flavonoids in hops and beer that may be potentially useful in the prevention of human disease attributed to free radical damage. The observation that prenyl groups are important in conferring antioxidant activity to certain flavonoids may lead to the discovery or synthesis of novel prenylated flavonoids as preventive or therapeutic agents against human diseases associated with free radicals. Our encouraging results with xanthohumol suggest that this prenylchalcone should be further studied for its antioxidant action and protective effects against free radical damage in animals and humans. Preliminary studies have shown that xanthohumol is absorbed from the digestive tract in rats, and more studies are needed to evaluate the bioavailability of these interesting flavonoids in people.

Further studies are also needed to establish the safety of xanthohumol or other flavonoids for use as dietary supplements since high doses of these compounds may produce adverse effects in humans, according to recent findings by Dr. Martyn Smith, professor of toxicology, University of California at Berkeley.

11

GLYCOSIDE

In chemistry, glycosides are certain molecules in which a sugar part is bound to some other part. Glycosides play numerous important roles in living organisms. Many plants store important chemicals in the form of inactive glycosides; if these chemicals are needed, the glycosides are brought in contact with water and an enzyme, and the sugar part is broken off, making the chemical available for use. Many such plant glycosides are used as medications. In animals (including humans), poisons are often bound to sugar molecules in order to remove them from the body.

Formally, a glycoside is any molecule in which a sugar group is bonded through its anomeric carbon to another group via an O-glycosidic bond or an S-glycosidic bond; glycosides involving the latter are also called thioglycosides. The given definition is the one used by IUPAC. Many authors require in addition that the sugar be bonded to a non-sugar for the molecule to qualify as a glycoside, thus excluding the polysaccharides. The sugar group is then known as the glycone and the non-sugar group as the aglycone or genin part of the glycoside. The glycone can consist of a single sugar group (monosaccharide) or several sugar groups (oligosaccharide).

Related Compounds

Molecules containing an N-glycosidic bond are known as glycosylamines and are not discussed in this article. (Many authors in biochemistry call these compounds N-glycosides and group them with the glycosides; this is considered a misnomer and discouraged by IUPAC.)

Chemistry

Much of the chemistry of glycosides is explained in the article on glycosidic bonds. For example, the glycone and aglycone portions can be chemically separated by hydrolysis in the presence of acid. There are also numerous enzymes that can form and break glycosidic bonds. The most important cleavage enzymes are the glycoside hydrolases, and the most important synthetic enzymes in nature are glycosyl transferases. Mutant enzymes termed glycosynthases have been developed that can form glycosidic bonds in excellent yield.

There are a great many ways to chemically synthesize glycosidic bonds. Fischer glycosidation refers to the synthesis of glycosides by the reaction of unprotected monosaccharides with alcohols (usually as solvent) in the presence of a strong acid catalyst. The Koenigs-Knorr reaction is the condensation of glycosyl halides and alcohols in the presence of metal salts such as silver carbonate or mercuric oxide.

Classification

We can classify glycosides by the glycone, by the type of glycosidic bond, and by the aglycone.

By Glycone

If the glycone group of a glycoside is glucose, then the molecule is a glucoside; if it is fructose, then the molecule is a fructoside; if it is glucuronic acid, then the molecule is a glucuronide; etc. In the body, toxic substances are often bonded to glucuronic acid to increase their water solubility; the resulting glucuronides are then excreted.

By Type of Glycosidic Bond

Depending on whether the glycosidic bond lies "above" or "below" the plane of the cyclic sugar molecule, glycosides are classified as a-glycosides or ß-glycosides. Some enzymes such as a-amylase can only hydrolize a-linkages; others, such as emulsin, can only affect ß-linkages.

By Aglycone

Glycosides are also classified according to the chemical nature of the aglycone. For purposes of biochemistry and pharmacology, this is the most useful classification.

Alcoholic Glycosides

An example of an alcoholic glycoside is salicin which is found in the genus salix. Salicin is converted in the body into salicylic acid, which is closely related to aspirin and has analgesic, antipyretic and antiinflammatory effects.

Anthraquinone Glycosides

These glycosides contain an aglycone group that is a derivative of anthraquinone. They are present in senna, rhubarb and aloes; they have a laxative effect.

Coumarin Glycosides

Here the aglycone is coumarin. An example is apterin which is reported to dilate the coronary arteries as well as block calcium channels. Those obtained from dried leaves of Psoralia corylifolia have Main glycosides psoralin and corylifolin.

Cyanogenic Glycosides

In this case, the aglycone contains a cyanide group, and the glycoside can release the poisonous hydrogen cyanide if acted upon by some enzyme. An example of these is amygdalin from almonds. Cyanogenic glycosides can be found in the fruits (and wilting leaves) of the rose family (including cherries, apples, plums, almonds, peaches, apricots, raspberries, and crabapples). Cassava, an important food plant in Africa and South America, contains cyanogenic glycosides and therefore has to be washed and ground under running water prior to consumption. Sorghum (*Sorghum bicolor*) expresses cyanogenic glycosides in its roots and thus is resistant to pests such as rootworms (*Diabrotica* spp.) that plague its cousin maize (*Zea mays L.*).

Flavonoid Glycosides

Here the aglycone is a flavonoid. This is a large group of flavonoid glycosides. Examples include:

- *Hesperidin* (aglycone: Hesperetin, glycone: Rutinose)
- *Naringin* (aglycone: Naringenin, glycone: Rutinose)
- *Rutin* (aglycone: Quercetin, glycone: Rutinose)
- *Quercitrin* (aglycone: Quercetin, glycone: Rhamnose)

Among the important effects of flavonoids are their antioxidant effect. They are also known to decrease capillary fragility.

Phenolic Glycosides (Simple)

Here the aglycone is a simple phenolic structure. An example is arbutin found in the Common Bearberry Arctostaphylos uva-ursi. It has a urinary antiseptic effect. Rutin found in rooibos tea.

Saponins

These compounds give a permanent froth when shaken with water. They also cause hemolysis of red blood cells. Saponin glycosides are found in liquorice. Their medicinal value is due to their expectorant effect.

Steroidal Glycosides or Cardiac Glycosides

Here the aglycone part is a steroidal nucleus. These glycosides are found in the plant genera Digitalis, Scilla, and

Strophanthus. They are used in the treatment of heart diseases e.g. congestive heart failure (historically as now recognised does not improve survivability; other agents are now preferred] and arrhythmia.

Steviol Glycosides

These sweet glycosides found in the stevia plant Stevia rebaudiana bertoni have 40-300 times the sweetness of sucrose. The two primary glycosides, stevioside and rebaudioside A, are used as natural sweeteners in many countries. These glycosides have steviol as the aglycone part. Glucose or rhamnose-glucose combinations are bound to the ends of the aglycone to form the different compounds.

Thioglycosides

As the name implies (q.v. thio-), these compounds contain sulfur. Examples include sinigrin, found in black mustard, and sinalbin, found in white mustard.

GLYCOSIDE HYDROLASE

Glycoside hydrolases (also called glycosidases) catalyze the hydrolysis of the glycosidic linkage to generate two smaller sugars. They are extremely common enzymes with roles in nature including degradation of biomass such as cellulose and hemicellulose, in anti-bacterial defense strategies (eg lysozyme), in pathogenesis mechanisms (eg viral neuraminidases) and in normal cellular function (eg trimming mannosidases involved in N-linked glycoprotein biosynthesis).

Occurrence and Importance

Glycoside hydrolases are found in essentially all domains of life. In bacteria and prokaryotes, they are found both as intracellular and extracellular enzymes that are largely involved in nutrient acquisition. One of the important occurrences of glycoside hydrolases in bacteria is the enzyme beta-galactosidase (LacZ), which is involved in regulation of expression of the lac operon in E. coli. In higher organisms glycoside hydrolases are found within the endoplasmic reticulum and Golgi apparatus where they are involved in processing of N-linked glycoproteins, and in the lysozome as enzymes involved in the degradation of carbohydrate structures. Deficiency in specific lysozomal glycoside hydrolases can lead to a range of lysosomal storage disorders that result in developmental problems or death. Glycoside hydrolases are found in the intestinal tract and in saliva where they degrade complex carbohydrates such as lactose, starch, sucrose and trehalose. In the gut they are found as glycosylphosphatidyl anchored enzymes on endothelial cells. The enzyme lactase is required for degradation of the milk sugar lactose and is present at high levels in infants, but in most populations will decrease after weaning or during infancy, potentially leading to lactose intolerance in adulthood. The enzyme O-GlcNAcase is involved in removal of N-acetylglucoamine groups from serine residues in the cytoplasm and nucleus of the cell. The glycoside hydrolases are involved in the biosynthesis and degradation of glycogen in the body.

Classification

Glycoside hydrolases are classified into EC 3.2.1 as enzymes catalyzin the hydrolysis of O- or S-glycosides. Glycoside hydrolases can as be classified according to the stereochemical outcome of the hydrolysis reaction: thus they can be classified as either retaining or inverting enzymes. Glycoside hydrolases can also e classified as exo or endo acting, dependent upon whether they act at the (usually non-reducing) end or in the middle, respectively, of an oligo/polysaccharide chain. Glycoside hydrolases may also be classified by sequence based methods.

Sequence-based Classification

Sequence-based classifications are among the most powerful predictive method for suggesting function for newly sequenced enzymes for which function has not been biochemically demonstrated. A classification system for glycosyl hydrolases, based on sequencamilies. This classification is available on the CAZy (Carbohydrate-Active Enzymes) web site The database provides a series of regularly updated sequence based classification the allow reliable prediction of mechanism (retaining/inverting), active site residues and possible substrates. Based on three dimensional structural similarities, the sequence-based families have been classified into 'clans' of related structure. Recent progress in glycosidase sequence analysis and 3D structure comparison has allowed the proposal of an extended hierarchical classification of the glycoside hydrolases.

Inverting Glycoside Hydrolases

Inverting enzymes utilize two enzymic residues, typically carboxylate residues, that act as acid and base respectively, as shown below for a ß-glucosidase.

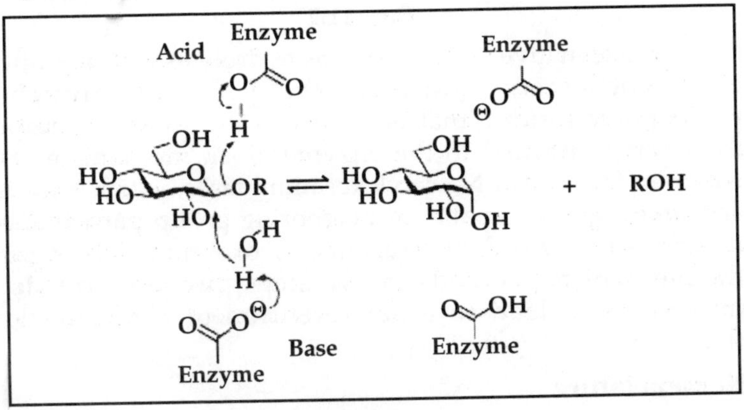

Fig. 11.1

Retaining Glycoside Hydrolases

Retaining glycosidases operate through a two-step mechanism, with each step resulting in inversion, for a net retention of chemistry. Again, two residues are involved, which are usually enzyme-borne carboxylates. One acts as a nucleophile and the other as an acid/base. In the first step the nucleophile attacks the anomeric centre, resulting in the formation of a glycosyl enzyme intermediate, with acidic assistance provided by the acidic carboxylate. In the second step the now deprotoned acidic carboxylate acts as a base and assists a nucleophilic water to hydrolyze the glycosyl enzyme intermediate, giving the hydrolyzed product. The mechanism is illustrated below for hen egg white lysozyme (Fig. 11.2).

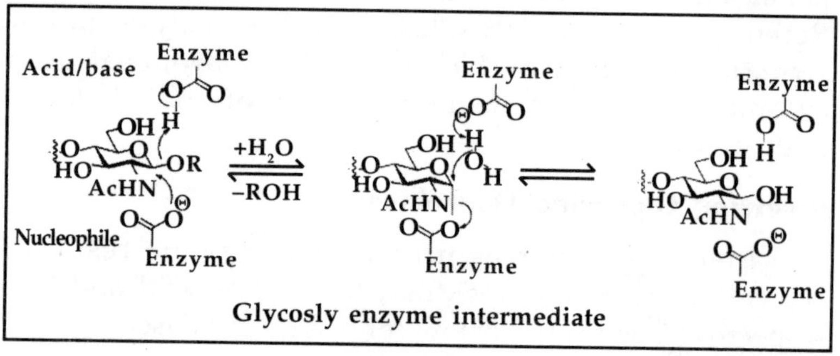

Fig. 11.2

An alternative mechanism for hydrolysis with retention of stereochemistry can occur that proceeds through a nucleophilic residue that is bound to the substrate, rather than being attached to the enzyme. Such mechanisms are common for certain N-acetylexosaminidases, which have an acetamido group capable of neigboring group participation to form an intermediate oxazoline or oxolinium ion. Again, the mechanism proceeds in two steps through individual inversions to lead to a net retention of configuration (Fig. 11.3).

Nomenclature

Glycoside hydrolases are typically named after the substrate that they act upon. Thus glucosidases catalyze the hydrolysis of glucosides and xylanases catalyze the cleavage of the xylose based homopolymer xylan. Other examples include lactase, amylase, chitinase, sucrase, maltase, neuraminidase, invertase, hyaluronidase and lysozyme.

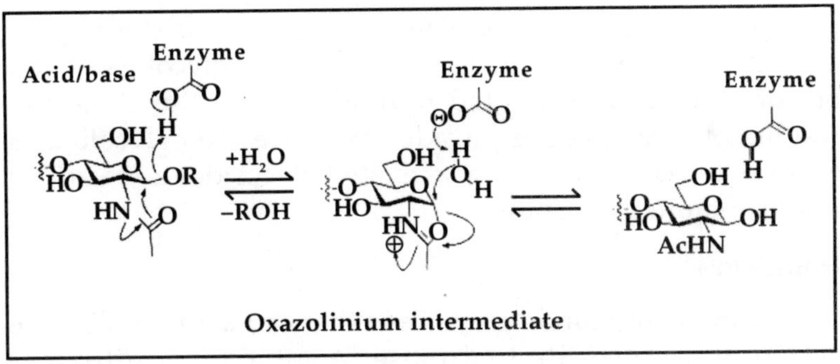

Oxazolinium intermediate

Fig. 11.3

Uses

Glycoside hydrolases have a variety of uses including degradation of plant materials (eg cellulases for degrading cellulose to glucose, which can be used for ethanol production), in the food industry (invertase for manufacture of invert sugar, amylase for production of maltodextrins), and in the paper and pulp industry (xylanases for removing hemicelluloses from paper pulp). Cellulases are added to detergents for the washing of cotton fabrics and assist in the maintenance of colours through removing microfibres that are raised from the surface of threads during wear.

In organic chemistry, glycoside hydrolases can be used as synthetic catalysts to form glycosidic bonds through either reverse hydrolysis (kinetic approach) where the equilibrium position is reversed; or by transglycosylation (kinetic approach) whereby retaining glycoside hydrolases can catalyze the transfer of a glycosyl moiety from an activated glycoside to an acceptor alcohol to afford a new glycoside.

Mutant glycoside hydrolases termed glycosynthases have been developed that can achieve the synthesis of glycosides in high yield from activated glycosyl donors such as glycosyl fluorides. Glycosynthases are typically formed from retaining glycoside hydrolases by site-directed mutagenesis of the enzymic nucleophile to some other less nucleophilic group, such as alanine or glycine. Another group of mutant glycoside hydrolases termed thioglycoligases can be formed by site-directed mutagenesis of the acid-base residue of a retaining glycoside hydrolase. Thioglycoligases catalyze the condensation of activated glycosides and various thiol containing acceptors.

Inhibitors

Many compounds are known that can act to inhibit the action of a glycoside hydrolase. A number of nitrogen-containing 'sugar-shaped' heterocycles have been found in nature including deoxynojirimycin, swainsonine, australine and castanospermine. From these natural templates many other inhibitors have been developed including is of agomine and deoxygalactonojirimycin, and various unsaturated compounds such as PUGNAc. Several drugs in clinical use are inhibitors of glycoside hydrolases including acarbose, Relenza (zanamivir), miglitol and Tamiflu (oseltamivir). Some proteins have been found to act as glycoside hydrolase inhibitors.

12

PLANT ALKALOIDS

During the past 130 million years, flowering plants have colonized practically every habitat on earth, from arid deserts, boggy meadows and windswept alpine summits, to sun-baked grasslands, lush rain forests and wave-battered rocky shores. They have replaced most of the ancient ferns and seed plants that dinosaurs subsisted on, and developed a complex and fascinating relationship with insects and mammals. During these countless centuries of time, flowering plants have gradually evolved all sorts of ingenious protective devices to discourage hungry herbivorous animals. Leaves and stems have developed a variety of vicious spines and stinging hairs (trichomes). In some plants, the dense covering of silvery hairs may also provide other ecological advantages such as solar reflection and insulation in arid environments. But mechanical defenses, such as spines and trichomes, are of limited value and probably would not deter all hungry herbivores, particularly the chewing and sucking insects. Therefore, plants have developed a "chemical warfare," a defense strategy based on a vast arsenal of chemicals which are toxic or distasteful to animals. According to Daniel Janzen, noted authority of the Costa Rican rain forest, developing seeds of the tropical liana Mucuna (including *M. urens* and *M. pruriens*) are nearly free from seed predators. In addition to a dense covering of stinging trichomes, the pods of Mucuna are rich in the potentially toxic amino acid L-dopa. Just as genetic variability and time allow agricultural pests to tolerate pesticides, so can some herbivores circumvent a plant's natural chemical defenses. This "predatory pressure" has resulted in the evolution of an endless array of complex plant molecules, from gums and terpenes to alkaloids and phenolic compounds. For example, in nettles (*Urtica species*) the sophisticated defense chemicals acetylcholine and histamine are employed in an ingenious system of "injection hairs" strategically placed throughout the plant. When we touch these plants, we may be accidental casualties in a chemical warfare between plants and herbivores that has waged through countless millennia.

One of the largest groups of chemical arsenals produced by plants are the alkaloids. Many of these metabolic by-products are derived from amino acids and include an enormous number of bitter, nitrogenous compounds. More than 10,000 different alkaloids have been discovered in species from over 300 plant families. Alkaloids often contain one or more rings of carbon atoms, usually with a nitrogen atom in the ring. The position of the nitrogen atom in the carbon ring varies with different alkaloids and with different plant families. In some alkaloids, such as mescaline, the nitrogen atom is not within a carbon ring. In fact, it is the precise position of the nitrogen atom that effects the properties of these alkaloids. Although they undoubtedly existed long before humans, some alkaloids have remarkable structural similarities with neuro-transmitters in the central nervous system of humans, including dopamine, serotonin and acetylcholine. The amazing effect of these alkaloids on humans has led to the development of powerful pain-killer medications, spiritual drugs, and serious addictions by people who are ignorant of the properties of these powerful chemicals.

Thousands of different alkaloids have been discovered from throughout the plant kingdom, but there are some species that do not contain any of these bitter, nitrogenous compounds. One of the most remarkable examples of the "competitive disadvantage" of a tree unable to produce alkaloids is the bullhorn acacia (*Acacia cornigera*) of Central America. The common name of "bullhorn" refers to the large, swollen thorns (technically called stipular spines) that occur in pairs at the base of leaves, and superficially resemble the horns of a steer. In fact, the thorns of *A. cornigera*, and a related species *A. collinsii*, are so striking that they are often strung into unusual necklaces and belts. In El Salvador the horn-shaped thorns provide the legs for small ballerina seed dolls which are worn as decorative pins.

According to researchers, other species of *Acacia* growing in the same region of Central America (including *A. chiapensis* and *A. macrantha*) produce alkaloids, but grow much more slowly and live in drier areas than *A. cornigera*. Apparently these other species of Acacia pay the price for their alkaloid defense system in terms of a slower growth rate, which enables them to compete only in the drier regions where the growth of competing vegetation is also slower and less vigorous. The ability of A. cornigera to enter more moist, lush vegetation areas is apparently related to its evolution of another defense system that depends on a little hymenopteran helpmate rather than the production of bitter alkaloids.

The "swollen-thorn" acacias of Central America are truly remarkable trees. In the wild, their enlarged, hollowed-out stipular spines are occupied by fiercely biting-stinging ants that protect them from browsing herbivores and epiphytic plants that might shade them out. The swollen thorns are not galls, they are not produced in response to chemical or physical stimuli from invasive insects imbedded in their tissues. The amazing thorns are genetically-programmed structures that are formed with or without the presence of symbiotic ants. On wild trees they are inhabited by colonies of *Pseudomyrmex ferruginea*, very aggressive ants with a painful sting. Disturbed ants release an alarm pheromone and rush out of their thorn "barracks" in great numbers. According to Daniel Janzen, livestock can apparently smell the pheromone and avoid these acacias day and night. Getting stung in the mouth and tongue is an effective deterrent to browsing on the tender foliage. In addition to protecting *A. collinsii* from leaf-cutting ants and other unwanted herbivores, the ants also clear away invasive seedlings around the base of the tree that might overgrow it and block out vital sunlight. According to Daniel Janzen, the Central American swollen-thorn acacias lack the chemical defenses of most other acacias to discourage ravaging insect predators and competition, and symbiotic ants have taken over this vital role. The acacias reward their ant helpmates with thorn "condos" to live in, carbohydrate-rich nectar from glands on the leaf stalks, and nourishing, protein-lipid morsels called Beltian bodies on the leaflet tips. There is no known function for Beltian bodies, except to provide food for symbiotic ants.

Prior to settling on a thorn acacia, the winged virgin queen ant goes on a mating flight to the highest treetop or nearby hill. Here she gets inseminated by a winged male and then hunts for an acacia in which to lay her eggs. The queen ant cuts an entrance hole into a green thorn, hollows it out, and then deposits her eggs. Subsequent entrance holes are cut by the new generations of worker ants. All this astonishing, complicated behavior has evolved in a tree that for some reason doesn't synthesize alkaloids.

Chile peppers in the wild may also benefit from a naturally-occurring alkaloïd present in their fruits. The active ingredient causing the intense burning pain when you chew into the walls of these fruits, especially the placental region where the seeds are attached, is the alkaloid capsaicin. So potent is this alkaloid that one millionth of a drop can be detected by the human tongue. Capsaicin is not broken down during the digestion process—this is why you often get burned several hours later after dining on chile peppers. Like other alkaloids in the chemical arsenal of plants, capsaicin may serve to discourage mammalian fruit predators. Botanists believe that birds are immune to the burning sensation of capsaicin, and may serve to disperse the seeds. Capsaicin may prevent hungry mammals from devouring the fruits, so that they can be eaten by fruit-eating birds who are attracted to bright red fruits. Passing through the bird's digestive tract relatively unharmed, the small seeds are dispersed to other favorable regions. According to D. Dewitt and P. W. Bosland, there are 5 species of Capsicum peppers native to the New World: *C. pubescens*, *C. baccatum*, *C. annuum*, *C. frutescens* and *C. chinense*. The hottest chile peppers belong the *C. chinense* group, including the notorious habanero. Although this species is named "*chinense*," it is not from China. Actually, its center of origin is thought to be the Amazon Basin of South America.

THE DEADLY DATURA

There are approximately 25 different species of Datura throughout the world, including Europe, Africa, southeast Asia, Central and South America, Mexico and the United States. They are often called jimsonweed or "thornapple." The latter name refers to the spiny seed-bearing capsules. Most of the species are low, shrubby or sprawling annuals or perennials, but some tree-like forms may reach 11 metres (36 feet) in height. The tree-like forms are occasionally cultivated as ornamentals and are usually placed in the genus *Brugmansia*. They generally have the same characteristic trumpet-shaped flowers as *Datura* with striking color variations of red, pink and yellow. Both genera belong to the Nightshade Family (Solanaceae), along with the deadly nightshade (*Solanum dulcamara*), tomato (*Lycopersicum esculentum*), eggplant (*Solanum melongena*) and potato

(*S. tuberosum*). Many species of *Solanum* (called nightshades) are quite poisonous to humans if eaten raw. Incidentally, the new sprouts of potato tubers contain the toxic alkaloids solanine and solanidine. Until about a century ago the tomato was thought to be poisonous because of its toxic relatives.

The common native *Datura* of the western United States, with rank-smelling foliage and large, white flowers up to 20 centimetres (8 inches) long is *D. wrightii*. Sometimes the flowers are tinged with purple and resemble oversized petunia or morning glory blossoms. It is a sprawling perennial with an enormous taproot that may extend more than 60 centimeters (2 feet) into the ground. *D. wrightii* has a large geographic range, including California, Utah, Arizona, New Mexico and Texas. It is often listed in older references as D. meteloides, a name that actually applies to a similar Mexican species, *D. inoxia* sp. *inoxia*. Another species with smaller flowers, *D. discolor*, is native to desert washes and riverbeds of southeastern California and Arizona.

A third species, *Datura stramonium*, is naturalized throughout the United States. Most older references list *D. stramonium* as an Old World species naturalized as an weed in North America. According to Dr. Robert Bye of the Universidad Nacional Autonoma de Mexico, *D. stramonium* probably originated in the New World and migrated to the Old World during pre-Columbian time. It can readily be distinguished from *D. wrightii* by its more erect habit, smaller flowers and distinctive angular or prismatic calyx. It is a cosmopolitan annual weed and prolific seed-producer. A dozen viable seeds planted in fertile soil in spring may give rise to nearly 50,000 seeds by late summer, an increase of more than 400,000 per cent.

Although jimsonweed is synonymous with several species of *Datura*, this unusual common name is actually derived from *D. stramonium*. In 1676 British soldiers stationed in Jamestown, Virginia became intoxicated by

D. stramonium when it was inadvertently included in their salads by the regimental cooks. The episode was widely publicized and the plant culprit became known as "Jamestown weed", and later as jimsonweed.

The leaves, stem, root and fruits of *Datura* contain a battery of tropane alkaloids, the most potent of which are atropine, hyoscyamine and scopolamine. These alkaloids affect the central nervous system, including nerve cells of the brain and spinal cord which control many direct body functions and the behavior of men and women. They may also affect the autonomic nervous system, which includes the regulation of internal organs, heartbeat, circulation and breathing. One autonomic response of atropine is the dilation of pupils, once considered to be a beautiful and mysterious look in Italian women. In fact, belladonna means "beautiful lady," so named because sap from the closely related belladonna plant (*Atropa belladonna*) was used as eye drops to dilate the pupils.

The action of tropane alkaloids at the cellular level is complex. It is summarized by R.E. Schultes and A. Hofmann in the Botany and Chemistry of Hallucinogens and in Medical Botany by W.H. Lewis and M.P.F. Elvin-Lewis. Tropane alkaloids are found in many other poisonous plants, including henbane (*Hyoscyamus niger*), pituri (*Duboisia* sp.), and mandrake (*Mandragora officinarum*), all of which were used extensively in witches' brews and folk medicines.

A common property of tropane alkaloids is a methylated nitrogen atom N-CH_3 at one end of the molecule. This chemical structure is also found in the neurotransmitter acetylcholine, which transmits impulses between nerves in the brain and neuromuscular junctions.

The anesthetic properties of tropane alkaloids may relate to their interference with acetylcholine, perhaps by competing with it at the synaptic junctions, thus blocking or inhibiting nerve impulses. It is interesting to note that the infamous tropane alkaloid, cocaine, is also a local anesthetic when injected into skin or muscle tissue. This property led to the discovery and synthesis of the more potent compound, novocain, widely used in dentistry.

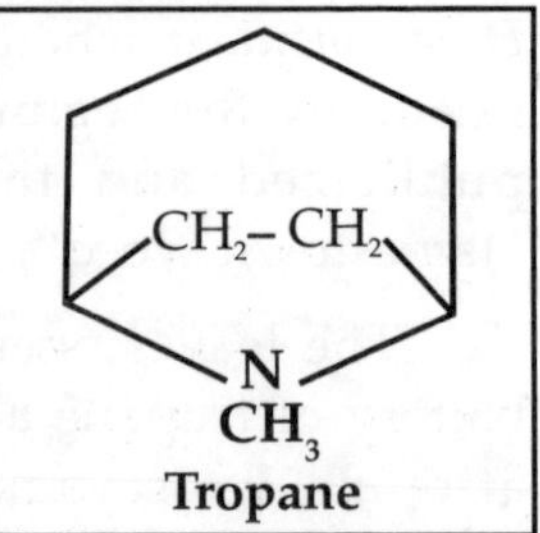

Tropane

Without getting into complicated anatomy and physiology, one nerve cell (neuron) connects to an adjacent neuron by a long extension called an axon. The axon branches into axonal endings, each of which attaches to the adjacent neuron at a synaptic knob filled with acetylcholine. The minute gap or synaptic cleft within this knob is only about 0.02 micrometres. As a nerve impulse (wave of depolarization or action potential) reaches this gap, acetylcholine diffuses across the synaptic cleft and activates the adjacent neuron. Acetylcholine in the synaptic cleft is deactivated or broken down by the enzyme acetylcholinesterase, thus shutting off the action potential. Organophosphate insecticides, such as malathion and parathion, bind to active sites on this enzyme, thus preventing the normal shut down of nerve impulses and destroying the nervous control of insects. Nerve gasses developed during World War II have a similar effect on the nervous system. Gulf War soldiers carried an atropine syrette to counter the possible effects of nerve gas.

Depending on the dosages, several tropane alkaloids of Datura (when absorbed together) may have synergistic properties resulting in extreme hallucinations, delirium and death. Since the alkaloids are fat soluble they are readily absorbed through the skin and mucous membranes. Volumes have been written about the uses and properties of *Datura* in the Middle Ages. Most of the uses involved the consumption of potions or concoctions made from various parts of the plant.

During ancient religious rituals in India, seeds were eaten by priests to induce hallucinogenic, prophetic and oracular states. European priests apparently drank Datura for the same reason. Some authorities believe the intoxicating smoke inhaled by Greek priests over 2000 years ago at the Oracle of Delphi was *Datura*. Thieves in India and Europe used *Datura* for centuries as "knockout drops" to rob their stupefied victims. The plant was also known in China, where a law prohibited mixing it with wine and other drinks.

In the East Indies, women fed *Datura* leaves to beetles, and then fed the poisonous dung to faithless lovers. Prostitutes in India added the seeds to their patron's drinks to induce sexual excitement. In fact, the use of *Datura* as an aphrodisiac spread throughout India, the Far East and Europe, and was an important ingredient in love potions and witches' brews. Specially prepared salves and ointments were also applied to various parts of the body. The famous seventeenth century Dutch artist, David Teniers the Younger, made several paintings of witches preparing for their demonic orgy or sabbat. The scenes frequently depicted a nude witch being anointed while she straddled a broom. According to M.J. Harner, writing in Hallucinogens and Shamanism, the use of a broom or staff was undoubtedly more than a symbolic Freudian act, for it served to apply the salves to sensitive vaginal membranes.

Clay tablets from Babylonian and Assyrian ruins indicate that *Datura* was used medically in ancient civilizations several thousand years ago. Greek and Roman physicians used *Datura* mixed with opium as a sedative and general anesthetic during surgery. In fact, the use of scopolamine (one of the alkaloids in Datura) plus morphine as an effective pain reliever and sleep inducer was common practice until the nineteenth century.

One of the most interesting medical cases of the 20th century involved a German physician, Dr. Carl Gauss, and the Lutheran Church. In 1905, Dr. Gauss used extracts from Datura and morphine to induce twilight sleep treatment for women experiencing difficult child birth. The church elders denounced Dr. Gauss because the *Old Testament* said that women were to bring forth in pain (Genesis 3:16). The combination of scopolamine (one of the active alkaloids found in *Datura*) plus morphine was used for years as an effective pain reliever and sleep inducer; however, it is generally considered unsatisfactory for women in labor because of hallucinogenic side effects on the mother, and it may repress breathing of the newborn.

Datura had a number of uses among Indian tribes of the United States, as well as Mexico and South America. In fact, it is difficult to find a tribe that didn't use a species of *Datura* from their region in one way or another. The hallucinogenic uses involved drinking an infusion made from the crushed roots or sometimes the crushed seeds fermented in water. Some aboriginal Indians in South America gave a *Datura*-alcohol beverage to wives and slaves of dead warriors and chieftains. The powerful brew induced stupor before they were buried alive to accompany their dead husbands and masters on the long journey to heaven. The high priests of some tribes took *Datura* in order to communicate with spirits of the dead and with their gods. The brilliant red-flowered tree *Datura* (*Brugmansia sanguinea*) is used today by herbal healers called "curanderos" in several countries of South America.

Probably the best known use of *Datura* by several North American Indian tribes was the puberty ceremonial dances involving the drinking of a "toloache" (*Datura*) infusion by young boys preparing to enter manhood. The ceremonies generally involved wild erratic dancing, varied hallucinations, and finally unconsciousness.

Datura alkaloids even have modern medicinal uses. The fat solubility of tropane alkaloids is employed in a remarkable remedy for seasick mariners called Transderm Scop®. A small, medicated disc resembling a circular Band-Aid® releases small amounts of scopolamine into the bloodstream for up to 3 days. The anti-nausea effects of scopolamine may relate to its anticholinergic action on the central nervous system, which results in inhibition of the vomiting reflex.

Jimsonweed Junkie Moth

The nocturnal blossoms and pollination ecology of *Datura wrightii* are among the most ingenious and unusual of all wildflowers of western North America. The entire corolla is neatly folded or pleated (plicate) and twisted (convolute) in the bud forming a compact cylinder. Each day at dusk during the summer months the buds begin to gradually unfold. Each corolla slowly unfurls and then suddenly snaps open as the intertwined lobes come lose from one another. At this instant a powerful fragrance is emitted.

Five long stamen filaments are attached to the funnelform corolla at the throat. The filaments extend as ridges down the inner corolla tube, forming 5 narrow canals to the base of the ovary where the disc-shaped nectary is located. The nectar canals can best be seen by examining a corolla tube in cross section. The curious name "revolver flower" refers to nectar canals which resemble the cylinder chambers of a 5-shot revolver. At night the nectar oozes along the length of the canals within the corolla tube.

During mid and late summer the white, fragrant blossoms are frequently visited by large nocturnal hawk moths (family Sphingidae). They are sometimes called sphinx moths because the alarm posture of the larva resembles the Egyptian sphinx. Several species of hawk moths are known to visit blossoms of *Datura wrightii*, but two of the most common are *Manduca quinquemaculata* and *M. sexta*. The larval forms of both are better known as tomato and tobacco hornworms.

Since *Datura*, tomatoes and tobacco all belong to the Nightshade family (Solanaceae), the larvae are apparently content to feed on whichever plant is available to them. The larvae are remarkably camouflaged with green markings and are difficult to spot as they rapidly devour your tomato plants. After feasting on *Datura* (or your tomato plants) all summer, the robust, ravenous caterpillars crawl to the ground and burrow into the soil where they undergo pupation. Unlike many other moth larvae they do not spin a cocoon. Probably every tomato gardener has unearthed the large, carmel-colored pupa with its peculiar "jug handle" appendage, which is actually a case for the developing proboscis of the adult moth.

In warm regions there may be two generations per year: summer pupae produce adults after only a week or two; fall pupae remain in the ground until the following late spring or summer. The adult moth emerges from the pupal case and pushes out of the soil, eventually flying off into the night. After mating the gravid (pregnant) female lays her eggs on a convenient *Datura* plant—or on your prize-winning tomato plants while you sleep.

Adult moths have remarkable proboscides (tongues) up to 12 centimetres long (over 4 inches), long enough to reach the base of a 10-11 centimetre (4 inch) corolla tube. When the moth is not feeding the remarkable tongue rolls up into a neat, compact coil. The common white-lined sphinx moth (Hyles lineata) of the American southwest, with a medium proboscis of 3-5 centimetres (2 inches), can only reach nectar in the upper part of the nectar canals. Unlike the Manduca moths, its pupa lacks the characteristic "jug handle" appendage.

The hawk moth approaches the *Datura* flower with its proboscis extended, lands on the blossom, crawls onto the corolla throat, and inserts its proboscis into the nectar canal. This is somewhat unusual because on most types of flowers hawk moths feed from a hovering position. While feeding they often flap their wings against the corolla throat. The proboscis becomes moist and sticky after insertion into the nectar canal, and pollen from anthers adheres to it readily. Pollen also gets on the head and other furry body parts. Thus pollen is transferred from one flower to another as the moth rubs against sticky receptive stigmas at the tips of long exerted styles. According to the Grants, hawk moths are the only flower-visiting insect with mouthparts that fit the long, slender nectar canals of *Datura wrightii*.

Another fascinating aspect of the Grant's research concerns a rather unconventional type of floral reward for hawk moths visiting *Datura* blossoms. Several intoxicating alkaloids are known to occur in Datura, but heretofore have not been correlated with pollination. Apparently *Datura* nectar is "spiked" with alkaloids and the hawk moths seem to like it and come back for more. Sometimes they arrive early and hover around the flowers, impatiently waiting for the blossoms to "pop" open. Outside the windows at the Wayne's Word® headquarters we have observed what appear to be intoxicated moths flying erratically around D. wrightii, clumsily landing on blossoms and crashing into leaves or falling upon the ground. With a flashlight their eyes glow bright red in the darkness.

Although the coincidence of proboscis and floral lengths in hawk moths and Datura is quite remarkable, these coadapted partners have the ability to obtain nectar and set seeds in the absence of each other. Hawk moths may feed on a variety of bee flowers and hummingbird flowers, and pollen-collecting bees may visit Datura blossoms in late afternoon and early morning. The hippo staff at Wayne's Word® has observed large carpenter bees (*Xylocopa*) and bumble bees (*Bombus*) on the blossoms of *D. wrightii*, busily collecting pollen from the anthers.

Flowers of some *Datura* species are also homogamous (stamens and pistils mature at the same time) and are self-compatible and partially self-pollinating. It is thus possible for one partner to migrate beyond the range of the other partner for a time. According to Verne Grant, flexibility in the pollination system permits migrational and evolutionary change. During times of general flower scarcity, hawk moths are more dependent on Datura and related sphingophilous (hawk moth-loving) blossoms because of the reliable nectar source which is unavailable to other animals.

There are many other examples of large, white blossoms pollinated by nocturnal hawk moths, including the fragrant gardenias of French Polynesia and South Africa. In fact, to reach the nectar of a Madagascar orchid (*Macroplectrum sesquipedale*) requires a 30 centimetre (eleven inch) proboscis. This remarkable orchid is also known as *Angraecum sesquipedale*. Long before it was found in nature, both Charles Darwin and Alfred Wallace (founding fathers of the principles of evolution) predicted that it would be a hawk moth.

Although the potent alkaloids of Datura have produced untold suffering and psychedelic binges among people through countless generations, they may also be an ingenious strategy to insure repeat visits by long-tongued hawk moths through the medium of drug addiction. When the moths sober up they come straight back for more nectar. Only recently are scientists beginning to solve the mysteries of plant toxins and how they may serve as chemical defenses or attractants, rather than simply nonadaptive by-products of plant evolution.

OLD AND NEW WORLD HALLUCINOGENIC MUSHROOMS

Most fungi are not deadly to humans and many are perfectly edible (and are quite delicious); however, some species are poisonous and contain potent neurotoxins. Placing a silver coin in a pan of cooking mushrooms to see if it turns black is not a reliable method of testing poisonous mushrooms. Unless you understand fungal terminology and know how to use a good taxonomic key, the staff at Wayne's Word does not encourage self indulgence on wild mushrooms. The beautiful, red, fly agaric mushroom (*Amanita muscaria*) is unmistakable with its bright red cap covered with white scales. It contains the toxic alkaloid, muscimol, which is derived from ibotenic acid—an amino acid. In Europe the mushrooms were reportedly left in open dishes to kill flies; however, according to some authorities, the flies are merely stunned or stupefied by the toxin, and may even regain control and fly away. Although it is poisonous to humans, there are other species of Amanita that are much more dangerous and are potentially lethal if ingested. Some of these dangerously poisonous species are death cap (*A. phalloides*), death angel (*A. ocreata*), and panther amanita (*A. pantherina*). Fortunately these latter deadly poisonous species are not bright red and are seldom confused with *A. muscaria*; however, they may be confused with other edible mushrooms by inexperienced gourmets. This species may be one of the most common causes of mushroom poisoning in the Pacific Northwest.

When ingested by humans, *Amanita muscaria* may produce visions and delirium, and it is perhaps one of the oldest known hallucinogens. Recent studies suggest that this mushroom was the mysterious God-narcotic *"Divine Soma"* of ancient India. Thousands of years ago, Aryan conquerors who swept across India, worshipped *soma*, drinking it in religious ceremonies. Many hymns in the Indian *Rig-Veda* are devoted to *Soma* and describe the mushroom and its effects. According to the *Rig-Veda, Soma* is without leaves, seeds or branches, with a head and stalk or pillar; its dazzling red skin is like the hide of the bull; its dress like that of a sheep, with woolly fragments remaining when the envelop bursts. This is a remarkably accurate description of the fly agaric mushroom (*A. muscaria*). There are reports of Siberian tribesmen who ingested the mushroom to get intoxicated.

Since the active chemical (muscimol) passes through the body relatively unaltered, others would drink the urine from these men to get high. This way a few mushrooms could inebriate many people relatively safely and efficiently. Lapland shamans eat fly agaric mushrooms for enlightenment, and some authors have postulated that this may have given rise to the flying reindeer and the red- and white-costumed Santa Claus legends.

Apparently not everyone agrees that the *"Divine Soma"* is *Amanita muscaria*. The active alkaloid in fly agaric mushrooms (muscimol) doesn't produce the psychoactive effects described in the *Rig Veda* and other literature. Although the identity of the *Divine Soma*. Based on first-hand experience with these hallucinogens, he has suggested that a psilocybin "magic mushroom," such as *Stropharia cubensis*, is the true Divine Soma. In fact, he also states that the use of mind-altering psilocybin mushrooms by ancient humans in Africa may have been a catalyst in the development of language and religion in primitive cultures.

Amanita muscaria was apparently one of the sacred hallucinogenic mushrooms of the Incas, Mayans and Aztecs. For the Indians of Mexico, Central and South America, partaking of these mushrooms was a deeply religious experience, enabling them to communicate with their gods. Cortez reported a mushroom (resembling *Amanita muscaria*) being eaten during the coronation of Montezuma, and in Guatemala stone carvings dating back to 1000 BC depict curious figures with umbrella-like tops resembling the caps and stalks of an *Amanita* mushroom. Mushrooms are also depicted in ancient Peruvian vessels and in the Mexican Codices. One drawing shows an animal-like messenger from god offering the sacred Amanita to a ruler seated on a throne. And a fresco in a Roman Catholic Church in Plaincouralt (Indre), France depicts Adam and Eve on either side of a tree of knowledge that is unequivocally a branched *Amanita* mushroom. Some scholars believe that the original story of Alice's Adventures in Wonderland, where Alice speaks to a green caterpillar who is seated on a red- and white-capped mushroom, is actually the interpretation of a mushroom.

Mushrooms Containing Natural LSD

A number of other hallucinogenic mushrooms are used by shamans in Mexico, Central and South America, including the four genera *Psilocybe, Paneolus, Conocybe* and *Stropharia*. The exact species selected by different shamans is determined partly by personal preference and partly by the purpose of their use. Since mushrooms are often seasonal, their regional availability may also be a factor in the selection process. The Aztecs referred to these mushrooms as "teonanacatl" (flesh of the gods).

When the Spaniards conquered Mexico, they were appalled to find the natives worshipping their deities with the help of inebriating plants. Although the Spanish conquerors hated and attacked the religious use of all hallucinogens, including "peyotyl" (peyote), "ololiuqui" (morning glory), and "toloache" (*Datura*), they especially resented the psilocybin mushrooms "teonanacatl." In order for the Aztecs to carry on their cultural traditions without persecution, the use of some of these hallucinogens went "underground." The Aztecs may have tried to protect their real sacred plant (peyote) by convincing the Spaniards that all their teonanacatl were dried mushrooms, when actually many of the "mushrooms" were really the dried, shriveled crowns of a sacred peyote cactus. The Spaniards first misidentified peyote as a mushroom in the sixteenth century when they stated that the Aztec substance "teonanacatl" and peyote were the same. It is easy to see how the Spanish authorities could have mistaken the dried crowns or tops (buttons) of peyote cactus for the caps of teonanacatl mushrooms. The Aztecs may have fooled their conquerors into thinking that these religious plants were mushrooms, while the identity of one of their most spiritual and sacred plants (peyote) was a cactus. Even in the 1900s, botanists and anthropologists concluded that teonanacatl and peyote were the same drug. This mistake was perpetuated until 1936 when hallucinogenic mushrooms were rediscovered and definitely linked to early Mexican ceremonies.

The psychoactive alkaloid in the teonanacatl mushrooms is psilocybin, a potent indole alkaloid. Psilocin, a dephosphorylated version of psilocybin, is about 10 times stronger. After ingestion by humans, psilocybin is automatically converted into psilocin. Most psilocybin-containing mushrooms have only a trace of psilocin. The common psilocibin mushroom of the Pacific coast of North America, Psilocybe cyanescens has a higher concentration of natural psilocin and is appropriately named "potent psilocybe." Although two of the most famous species of psilocybin mushrooms are *Psilocybe mexicana* and *Stropharia cubensis*, there are literally dozens of other species in the above 4 genera with similar hallucinogenic properties. In fact, Paul Stamets describes all of the species and includes color photographs. Like so many LBM's (Little Brown Mushrooms), they are difficult to identify unless you are familiar with mushroom structure and spore taxonomy, and have a good compound microscope at your disposal. In fact, two deadly look-alike LBM's (*Galerina autumnalis* and *Pholiotina filaris*) resemble certain species of Psilocybe. The small ring on their stems (called an annulus) and rusty brown spores (rather than black spores) are "dead" give aways to avoid these potentially lethal mushrooms.

Indole alkaloids contain the indole carbon-nitrogen ring which is also found in the fungal alkaloids ergine and psilocybin, the neurotransmitter serotonin, and the mind-altering drug LSD. These alkaloids may interfere or compete with the action of serotonin in the brain.

Ergot: Fungus Disease of Rye

One of the most amazing stories about naturally-occurring alkaloids in fungi concerns ergot (*Claviceps purpurea*), a fungus that infects grains of rye and related grasses. One of the psychoactive components of ergot fungus is the alkaloid ergine (d-lysergic acid amide), better known as natural LSD. The more potent synthetic LSD, (d-lysergic acid diethylamide), also known as LSD 25, is one of the most powerful psychoactive drugs known. LSD 25 was originally synthesized from natural pshchoactive alkaloids in ergot. Natural LSD (ergine) is also found in the seeds of two species of Mexican morning glory vines which are still ingested by native Indians in an important medicinal and religious ritual.

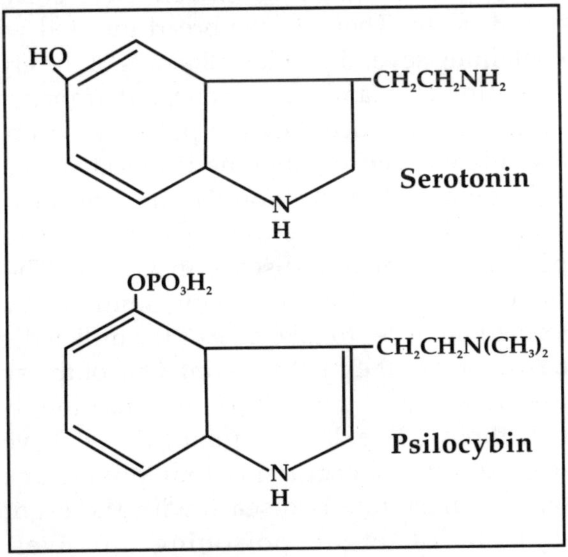

HO
$CH_2CH_2NH_2$
N
H
Serotonin

OPO_3H_2
$CH_2CH_2N(CH_3)_2$
N
H
Psilocybin

Ergot forms a dark, compact, fungal mass called a sclerotium where the grain would normally develop. One or several of these pelletlike sclerotia can be seen in an infected grain spike, typically extending out from the bracts (glumes). When separated from the grain spike, the sclerotia superficially resemble rat droppings (rat pellets). The sclerotia are the source of the potent alkaloids in Claviceps purpurea. In late spring, when rye plants are in bloom, the overwintering sclerotia from the previous year's crop produce stalked ascocarps resembling microscopic fungal fruiting bodies. The head of each ascocarp contains many embedded perithecia. The perithecia contain numerous saclike asci, each with eight ascospores. The ascospores infect the young, developing grains (ovaries) of rye plants, eventually replacing them with purplish-black sclerotia. Because it produces ascospores within saclike asci, Claviceps is placed in the fungal Class Ascomycetes.

During the Middle Ages, tens of thousands of people in Europe were afflicted with ergotism, a malady characterized by gangrenous extremities, convulsions, madness and death. They ate rye bread infested with ergot fungus containing several peptide alkaloids of the ergotamine group (including ergotamine, ergosine and ergocristine) that affect blood vessels. Since they are potent vasoconstrictors, these alkaloids can cause gangrene if ingested in sufficient dosages. Known as "St. Anthony's Fire," ergotism was a dreaded disease in Europe. Between 990 and 1129, more than 50,000 people died of this disease in France. The disease became so devastating that in 1093 in southern France the people formed an order to take care of the afflicted, and they chose St. Anthony as their patron saint. One of the symptoms of the disease was an intense burning sensation, hence the name St. Anthony's Fire. It wasn't until 1597 (500 years after the first epidemic of ergotism) that physicians finally associated this horrendous disease with the ergot on rye. Another form of ergot poisoning involves severe hallucinations and madness, caused by pschoactive alkaloids in the sclerotia.

A number of important medical discoveries have come from the study of ergot fungus and ergotism. In 1935 the alkaloid ergonovine was isolated from ergot. Since it causes strong muscular contractions, it has been used to induce labor and to control hemmorrhaging. The alkaloid ergotamine has been used extensively to relieve migraine headaches through the constriction of blood vessels. Thousands of pounds of ergot sclerotia are harvested each year from midwestern rye farms, and are used for various prescription drugs. When he added diethylamide he produced lysergic acid diethylamide, better known as LSD. While working on this new compound, Hoffman discovered that its strong hallucinogenic effects were similar to that of natural lysergic acid alkaloids in the seeds of "ololiuqui," morning glories used by the Aztecs in their religious ceremonies.

A Hallucinogen Alkaloid Found in Seeds and Toads

Another fascinating indole alkaloid called bufotenine occurs in the seeds of Yopo or Paricá (*Anadenanthera peregrina*), a South American leguminous tree of the Orinoco River basin (not to be confused with the leguminous genus Adenanthera). Indians of this region prepare a powder from the ground seeds which they use as a hallucinogenic snuff. Bufotenine (5-hydroxydimethyltryptamine) is a derivative of the indole alkaloid tryptamine, which is derived from the essential amino acid tryptophan. Tryptophan is one of the 8 (9) essential dietary amino acids in humans (which we cannot synthesize), and is widely distributed in the animal kingdom. Interestingly enough, bufotenine is also present in the skin secretion of certain toads of the genus Bufo, and explains the practice of licking toads by some people. The popular dietary supplement 5-HTP, sold at natural food stores, is 5-hydroxytryptophan. It is made from an extract of *Griffonia simplicifolia* seeds from coastal West Africa. 5-HTP is a metabolic precursor of serotonin and is taken as a treatment for depression and sleeping disorders. This herb may conflict with other antidepressant medications, and it would be wise to consult with a knowledgeable physician before taking it.

The Morning Glories

The morning-glory family (Convolvulaceae) contains at least 50 genera and more than 1000 species, from high-climbing vines and woody lianas of the tropical rain forest to prostrate, trailing perennials. They decorate our fences, trellises and walls with lush green foliage and colorful funnel-shaped blossoms, and form lovely green carpets of dichondra lawn. Several vines of this family provide us with valuable and nutritious root crops, including jicama and sweet potatoes. Although the Morning-Glory Family is usually associated with climbing vines, it also includes erect herbs, shrubs and a few trees. One unusual genus includes the parasitic dodders (Cuscuta) which smother their host with masses of twining, spaghetti-like orange stems. Other morning glories have invaded cultivated fields and have become troublesome weeds. Called "bindweeds," they literally twine themselves over other plants that happen to be in their growth path. Some morning glories, including the infamous Mary's bean (Merremia discoidesperma) are excellent seed voyagers and have colonized the distant beaches of tropical islands and atolls.

Seeds of two infamous Mexican morning glories, *Ipomoea tricolor* (syn. *I. violacea*) and the white-flowered *Turbina corymbosa* (syn. *Ipomoea burmanni*), were taken in a drink by Aztec priests in order to commune with their gods. The ground seeds were only ingested by experienced persons who understood the proper "spiritual dosage." The seeds from the white-flowered morning glory Turbina corymbosa are called *"ololiuqui"* (pronounced *o-low-lee-oo-key*) by native Indians of Mexico, and to this day provide them with an important medicinal and religious ritual in their cultures. The black, angular seeds from the pink-flowered Ipomoea tricolor are called *"tlitliltzin."* An intoxicating drink made from the ground seeds of these species is administered by a shaman and is used by a number of different tribes for the devine recovery of illness.

Like other sacred, mind-altering plants used by the Aztecs for worshipping their gods, the use of ololiuqui was forbidden by the Spaniards. Spanish attempts to eradicate the use of these plants resulted in secrecy by the Aztecs. As in the teonanacatl mushrooms, the identity of the plants known as ololiuqui was shrouded in mystery. Because of the similar, trumpet-shaped (funnel-shaped) blossoms, the plant was thought to be Datura, a known hallucinogen still used in Mexico. Finally in the 1930s, the seeds were clearly linked to species of morning glories.

Synthetic LSD has two additional ethyl groups (C_2H_5) and is about 100 times more potent. Before it was discovered in morning glories, ergine was only known from ergot (*Claviceps purpurea*), a rust fungus that infects grains. Psychoactive alkaloids, such as ergine and psilocybin (from the mushrooms Psilocybe, Stropharia, Paneolus and Conocybe) contain the indole structure, a double carbon-nitrogen ring also found in the natural neurotransmitter serotonin. These alkaloids may interfere or compete with the action of serotonin in the brain, causing psychedelic visions, delusions and hallucinations.

Wild and Crazy Plants: Locoweeds

Unlike the previous mind-altering plants, the next group to be discussed are not taken as drugs plants. If ingested they can cause serious and permanent damage to the central nervous system. Nonetheless, their poisonous effects on unfortunate herbivores is quite fascinating and may lead to a better understanding of certain human genetic disorders. These plants are most commonly associated with abnormal behavior in livestock and other range animals, and are often referred to as locoweeds. They belong to the large and diverse genus of flowering plants, Astragalus. A few western locoweeds also belong to the closely related genus, Oxytropis. Literally hundreds of different species of locoweeds grow in almost every conceivable habitat, from coastal bluffs, grasslands and deep desert canyons to sun-baked sand dunes and rocky alpine summits. In fact, Astragalus is one of the largest genera of flowering plants with approximately 2,000 different species in the northern hemisphere. Just trying to identify all the different kinds of locoweeds in the western states can be truly overwhelming. Although most North American species are poisonous, several kinds were apparently eaten by native Americans and some are actually good forage plants.

Locoweeds belong to the enormous legume family (Fabaceae), along with beans, peas, clover, alfalfa and more than 15,000 other related species. They are sometimes called milk vetches from the notion that milk secretion in goats was increased when they fed on the common Old World forage species (*Astragalus cicer*). Like many legumes, the leaves are typically divided into a dozen or more leaflets, and the flowers resemble small pea blossoms. Some species produce inflated seed pods that make a distinct popping sound if you step on them. Locoweeds are also called 'rattleweed' because of the bladder-like, inflated pods, particularly when a gust of wind rattles the seeds inside. *Astragalus* is derived from a Greek word meaning anklebone, the plural of which means dice. Perhaps the dice connotation refers to the rattling of seeds inside papery pods, like the sound of dice in a thrower. In anatomy, the astragalus or talus is one of seven bones in the ankle joint. Anklebones were apparently used for dice by ancient Greeks, and to this day, veteran crapshooters in Las Vegas refer to dice as "bones." Since adult astragalus bones are a little too large for dice, some of the smaller, cuboidal or cuneiform anklebones were probably used.

Many species of locoweeds native to the western United States are known to be poisonous to livestock. The actual mechanism of locoweed poisoning may involve:

1. toxic levels of selenium absorbed from the soil;
2. titrogen-containing sugar compounds called nitro-glycosides; and
3. potent swainsonine alkaloids causing a condition called "locoism."

Of the 372 species of Astragalus in North America, about 25 species contain toxic levels of selenium, 263 contain poisonous nitroglycosides, and 13 cause locoism. Some of the poisonous species may be placed in more than one of the above three categories. Bee keepers in Nevada have reported serious honey bee losses after working the flowers of spotted locoweed (*Astragalus lentiginosus*). The toxicity of Astragalus to bees is unusual because relatively few plants produce nectar or pollen which is poisonous to honey bees. The notoriously toxic "diablo locoweed" (*A. oxyphysus*) is well-known in California and some ranchers have attempted to eradicate it from their property.

Some species of *Astragalus accumulate* toxic levels of selenium and often have a peculiar malodorous foliage. In fact, specimens of *A. bisulcatus* and the desert species *A. crotalariae* can produce the dominant scent in herbarium cabinets for many years. Locoweed indicators of selenium-rich soils are sometimes referred to as "poison vetches," and may contain selenium levels of several hundred to 10,000 ppm (parts per million). Several names have been applied to selenium poisoning in cattle, including "blind staggers" and "alkali disease." In severe cases, the animals become lame and emaciated, and often fall into a kneeling position from which they are unable to rise. Toxic levels of selenium also occur in other wild plants of western North America, such as species of Stanleya, colorful shrubby perennials in the mustard family (Brassicaceae). Selenium poisoning of fish and waterfowl from has been well documented in California's Central Valley. In the human body, the trace element selenium is needed for the function of certain enzymes, and may serve as a cellular antioxidant thought to suppress certain tumors. Natural sources of selenium come from the allium vegetables, including onions and garlic.

The majority of locoweed species poisonous to livestock contain toxic nitroglycosides. The extreme toxicity of nitroglycosides, such as miserotoxin, in livestock is caused by the production 3-nitropropionic acid (NPA) through a complex metabolic pathway involving enzymes of rumen microbes and the liver. Another toxic reaction involves the oxidation of hemoglobin by nitrites produced by the hydrolysis of miserotoxin. The oxidized hemoglobin (called methemoglobin) is incapable of carrying oxygen. NPA is lethal to animals because it inhibits the vital enzyme succinate dehydrogenase inside mitochondria, thus blocking ATP synthesis and ultimately causing cellular death. In some animals with different gastrointestinal microbes, such as rats and rabbits, the miserotoxin is not converted into lethal NPA; however, studies indicate that death in rabbits is due to nitrite poisoning. Symptoms of acute livestock poisoning involve general weakness and loss of neural control, convulsions, blindness, coma, and death. More than 200 species of Astragalus in North America contain nitroglycosides, including A. cibaria, A. falcatus, and A. miser. The latter species has also been known to cause high mortality in foraging honey bees.

One of the most destructive types of livestock poisoning by locoweed ingestion is called "loco disease" or locoism. It is caused by at least two very potent indolizidine alkaloids, swainsonine and swainsonine-N-oxide, and impels horses and cattle to act in a wild and crazy manner. Some authorities only apply the term "locoweed" to species of Astragalus and Oxytropis containing these alkaloids, such as *A. lentiginosus*, *A. mollissimus*, *A. wootonii*, *O. lambertii*, and *O. sericea*. Swainsonine was originally isolated from the Australian darling pea (Swainsona) and more recently from the spotted locoweed (Astragalus lentiginosus). Consumption of locoweeds for two weeks to a month is necessary before obvious signs of poisoning are evident. Animals suffering from locoism may exhibit depression, a staggering gait, and general muscular incoordination. They may withdraw from other animals and become solitary. The final stages are characterized by difficulty in eating or drinking, paralysis and death. Afflicted animals often become nervous, or easily aggravated, and exhibit a complete loss of depth perception. There are reports of animals being injured or killed by running through fences or falling into ponds and streams. When plenty of other forage is available, animals tend to avoid locoweed; however, poisoned animals apparently acquire a taste for it and actually seek it out.

The cause of locoism at the cellular level is very complex. The swainsonine alkaloids inhibit or tie up the key enzyme mannosidase resulting in the accumulation of mannose sugar in nerve cells and irreparable damage to brain tissue. This condition is remarkably similar to a genetic deficiency of the same vital enzyme in humans called mannosidosis. Mannosidosis is a genetic disorder called a lysosomal storage disease, in which cells of the central nervous system become filled with cytoplasmic vacuoles of mannose due to the lack of the vital enzyme mannosidase that is essential in breaking down mannose. The actual vacuoles are swollen organelles called lysosomes where the enzymatic breakdown process normally occurs. Lysosomal storage diseases, such as mannosidosis, are often caused by recessive genes and result in paralysis and death within a few years following birth. Perhaps one of the better known storage diseases is Tay Sachs Disease, in which nerve cells fill up with a lipid called ganglioside or GM2 because they lack the vital enzyme HEX A needed to break down GM2. Studies of the biochemical effects of locoweed poisoning on the central nervous system of cattle may lead to a better understanding of these tragic human neurological disorders.

Native American Indians were apparently aware of the poisonous properties of some locoweeds and avoided them. Other drug plants are occasionally called locoweeds, such as the hallucinogenic jimsonweed (*Datura*), and some of these were commonly utilized by Indians during ceremonial rituals. In the southwest, Cahuilla Indians utilized the pods of at least one unknown Astragalus locoweed. The pods were pounded up and mixed with beans and other foods, perhaps as a spice or flavor enhancer. An Arizona locoweed (A. ceramicus), with beautiful brown-mottled pods, produces sweet, edible rootstocks which are reportedly eaten in spring by Hopi children. Another locoweed of the prairie and plains states (*A. crassicarpus*) produces edible fleshy pods. It is known locally as ground plum, Indian pea, or buffalo bean, and the pods were eaten, raw or cooked, by Indians and white settlers. The perennial roots of three species, including *A. canadensis*, *A. caryocarpus*, and *A. pictus-filifolius*, were eaten raw or cooked by Blackfoot Indians of Montana and Hopi of Arizona. Not all locoweeds are poisonous to people; however, because of the difficulty in identifying some species, it would definitely not be advisable to try any of them in gourmet dishes. It would actually be easier to select edible mushrooms from the deadly species, especially with all of the pictorial mushroom guides available today.

Mescaul Bean and Peyote Cactus

Probably the most famous New World hallucinogenic plant is peyote (*Lophophora williamsii*), a small, spineless cactus native to the Rio Grande valley of Texas and the northern and central parts of the Mexican plateau region. Another species (*L. diffusa*) is native to the Mexican state of Queretaro. The rounded, gray-green stem crown (top) is radially-divided into sections, each bearing a small meristematic region (called an areole) from which arises a tuft of hairs. The crown tapers into a thick carrot-like root that extends into the ground.

Called "peyotyl" by the Aztecs, this was truly a sacred plant used in religious ceremonies where they communicated with their gods. The spiritual, religious usage of peyote persists to this day by the Tarahumara, Huichol and other Mexican Indians, as well as by members of the Native American Church in the United States and western Canada. The Indians cut off the crowns and sundry them into brown, mushroom-shaped "mescal buttons" that last for long periods and can be shipped to distant places for use. After the crown (button) dries, the soft, fleshy tissue is reduced in volume. For this reason the tufts of hairs appear much larger and occupy a larger proportion of the button. The Aztec word peyotyl means "caterpillar cocoon," referring to the white, woolly tufts of hairs. When the top is severed, the plant often resprouts with new crowns so that many-crowned peyote plants are common. Except for the woolly hairs, the dried, peyote buttons superficially resemble the cap of a dried mushroom.

Spanish conquerors tried to ban the use of peyote by native Indians. By 1720 the eating of peyote was prohibited throughout Mexico, but peyote was so strongly rooted in native Indian lore that its use actually spread to other tribes. The Spanish thought the peyote buttons used by Aztecs were mushrooms, and it wasn't until the 1930s that researchers finally discovered that the Aztecs were actually using both peyote (peyotyl) and psilocybin mushrooms (teonanacatl) in their religious ceremonies.

The peyote cactus contains more than 50 different alkaloids, but the most active hallucinogen is mescaline. The chemistry, botany and history of peyote is discussed in a fascinating book by E.F. Anderson. Mescaline has a chemical structure similar to the brain neurotransmitter dopamine. It is also structurally similar to the neurohormone norepinephrine (noradrenalin) and to the stimulant amphetamine. In the peyote cactus, mescaline is formed in a complex pathway from the amino acid tyrosine. A similar pathway in humans produces epinephrine (adrenalin) and its demethylated precursor norepinephrine from tyrosine. Dopamine and its precursor L-dopa are also derived from a tyrosine pathway. The following illustration shows the remarkable molecular similarity between mescaline and dopamine.

Mescaline also occurs in several other cactus species, including the commonly cultivated, night-blooming, South

American San Pedro cactus (*Trichocereus pachanoi*). In the Andes of Peru, Ecuador and Bolivia the natives call this tall, columnar cactus "aguacolla" or "giganton." An intoxicating drink called "cimora" is made from the boiled stems. The drink may be spiked with other potent hallucinogens, including species of Brugmansia (*Datura*). The cut stems are sometimes seen in market places of the northern Peruvian Andes in neatly stacked piles. There are about 25 species of Trichocereus native to South America. They are typically large, tree-like cacti with cylindrical, ribbed stems and large, nocturnal, white blossoms. Other species within this fascinating genus may also contain mescaline.

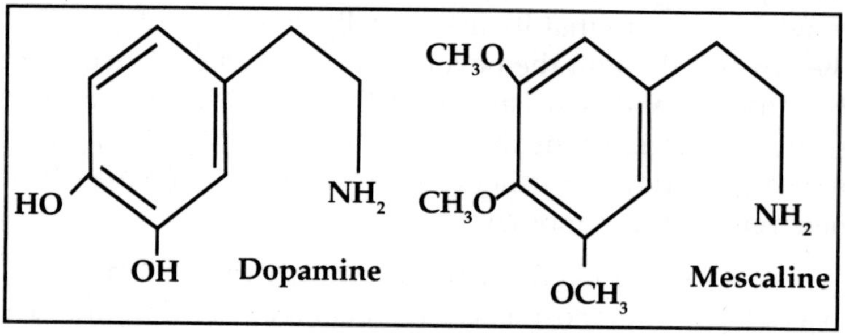

HO, OH, NH_2 — Dopamine

CH_3O, CH_3O, OCH_3, NH_2 — Mescaline

Contrary to popular rumors, mescaline is not found in the bright red, poisonous seeds of the beautiful, drought-resistant shrub called mescal bean (*Sophora secundiflora*); however, they do inhabit a similar range in the arid lands of the southwestern United States and Mexico. Mescaline is also not related to the highly intoxicating beverage called "mescal" or "mezcal," made from the fermented and distilled juices of several North American species of Agave, including *A. americana* and *A. atrovirens*. Incidentally, the fermented juice is called pulque, and the highly-alcoholic distilled products include mezcal and tequila. The seeds of mescal bean contain another potent and dangerously poisonous alkaloid, cytisine, which was ingested by some North American Indian tribes in a vision-seeking "Red Bean Dance" prior to the widespread use of peyote. Mescal beans have been discovered in Indian sites dating before AD 1000, and from one site dating back to 1500 BC. In fact, to this day the leader of the peyote ceremony in some of these tribes (called the "roadman") wears a necklace made from bright red mescal beans.

One of the most interesting stories concerning the use of peyote north of Mexico concerns Quanah Parker, son of a Comanche war chief (Nokoni) and Cynthia Parker (a white woman who was captured by the Indians). The Last Comanche Chief: The Life and Times of Quanah Parker, and Weston La Barre. In 1884, Quanah Parker became seriously ill and was treated by a Mexican curandera. Quanah regained his health and recognized that peyote could be a useful factor in binding his people together. The latter half of the 19th century (post-Civil War period) was a time of turmoil and humiliation for the American Indian tribes. Their pristine hunting lands were gradually being taken away from them; they were swindled by federal authorities; they were forced to move to reservations far from their homes; they were forced to attend schools that denied their heritage; they were corrupted by the white man's "firewater" (alcohol); and they had Christianity forced upon them by missionaries. Quanah fashioned a series of ceremonies, with cultural elements from Comanche, Kiowa, Apache, and parts of Christianity. This was a good time for the peyote religion—to bring native people dignity and hope of survival, and to bring them spiritual sustenance. The peyote religion spread rapidly during the late 1800s and early 1900s. With the assistance of James Mooney, an ethnologist with the Smithsonian Institution, the Native American Church was finally established in 1918.

13
HERBAL MEDICINE

What is Herbal Medicine?

Herbal medicine, also called botanical medicine or phytomedicine, refers to the use of any plant's seeds, berries, roots, leaves, bark, or flowers for medicinal purposes. Long practiced outside of conventional medicine, herbalism is becoming more mainstream as up-to-date analysis and research show their value in the treatment and prevention of disease.

What is the History of Herbal Medicine?

Herbal medicine had been used for medicinal purposes long before recorded history. For example, ancient Chinese and Egyptian papyrus writings describe medicinal plant uses. Indigenous cultures (e.g., African and Native American) used herbs in their healing rituals, while others developed traditional medical systems (e.g., Ayurveda and Traditional Chinese Medicine) in which herbal therapies were used systematically. Scientists found that people in different parts of the globe tended to use the same or similar plants for the same purposes.

In the early 19th century, when methods of chemical analysis first became available, scientists began extracting and modifying the active ingredients from plants. Later, chemists began making their own version of plant compounds, beginning the transition from raw herbs to synthetic pharmaceuticals. Over time, the use of herbal medicines declined in favor of pharmaceuticals.

Recently, the World Health Organization estimated that 80% of people worldwide rely on herbal medicines for some aspect of their primary healthcare. In the last twenty years in the United States, increasing public dissatisfaction with the cost of prescription medications, combined with an interest in returning to natural or organic remedies, has led to an increase in the use of herbal medicines. In Germany, roughly 600 to 700 plant-based medicines are available and are prescribed by approximately 70% of German physicians.

How do Herbs Work?

For most herbs, the specific ingredient that causes a therapeutic effect is not known. Whole herbs contain many ingredients, and it is likely that they work together to produce the desired medicinal effect. Many factors affect how effective an herb will be. For example, the type of environment (climate, bugs, soil quality) in which a plant grew will affect its components, as will how and when it was harvested and processed.

How are Herbs used?

For the reasons described in the previous section, herbalists prefer using whole plants rather than extracting single components from them. Whole plant extracts have many components. These components work together to produce therapeutic effects and also to lessen the chances of side effects from any one component. Several herbs are often used together to enhance effectiveness and synergistic actions and to reduce toxicity. Herbalists must take many things into account when prescribing herbs. For example, the species and variety of the plant, the plant's habitat, how it was stored and processed, and whether or not there are contaminants.

What Happens during a Visit to an Herbalist?

When you visit an herbalist, the treatment goals are often more broad than stopping a single complaint. Herbalists aim to correct imbalances, resolve patterns of dysfunction, and treat the underlying cause of your complaint. Specific symptoms may also be treated if necessary.

A session with an herbalist typically lasts one hour. You may be physically examined and asked about your medical history and your general well-being (that is, how well you sleep, what you eat, if you have a good appetite, good digestion and elimination, how often you exercise, and what you do to relax). The herbalist might recommend one or more herbs, dietary changes, and life-style modifications. Because herbal medicines are slower acting than pharmaceuticals, you might be asked to return for a follow-up in two to four weeks.

What is Herbal Medicine Good for?

Herbalists treat many conditions such as asthma, eczema, premenstrual syndrome, rheumatoid arthritis, migraine, menopausal symptoms, chronic fatigue, and irritable bowel syndrome, among others. Herbal preparations are best taken under the guidance of a trained professional. Be sure to consult with your doctor or an herbalist before self-treating. Some common herbs and their uses are discussed below. Please see our monographs on individual herbs for detailed descriptions of uses as well as risks, side effects, and potential interactions.

Ginkgo (Ginkgo biloba), particularly a standardized extract known as EGb 761, appears to produce improvements in awareness, judgment, and social function in people with Alzheimer's disease and dementia. In a year-long study of 309 people with Alzheimer's disease, those taking EGb 761 consistently improved while those on placebo worsened.

Kava kava (Piper methysticum) has become popular as a treatment for anxiety, but recent reports have traced liver damage to enough people who have used kava that the U.S. FDA has issued a warning regarding its use and other countries, such as Germany and Canada, have taken kava off of the market.

St. John's wort (Hypericum perforatum) is well known for its antidepressant effects, and an analysis of 27 studies involving more than 2,000 people confirmed that the herb is an effective treatment for mild to moderate depression.

Valerian (Valeriana officinalis) has had a long tradition as a sleep-inducing agent, with the added benefit of producing no hangover feeling the next day.

Echinacea preparations (from Echinacea purpurea and other Echinacea species) may bolster immunity. In a study of 160 volunteers with flu-like symptoms, echinacea extract reduced both the frequency and severity of cold symptoms.

Is there Anything I should Watch out for?

Used correctly, many herbs are considered safer than conventional medications, but because they are unregulated, herbal products are often mislabeled and may contain undeclared additives and adulterants. Some herbs are associated with allergic reactions or interact with conventional drugs. Self-prescribing herbal products will increase your risk, so it is important to consult your doctor and an herbalist before taking herbal medicines. Some examples of adverse reactions from certain popular herbs are described below.

St. John's wort causes sensitivity to the sun's ultraviolet rays, and ma stration (FDA) has issued a public health advisory concerning many of these interactions.

Kain, kava has been taken off the market in several countries because of the liver toxicity.

Valerian may cause oversedation, and in some people it may even have the unexpected effect of overstimulating instead of sedating.

Feverfew (Tanacetum parthenium) may cause agitation.

Bleeding time may be altered with the use of garlic, ginkgo, feverfew, ginger (Zingiber officinale) and ginseng.

Who is using Herbal Medicine?

Early one-third of Americans use herbs and it is estimated that in 1998 alone $4 billion was spent on herbal products in this country. Unfortunately, a recent study in the New England Journal of Medicine indicated that nearly 70% of individuals taking herbal medicines (the majority of which were well educated and had a higher-than-average income) were reluctant to reveal their use of complementary and alternative medicine to their doctors. Because herbal medicines contain a combination of chemicals, each with a specific action, many are capable of eliciting complex physiological responses—some of which may create unwanted or unexpected results when combined with conventional drugs. Be sure to consult your doctor before trying any herbal products.

How is Herbal Medicine Sold in Stores?

The herbs available in most stores come in several different forms: teas, syrups, oils, liquid extracts, tinctures, and dry extracts (pills or capsules). Teas are simply dried herbs left to soak for a few minutes in boiling water. Syrups, made from concentrated extracts and added to sweet-tasting preparations, are frequently used for sore throats and coughs. Oils are extracted from plants and often used as rubs for massage, either alone or as part of an ointment or cream. Tinctures and liquid extracts are solvents (usually water, alcohol, or glycerol) that contain the active ingredients of the herbs. Tinctures are typically a 1:5 or 1:10 concentration, meaning that one part of the herbal material is prepared with five to ten parts (by weight) of the liquid. Liquid extracts are more concentrated than tinctures and are typically a 1:1 concentration. A dry extract form is the most concentrated form of an herbal product (typically 2:1 to 8:1) and is sold as a tablet, capsule, or lozenge.

Currently, no organization or government body regulates the manufacture or certifies the labeling of herbal preparations. This means you can't be sure that the amount of the herb contained in the bottle, or even from dose to dose, is the same as what is stated on the label. Some herbal preparations are standardized, meaning that the preparation is guaranteed to contain a specific amount of the active ingredients of the herb. However, it is still important to ask companies that are making standardized herbal products the basis for their product's guarantee. If consumers insist on an answer to this question, manufacturers of these herbal products may begin to implement more quality control processes, like microscopic, chemical, and biological analyses. Again, it is important to consult your doctor or an expert in herbal medicine for the recommended doses of any herbal products you are considering.

Are there Experts in Herbal Medicine?

Herbalists, chiropractors, naturopathic physicians, and practitioners of Traditional Chinese Medicine all use herbs to treat illness. Naturopathic physicians believe that the body is continually striving for balance and that natural therapies can be used to support this process. They are trained in four-year, postgraduate institutions that combine courses in conventional medical science (such as pathology, microbiology, pharmacology, and surgery) with clinical training in herbal medicine, homeopathy, nutrition, and life-style couseling.

What is the Future of Herbal Medicine?

Although a renaissance is occurring in herbal medicine in the United States, the FDA still classifies herbs as dietary supplements and forbids manufacturers to claim that their products are able to treat or prevent specific diseases. In some countries in Europe, however, herbs are classified as drugs and are regulated. The German Commission E, an expert medical panel, actively researches their safety and effectiveness.

Phytochemical

Phytochemicals are plant-derived chemical compounds under scientific research for their potential health-promoting properties. Phytochemicals (or "phytonutrients") are non-essential nutrients, but still they have been scientifically confirmed as being important to human health.

Phytochemicals as Therapeutics

There is evidence from laboratory studies that phytochemicals in fruits and vegetables may reduce the risk of cancer, possibly due to dietary fibers, polyphenol antioxidants and antiinflammatory effects. Specific phytochemicals, such as fermentable dietary fibers, meet significant scientific agreement to be allowed limited health claims by the US Food and Drug Administration (FDA) synthetically produced to become the staple over-the-counter drug called Aspirin.

An important cancer drug, Taxol (paclitaxel), is a phytochemical initially extracted and purified from the Pacific yew tree.

Papillomatosis tumors (caused by the human papilloma virs), is in Phase III clinical trials for cervical dysplasia (a precancerous condition caused by the human papilloma virus) and is in clinical trials sponsored by the National Cancer Institute of the United States for a variety of cancers (breast, prostate, lung, colon, and cervical). The compound is being studied for anti-viral, anti-bacterial and anti-cancer properties through a variety of pathways and has been shown to synergize with Taxol in its anti-cancer properties, making it a possible anti-cancer phytochemical as taxol resistance is a major problem for cancer patients.

Some phytochemicals with physiological properties may be elements rather than complex organic molecules. Abundant in many fruits and vegetables, selenium, for example, is involved with major metabolic pathways, including thyroid hormone metabolism and immune function. Particularly, it is an essential nutrient and cofactor for the enzymatic synthesis of glutathione, an endogenous antioxidant.

Clinical Trials and Health Claim Status

There are currently many phytochemicals possibly having medicinal properties in clinical trials for a variety of diseases. Lycopene, for example, from tomatoes has been tested in clinical trials for cardiovascular diseases and prostate cancer. These studies, however, did not attain sufficient scientific agreement to conclude an effect on any disease The FDA position reads:

> "Very limited and preliminary scientific research suggests that eating one-half to one cup of tomatoes and/or tomato sauce a week may reduce the risk of prostate cancer. The FDA concludes that there is little scientific evidence supporting this claim."

Likewise, although lutein and zeaxanthin may affect visual performance and inhibit macular degeneration and cataracts, there was insufficient scientific evidence from clinical trials for such a specific effect or health claim.

Many phytochemicals have anti-inflammatory properties in vitro, including turmeric and chia. Inflammation is a factor in many diseases of aging including Alzheimer's and arthritis. Turmeric is also reported to be active against skin cancer (melanoma).

Clinical investigations continue to assess phytochemicals with medicinal properties.

Food Processing and Phytochemicals

Phytochemicals in freshly harvested plant foods may be destroyed or removed by modern processing techniques, possibly including cooking For this reason, industrially processed foods likely contain fewer phytochemicals and may thus be less beneficial than unprocessed foods. Absence or deficiency of phytochemicals in processed foods may contribute to increased risk of preventable diseases.

Interestingly, a converse example may exist in which lycopene, a phytochemical present in tomatoes, is either unchanged in conten or made more concentrated by processing to juice or paste, maintaining good levels for bioavailability.

List of Foods High in Phytonutrients

Foods high in phytonutrients, or superfoods are:

- soy – protease inhibitors, beta sitosterol, saponins, phytic acid, isoflavones
- tomato – lycopene, beta carotene, vitamin C.
- broccoli – vitamin C, 3, 3'-Diindolylmethane, sulphoraphane, lignans, selenium.
- garlic – thiosulphonates, limonene, quercitin.
- flax seeds and oil seeds – lignans.
- citrus fruits – monoterpenes, coumarin, cryptoxanthin, vitamin C, ferulic acid, oxalic acid.
- blueberries – tannic acid, lignans, anthocyanins.
- sweet potatoes – beta carotene.
- chilli peppers – capsaicin.
- legumes: beans, peas, lentils – omega fatty acids, saponins, catechins, quercetin, lutein, lignans.

Other Foods Rich in Phytonutrients or Superfoods

Some animal derived foods are also considered superfoods. Beginning in 2005, there has been a rapidly growing recognition of several common and exotic fruits recognized for their nutrient richness and antioxidant qualities, with over 900 new product introductions worldwide More than a dozen industry publications on functional foods and beverages have referred to various exotic or antioxidant species as superfruits, some of which are included in the list below.

- Apples – quercetin, catechins, tartaric acid.
- Açaí berries – dietary fiber, anthocyanins, omega-3, omega-6, omega-9, protein, beta-sitosterol, polyphenols. Açaí is the highest scoring plant food (spices excepted) for antioxidant ORAC value.

Dried Apricots

- Artichoke – silymarin, caffeic acid, ferulic acid
- Brassicates: kale, cabbage, brussels sprouts, cauliflower – lutein.
- Carrots – beta-carotene.
- Cocoa – flavonoids, epicatechin.
- Purple corn – anthocyanins.
- Cranberries – ellagic acid, anthocyanins.

Eggplant

- Gac – beta-carotene, lycopene.
- Goji (wolfberry) - ellagic acid, ß-carotene, ß-cryptoxanthin, zeaxanthin, lutein, lycopene, riboflavin, vitamin C, copper, selenium, zinc, protein.
- Pink grapefruit – lycopene.
- Red grapes and wine – quercitin, resveratrol, catechins, ellagic acid.
- Green tea – quercetin, catechins, oxalic acid.
- Mangos – cryptoxanthin.
- Mangosteen – xanthones.
- Nuts and seeds – resveratrol, phytic acid, phytosterols, protease inhibitors.

Porridge oats soluble fibre magnesium, zinc.

- Okra – beta carotene, lutein, zeaxanthin.
- Olive oil – monounsaturated fat, hydroxytyrosol, oleuropein, oleocanthal.
- Onions – quercetin, thiosulphonates.
- Papaya – cryptoxanthin.
- Bell peppers – beta-carotene, vitamin C.
- Pomegranate - vitamin C, tannins, especially punicalagins.
- Pumpkin – lignans, carotene.

Quinoa dietary fiber, protein without gluten with balanced essential amino acids

- Sea buckthorn - vitamin C, tocopherols, carotenoids, polyphenols, polyunsaturated fatty acids.
- Sesame - lignans.
- Shiitake mushrooms
- Spinach – oxalic acid, lutein, zeaxanthin, squash.
- Watermelon – lycopene zeaxanthin, sulphoraphane, indole-3-carbinol.
- Spirulina - beta-carotene.

The Superfood of the ages, now cultivated for mass distribution:

- Ganoderma lucidum lingzhi, Reishi mushroom - amino acids, over 100 triterpenoids (ganoderic acid) Terpenoid how density lipoproteins, high density polysaccharides, anticoagulant coumarin glycoside, alkaloids, organic germanium, beta-d-glucan, glucans, beta glucan (a polyglucose polysaccharide), lactones, ergosterols, mannitol, unsaturated fatty acids.

14

CELLULOSE

Cellulose is an organic compound with the formula ($C_6H_{12}O_6$), a polysaccharide consisting of a linear chain of several hundred to over ten thousand ß ($1 \rightarrow 4$) linked D-glucose units.

Cellulose is the structural component of the primary cell wall of green plants, many forms of algae and the oomycetes. Some species of bacteria secrete it to form biofilms. Cellulose is the most common organic compound on Earth. About 33 percent of all plant matter is cellulose (the cellulose content of cotton is 90 percent and that of wood is 50 per cent).

For industrial use, cellulose is mainly obtained from wood pulp and cotton. It is mainly used to produce cardboard and paper; to a smaller extent it is converted into a wide variety of derivative products such as cellophane and rayon. Converting cellulose from energy crops into biofuels such as cellulosic ethanol is under investigation as an alternative fuel source.

Some animals, particularly ruminants and termites, can digest cellulose with the help of symbiotic micro-organisms that live in their guts. Cellulose is not digestible by humans and is often referred to as 'dietary fibre' or 'roughage', acting as a hydrophilic bulking agent for faeces.

History

Cellulose was discovered in 1838 by the French chemist Anselme Payen, who isolated it from plant matter and determined its chemical formula Cellulose was used to produce the first successful thermoplastic polymer, celluloid, by Hyatt Manufacturing Company in 1870. Hermann Staudinger determined the polymer structure of cellulose in 1920. The compound was first chemically synthesized (without the use of any biologically-derived enzymes) in 1991, by Kobayashi and Shoda.

Commercial Products

Cellulose is the major constituent of paper and cardboard and of textiles made from cotton, linen, and other plant fibres.

Cellulose can be converted into cellophane, a thin transparent film, and into rayon, an important fibre that has been used for textiles since the beginning of the 20th century. Both cellophane and rayon are known as "regenerated cellulose fibres"; they are identical to cellulose in chemical structure and are usually made from viscose, a viscous solution made from cellulose. They environmentally friendly method to produce rayon is the Lyocell process.

Cellulose is the raw material in the manufacture of nitrocellulose (cellulose nitrate) which was historically used in smokeless gunpowder and as the base material for celluloid used for photographic and movie films until the mid 1930s.

Cellulose is used to make water-soluble adhesives and binders such as methyl cellulose and carboxymethyl cellulose which are used in wallpaper paste. Microcrystalline cellulose

(E460i) and powdered cellulose (E460ii) are used as inactive fillers in tablets and as thickeners and stabilizers in processed foods.

Cellulose is used in the laboratory as the stationary phase for thin layer chromatography. Cellulose fibres are also used in liquid filtration, sometimes in combination with diatomaceous earth or other filtration media, to create a filter bed of inert material. Cellulose is further used to make hydrophilic and highly absorbent sponges.

Cellulose insulation made from recycled newsprint is becoming popular as an environmentally preferable material for building insulation.

Cellulose Source and Energy Crops

The major combustible component of non-food energy crops is cellulose, with lignin second. Non-food energy crops are more efficient than edible energy crops (which have a large starch component), but still compete with food crops for agricultural land and water resources. Typical non-food energy crops include industrial hemp, switchgrass, Miscanthus, Salix (willow), and Populus (poplar) species.

Some bacteria can convert cellulose into ethanol which can then be used as a fuel; see cellulosic ethanol.

Structure and Properties

Cellulose has no taste, is odourless, is hydrophilic, is insoluble in water and most organic solvents, is chiral and it is biodegradable.

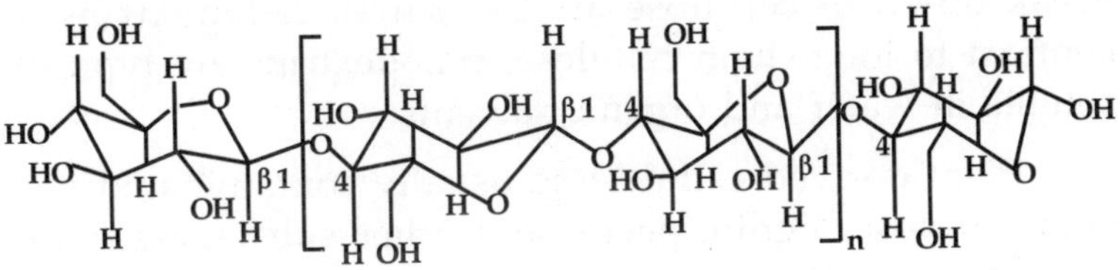

Fig. 14.1

Cellulose is derived from D-glucose units, which condense through ß(1 → 4)-glycosidic bonds. This linkage motif contrasts with that for α(1 → 4)-glycosidic bonds present in starch, glycogen, and other carbohydrates. Cellulose is a straight chain polymer: unlike starch, no coiling occurs, and the molecule adopts an extended and rather stiff rod-like conformation. The multiple hydroxyl groups on the glucose residues from one chain form hydrogen bonds with oxygen molecules on another chain, holding the chains firmly together side-by-side and forming microfibrils with high tensile strength. This strength is important in cell walls, where they are meshed into a carbohydrate matrix, conferring rigidity to plant cells.

Compared to starch, cellulose is also much more crystalline. Whereas starch undergoes a crystalline to amorphous transition when heated beyond 60-70 °C in water (as in cooking), cellulose requires a temperature of 320 °C and pressure of 25 MPa to become amorphous in water

Chemically, cellulose can be broken down into its glucose units by treating it with concentrated acids at high temperature.

Many properties of cellulose depend on its degree of polymerization or chain length, the number of glucose units that make up one polymer molecule. Cellulose from wood pulp has typical chain lengths between 300 and 1700 units; cotton and other plant fibres as well as bacterial celluloses have chain lengths ranging from 800 to 10,000 units. Molecules with very small chain length resulting from the break down of cellulose are known as cellodextrins; in contrast to long-chain cellulose, cellodextrins are typically soluble in water and organic solvents.

Plant-derived cellulose is usually contaminated with hemicellulose, lignin, pectin and other substances, while microbial cellulose is quite pure, has a much higher water content, and consists of long chains.

Molecular Structure

Cellulose is an insoluble molecule consisting of between 2000-14000 residues with some preparations being somewhat shorter. It forms crystals (cellulose Ia) where intra-molecular (O_3-HO_5' and O_6H-O_2') and intra-strand (O_6-HO_3') hydrogen bonds holds the network flat allowing the more hydrophobic ribbon faces to stack. Each residue is oriented 180° to the next with the chain synthesized two residues at a time. Although individual strand of cellulose are intrinsically no less hydrophilic, or no more hydrophobic, than some other soluble polysaccharides (such as amylose) this tendency to form crystals utilizing extensive intra- and intermolecular hydrogen bonding makes it completely insoluble in normal aqueous solutions (although it is soluble in more exotic solvents such as aqueous N-methylmorpholine-N-oxide (NMNO, ~0.8 mol water/mol, then up to 30% by wt cellulose at 100 °C [1060]), CdO/ethylenediamine (cadoxen), LiCl/N, N'-dimethylacetamide or near-supercritical water [1070]). It is thought that water molecules catalyze the formation of the natural cellulose crystals by helping to align the chains through hydrogen-bonded bridging.

Part of a cellulose preparation is amorphous between these crystalline sections. The overall structure is of aggregated particles with extensive pores capable of holding relatively large amounts of water by capillarity.

The natural crystal is made up from metastable Cellulose I with all the cellulose strands parallel and no inter-sheet hydrogen bonding. This cellulose I (that is, natural cellulose) contains two coexisting phases cellulose Ia (triclinic) and cellulose Iß (monoclinic) in varying proportions dependent on its origin; Ia being found more in algae and bacteria whilst Iß is the major form in higher plants.

Cellulose Ia and cellulose Iß have the same fibre repeat distance (1.043 nm for the repeat dimer interior to the crystal, 1.029 nm on the surface but differing displacements of the

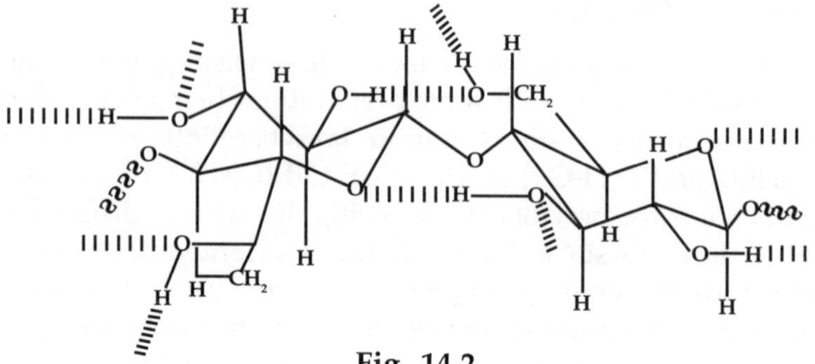

Fig. 14.2

sheets relative to one another. The neighboring sheets of cellulose Ia (consisting of identical chains with two alternating glucose conformers) are regularly displaced from each other in the same direction whereas sheets of cellulose Iß (consisting of two conformationally distinct alternating sheets, (as shown right where the 2-OH and 6-OH groups both change orientations so altering the hydrogen bonding pattern) each made up of crystallographically identical glucose conformers) are staggered . It has been found that cellulose (Iß) significantly alters the water structuring at its surface out to about 10 Å, which may affect its enzymatic digestion.

Cellulose Ia and cellulose Iß are interconverted by bending during microfibril formation and metastable cellulose Ia converts to cellulose Iß on annealing.

If it can be recrystallized (for example, from base or CS_2) cellulose I gives the thermodynamically more stable Cellulose II structure with an antiparallel arrangement of the strands and some inter-sheet hydrogen-bonding. Cellulose II contains two different types of anhydroglucose (A and B) with different backbone structures; the chains consisting of -A-A- or -B-B- repeat units Cellulose III is formed from cellulose mercerized in ammonia and is similar cellulose II but with the chains parallel, as in cellulose Ia and cellulose Iß . For a review of cellulose structure, see or the Centre de recherches sur les macromolécules végétales web site.

Assaying Cellulose

Given a cellulose-containing material, the portion that does not dissolve in a 17.5% solution of sodium hydroxide at 20 °C is a cellulose, which is true cellulose. Acidification of the extract precipitates ß cellulose. The portion that dissolves in base but does not precipitate with acid is? cellulose.

Cellulose can be assayed using a method described by Updegraff in 1969, where the fibre is dissolved in acetic and nitric acid to remove lignin, hemicellulose, and xylosans. The resulting cellulose is allowed to react with anthrone in sulfuric acid. The resulting coloured compound is assayed spectrophotometrically at a wavelength of approximately 635 nm.

In addition, cellulose is represented by the difference between acid detergent fibre (ADF) and acid detergent lignin (ADL).

Biosynthesis

In vascular plants cellulose is synthesized at the plasma membrane by rosette terminal complexes (RTC's). The RTC's are hexameric protein structures, approximately 25 nm in diameter, that contain the cellulose synthase enzymes that synthesise the individual cellulose chains Each RTC floats in the cell's plasma membrane and "spins" a microfibril into the cell wall.

The RTC's contain at least three different cellulose synthases, encoded by CesA genes, in an unknown stoichiometry Separate sets of CesA genes are involved in primary and secondary cell wall biosynthesis. Cellulose synthase utilizes UDP-D-glucose precursors to generate microcrystalline cellulose. Cellulose synthesis requires chain initiation and elongation, and the two processes are separate. CesA glucosyltransferase initiates cellulose polymerization using a steroid primer, sitosterol-beta-glucoside, and UDP-glucose A cellulase may function to cleave the primer from the mature chain.

Breakdown (Cellulolysis)

Cellulolysis is the process of breaking down cellulose into smaller polysaccharides called cellodextrins or completely into glucose units; this is a hydrolysis reaction. Because cellulose molecules bind strongly to each other, cellulolysis is relatively difficult compared to the break down of other polysaccharides.

Mammals do not have the ability to break down cellulose directly. Some ruminants like cows and sheep contain certain symbiotic anaerobic bacteria (like Cellulomonas) in the flora of the gut wall, and these bacteria produce enzymes to break down cellulose; the break down products are then used by the mammal. Similarly, lower termites contain in their hindguts certain flagellate protozoa which produce such enzymes; higher termites contain bacteria for the job. Fungi, which in nature are responsible for recycling of nutrients, are also able to break down cellulose.

The enzymes utilized to cleave the glycosidic linkage in cellulose are glycoside hydrolases including endo-acting cellulases and exo-acting glucosidases. Such enzymes are usually secreted as part of multienzyme complexes that may include dockerins and cellulose binding modules; these complexes are in some cases referred to as cellulosomes.

Hemicellulose

Hemicellulose is a polysaccharide related to cellulose that comprises ca. 20% of the biomass of most plants. In contrast to cellulose, hemicellulose is derived from several sugars in addition to glucose, including especially xylose but also mannose, galactose, rhamnose, and arabinose. Hemicellulose consists of shorter chains - around 200 sugar units as opposed to 7,000 - 15,000 glucose molecules in the average cellulose polymer. Furthermore, hemicellulose is branched, whereas cellulose is unbranched.

Derivatives

The hydroxyl groups of cellulose can be partially or fully reacted with various reagents to afford derivatives with useful properties. Cellulose esters and cellulose ethers are the most important commercial materials. In principle, though not always in current industrial practice, cellulosic polymers are renewable resources.

Among the esters are cellulose acetate and cellulose triacetate, which are film- and fibre-forming materials that find a variety of uses. The inorganic ester nitrocellulose was initially used as an explosive and was an early film forming material.

Ether derivatives include:

- Ethylcellulose, a water-insoluble commercial thermoplastic used in coatings, inks, binders, and controlled-release drug tablets;
- Methylcellulose;
- Hydroxypropyl cellulose;
- Carboxymethyl cellulose;
- Hydroxypropyl methyl cellulose, E464, used as a viscosity modifier, gelling agent, foaming agent and binding agent; and
- Hydroxyethyl methyl cellulose, used in production of cellulose films.

Sources for Cellulose

Cellulose is found in plants as microfibrils (2-20 nm diameter and 100-40 000 nm long). These form the structurally strong framework in the cell walls. Cellulose (E460) is mostly prepared from wood pulp. Cellulose is also produced in a highly hydrated form by some bacteria (for example, Acetobacter xylinum).

Functionality

Cellulose has many uses as an anticake agent, emulsifier, stabilizer, dispersing agent, thickener, and gelling agent but these are generally subsidiary to its most important use of holding on to water. Water cannot penetrate crystalline cellulose but dry amorphous cellulose absorbs water becoming soft and flexible. Some of this water is non-freezing but most is simply trapped. Less water is bound by direct hydrogen bonding if the cellulose has high crystallinity but some fibrous cellulose products can hold on to considerable water in pores and its typically straw-like cavities; water holding ability correlating well with the amorphous (surface area effect) and void fraction (that is, the porosity). As such water is supercoolable, this effect may protect against ice damage. Cellulose can give improved volume and texture particularly as a fat replacer in sauces and dressings but its insolubility means that all products will be cloudy.

Swelled bacterial cellulose (ex. Acetobacter xylinum), in its never-dried state with much smaller fibrils (~1%) than from plants, exhibits pseudoplastic viscosity like xanthan gels but this viscosity is not lost at high temperatures and low shear rates as the cellulose can retain its structure. Where individual cellulose strands are surrounded by water they are flexible and do not present contiguous hydrophobic surfaces. Bacterial cells may be removed by hot alkali and the clean wet cellulose used as a substrate for immobilizing biomolecules or for covering wounds On drying the properties of bacterial cellulose irreversibly lose their hydrated properties and tend to those of plant cellulose.

About a third of the world's production of purified cellulose is used as the base material for a number of water-soluble derivatives with pre-designed and wide-ranging properties dependent on groups involved and the degree of derivatization Derivatizing cellulose interferes with the orderly crystal-forming hydrogen bonding, described above, so that even hydrophobic derivatives may increase the apparent solubility in water. Methyl cellulose (made by methylating about 30% of the hydroxyl groups) is thermogelling, forming gels above a critical temperature due to hydrophobic interactions between high-substituted regions and consequentially stabilized intermolecular hydrogen bonding. Such gels break down on cooling In a manner similar to that causing the solubility minimum for non-polar gases; hydrophobic saccharides becoming less soluble as the temperature increases . This property is useful in forming films as barriers to water loss and for holding on to small gas bubbles.

Hydroxypropyl methylcellulose (HPMC, E464) has similar properties and uses but with added water interaction and surface activity Both methylcellulose and HPMC may be used in gluten-free bakery products as gluten substitutes. Hydroxypropyl cellulose (E463) possesses good surface activity but does not gel as it forms open helical coils. It is a water-soluble thickener, emulsifier and film-former often used in tablet coating. Another important derivative of cellulose is carboxymethylcellulose.

CELLULOSE ACETATE

Cellulose acetate, first prepared in 1865, is the acetate ester of cellulose. Cellulose acetate is used as a film base in photography, and as a component in some adhesives; it is also used as a synthetic fibre.

Acetate Fibre and Triacetate Fibre

Acetate and triacetate are mistakenly referred to as the same fibre; although they are similar, their chemical compounds differ. Triacetate is known as a generic description or primary acetate containing no hydroxyl group. Acetate fibre is known as modified or secondary acetate having a few hydroxyl groups. Triacetate fibres, although no longer produced in the United States, contain a higher ratio of acetate-to-cellulose than do acetate fibres.

Cellulose Acetate Film

Cellulose acetate film was introduced in 1934 as a replacement for the unstable and highly flammable cellulose nitrate film stock that had previously been standard. When exposed to heat, moisture or acids in the film base begin to deteriorate to an unusable state, releasing acetic acid with a characteristic vinegary smell, causing the process to be known as "vinegar syndrome." Acetate film stock is still used in some applications, such as camera negative for motion pictures. Since the 1980s, polyester film stock (sometimes referred to under Kodak's trade name "ESTAR Base") has become more commonplace, particularly for archival applications. Acetate film was also used as the base for magnetic tape, prior to the advent of polyester film.

Cellulose Acetate Computer Tape

Cellulose acetate magnetic tape was introduced by IBM in 1952 for use on their IBM 726 tape drive in the IBM 701 computer. It was much lighter and easier to handle than the metal tape introduced by UNIVAC in 1951 for use on their UNISERVO tape drive in the UNIVAC I computer. In 1956 cellulose acetate magnetic tape was replaced by the more stable PET film magnetic tape for use on their IBM 727 tape drive.

Fibre

Cellulose acetate or acetate rayon fibre (1924) is one of the earliest synthetic fibres and is based on cotton or tree pulp cellulose ("biopolymers"). These "cellulosic fibres" have passed their peak as cheap petro-based fibres (nylon and polyester) and have displaced regenerated pulp fibres.

It was invented by two Swiss brothers, Doctors Camille and Henri Dreyfus, who originally began chemical research in a shed behind their father's house in Basel, Switzerland. In 1905, Camille and Henri developed a commercial process to manufacture cellulose acetate. The Dreyfus brothers initially focused on cellulose acetate film, which was then widely used in celluloid plastics and film. By 1913, Camille and Henri's studies and experiments had produced excellent laboratory samples of continuous filament acetate yarn. In 1924, the first commercial acetate filament was spun in the United States and trademarked as Celanese.

Trade names for acetate include:

- Acele;
- Avisco;
- Celanese;
- Chromspun; and
- Etron.

Fibre Properties

Acetate is a very valuable manufactured fibre that is low in cost and has good draping qualities. Properties of acetate have promoted it as the "beauty fibre". Acetate is used in fabrics such as satins, brocades, and taffetas to accentuate luster, body, drape and beauty.

- Hand: soft, smooth, dry, crisp, resilient.
- Comfort: breathes, wicks, dries quickly, no static cling.
- Drape: linings move with the body linings conform to the garment.
- Color: deep brilliant shades with atmospheric dyeing meet colorfastness requirements.
- Luster: light reflection creates a signature appearance.
- Performance: colorfast to perspiration staining, colorfast to dry cleaning, air and vapor permeable.
- Tenacity: weak fibre with breaking tenacity of 1.2 to 1.4 g/d; rapidly loses strength when wet; must be dry cleaned.

- Environmentally friendly: made from wood pulp, a renewable resource.
- Abrasion: Poor Resistance
- Heat retention: poor thermal retention; no allergenic potential (hypoallergenic)
- Dyeability: (two methods) cross-dying method where yarns of one fibre and those of another fibre are woven into a fabric in a desired pattern; solution-dying method provides excellent color fastness under the effects of sunlight, perspiration, air contaminants and washing

Acetate usually requires dry cleaning.

Production

The Federal Trade Commission definition for acetate fibre is "A manufactured fibre in which the fibre-forming substance is cellulose acetate. Where not less than 92 per cent of the hydroxyl groups are acetylated, the term triacetate may be used as a generic description of the fibre."

Acetate is derived from cellulose by deconstructing wood pulp into a purified fluffy white cellulose. In order to get a good product special qualities of pulps - dissolving pulps - are used. A common problem with these is that the reactivity of the cellulose is uneven, and thereby will the quality of the cellulose acetate sometimes be damaged. The cellulose is then reacted with acetic acid and acetic anhydride in the presence of sulfuric acid. It is then put through a controlled, partial hydrolysis to remove the sulfate and a sufficient number of acetate groups to give the product the desired properties. The anhydroglucose unit is the fundamental repeating structure of cellulose and has three hydroxyl groups which can react to form acetate esters. The most common form of cellulose acetate fibre has an acetate group on approximately two of every three hydroxyls. This cellulose diacetate is known as secondary acetate, or simply as "acetate".

After it is formed, cellulose acetate is dissolved in acetone into a viscose resin for extrusion through spinnerets (which resemble a shower head). As the filaments emerge, the solvent is evaporated in warm air via dry spinning, producing fine cellulose acetate fibres.

Production Method

1. Purified cellulose from wood pulp or cotton linters.
2 Mixed with glacial acetic acid, acetic anhydride, and a catalyst.
3. Aged 20 hours- partial hydrolysis occurs.
4. Precipitated as acid-resin flakes.
5. Flakes dissolved in acetone.
6. Solution is filtered.
7. Spinning solution extruded in column of warm air. Solvent recovered.
8. Filaments are stretched and wound onto beams, cones, or bobbins ready for use.

Acetate Fibre Characteristics

- Cellulosic and thermoplastic.
- Selective absorption and removal of low levels of certain organic chemicals.
- Easily bonded with plasticizers, heat, and pressure.
- Acetate is soluble in many common solvents (especially acetone and other organic solvents) and can be modified to be soluble in alternative solvents, including water.
- Hydrophilic: acetate wets easily, with good liquid transport and excellent absorption; in textile applications, it provides comfort and absorbency, but also loses strength when wet.

- Acetate fibres are hypoallergenic.
- High surface area.
- Made from a renewable resource: wood pulp can be composted or incinerated.
- Can be dyed, however special dyes and pigments are required since acetate does not accept dyes ordinarily used for cotton and rayon (this also allows cross-dyeing).
- Resistant to mold and mildew.
- Easily weakened by strong alkaline solutions and strong oxidizing agents can usually be wet cleaned or dry cleaned and generally does not shrink.

Major Industrial Acetate Fibre Uses

- Apparel: linings, blouses, dresses, wedding and party attire, home furnishings, draperies, upholstery and slip covers.
- Industrial uses: cigarette and other filters, ink reservoirs for fibre tip pens.
- High absorbency products: diapers and surgical products.

  The original Lego bricks were manufactured from cellulose acetate from 1949 to 1963.
- Award Ribbon: Rosettes for equestrian events, dog/cat shows, corporate awards, advertising and identification products all use cellulose acetate ribbon.
- Kem High End Playing Cards used at the World Series of Poker & Major Casino Poker rooms are made of Cellulose Acetate.

History

Acetate was first introduced in 1904, when Camille Dreyfus and his younger brother Henri, did chemical research and development in a shed in their father's garden in Basle, Switzerland. Inasmuch as their father was interested in a chemical factory, his influence was probably a factor in their choice of careers. And since Basle was a center of the dyestuffs industry, it was natural that their first achievement should be the development of synthetic indigo dyes. In search of a field that offers really limitless potentialities, they deliberately selected that of cellulose acetate products, including fibres for textile use.

For five years, the Dreyfus brothers studied and experimented in a logical, systematic manner in Switzerland and France. By 1910, they had perfected acetate lacquers and plastic film and opened a factory in Basle capable of producing about three tons a day. This was largely sold to the celluloid industry in France and Germany, and to Pathe Fréres in Paris for non-flammable motion picture film base. A small but constantly growing amount of acetate lacquer, called "dope", was sold to the expanding aircraft industry to coat the fabric covering wings and fuselage.

After some twenty-odd thousand separate experiments, by 1913, the brothers produced excellent laboratory samples of acetate continuous filament yarn. The outbreak of the First World War postponed completion of development leading to successful commercial production until 1921. The war, of course, necessitated rapid expansion of the Basle factory which terminated its trade with Germany and exclusively supplied the Allied Governments with acetate "dope" for military aircraft.

In November 1914, the British Government invited Dr.Camille Dreyfus to come to England to manufacture acetate "dope". In 1917, the War Department of the United States Government invited Dr. Dreyfus to establish a similar factory in the US after their entry into war. After about six weeks, a contract was negotiated for sale of acetate "dope" to the War Department and a plant site was sought. Dr.

Dreyfus and his associates started construction of the American company at Cumberland, Maryland in 1918, but the war was over before the plant could be completed. The business with the Government was completed in due time, construction of the plant continued, the early nucleus of the management began to assemble, and the organization in England completed development of the first commercially successful acetate textile yarn. In England, in 1912, the British company produced the first commercial cellulose acetate yarn. The yarn was sold primarily for crocheting, trimming, and effect threads and for popular-priced linings.

The first yarn spun in America was on Christmas Day, 1924, at the Cumberland, Maryland Plant. The first yarn was of fair quality, but sales resistance was heavy, and silk associates worked zealously to discredit acetate and discourage its use. Acetate became an enormous success as a fibre for moiré because its thermoplastic quality made the moiré design absolutely permanent. The same characteristic also made permanent pleating a commercial fact for the first time, and gave great style impetus to the whole dress industry.

This was a genuine contribution. The mixing of silk and acetate in fabrics was accomplished at the beginning and almost at once cotton was also blended, thus making possible low-cost fabrics by means of a fibre which then was cheaper than silk or acetate. Today, acetate is blended with silk, cotton, wool, nylon, etc. to give to fabrics an excellent wrinkle recovery, good left, handle, draping quality, quick drying, proper dimensional stability, cross-dye pattern potential, at a very competitive price.

INDEX

D

E

F

G

H

N

O

P